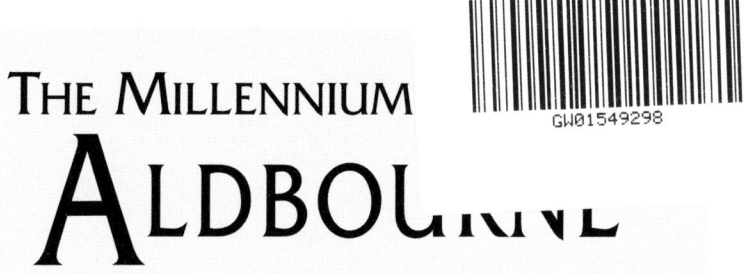

The Millennium
Aldbourne

A SNAPSHOT OF THE PARISH IN THE YEAR 2000

✥

Edited by David Lee and Malcolm Shuttleworth

Published in 2000 by Mrs P Hagerty, Copper Beeches, Southward Lane, Aldbourne, Wiltshire SN8 2DF on behalf of the Trustees of the Aldbourne Memorial Hall, Oxford Street, Aldbourne, Wiltshire.

© 2000 The Trustees of the Aldbourne Memorial Hall.

All rights reserved. No part of this publication may be reproduced or transmitted in any form or by any means, electronic or mechanical, including photocopy, recording, or any information storage and retrieval system, without permission in writing from the publisher.

British Library Cataloguing-in-Publication Data.
A catalogue record for this book is available from the British Library.

ISBN 0 9538013 0 6 Hardback
ISBN 0 9538013 1 4 Paperback

In Appreciation
The Trustees of the Aldbourne Memorial Hall and the Aldbourne Millennium Festival Committee express sincere thanks to the members of the Millennium Book of Aldbourne Working Party for the hard work and time freely given to produce this book.

The committees also wish to acknowledge and thank the Aldbourne Civic Society for all the help, advice and encouragement given.

The result is a truly wonderful record of the Parish of Aldbourne at the turn of the millennium, a book that will be treasured by future generations.

Chris Hill
Chairman
Aldbourne Millennium Festival Committee

Cover illustration: Aldbourne village pond in the 1840s, in 1926 and in 1999.

Book design consultant: Annette Findlay.

Cover design by Shane O'Dwyer from an idea by Alan Watson.

Scanning of photographs by Microset Imaging Limited, Witney, Oxfordshire.

Printed and bound by The Cromwell Press, Trowbridge, Wiltshire.

Editors' Acknowledgements
Our thanks are due to: Rufus Seager, our early inspiration; Barbara Croucher for her constuctive advice; New Horizon Trust, Cook Trust and Southward Wines for generous financial assistance; Ann and Giles Currie for fundraising; St Ivel Ltd; The Cromwell Press, The Crowood Press, Intergraph (UK) Ltd and D & N Publishing for their great patience in giving technical advice to enthusiastic amateurs.

Contents

	Contributors	4
	Foreword	5
	Introduction	6
One	The Square & The Green	7
Two	Up & Down Lottage Road	35
Three	The Roads off Lottage Road	63
Four	The Cook Road Estate	79
Five	Oxford Street & up the Hill	97
Six	South Street & the Roads off it	121
Seven	The Farm Lane Area	145
Eight	Marlborough Road & Onwards	177
Nine	Via Castle Street to Snap	197
Ten	The Whitley Estate	215
Eleven	West Street to Upham	231
	Index	255

Contributors

John Adey Marianne Adey Julie Alder Shirley Allen Michael Ancram Hazel Andrews Heather Athawes Pauline Badger Susan Bailey Anne Barnes Chris Barnes Ted Barnes Audrey Barrett Cyril Barrett Nancy Barrett Michael Bartrop Pat Batterson Wendy Beattie Mabel Beckingham Gwyneth Bell Peter Bell Peggy Bendle Peter Biggs Hugh Bland Peter Boaden Margaret Bowler Marion Bradley Louise Brenchly Anne Brown Betty Brown Barbara Brownell Jo Buckler Anthony Cain Glyn Chadwick John Coker Graham Cook John Cook Peta Cook Bill Cooper Peter Cotterell Steve Cox Sue Cox Jim Cullis Molly Cullis Allan Cummings Ann Currie Mark Davies Ray Day Peggy Delmé-Radcliffe Andy Devey Kate Digman Bev Dolman Ben Dowdeswell Meg Duckworth Brit Du Cros Rose Duddy John Dymond Liz Dymond Jane Ebbutt Alison Edmonds Charles Elms Fenella Elms Anthony Evans Jocelyn Evans Rhona Fletcher Jill Fremantle Dennis Fryer Charles Gape Helen Gape Howard Gibbs Shirley Gibbs Peter Gibson Sheila Gibson Claire Gillfeder Audrey Gilligan Terry Gilligan Dennis Goodyer Ron Hacker Penny Hagerty Brian Hale Charlie Hale Joan Hale Ann Hall Leigh Hancock Richard Handover Ceri Hanlon Gill Hanlon Gwen Hazell Michael Hellier Judy Henson Katie Henson Liz Heron Watson Chris Hill Jonathan Hill Roger Hill Suzanne Hill Diane Hillas Michael Hillas Joy Hobby Cathy Hughes Claire Hughes Chris Humphries Andrew Hunter Jill Hunter Jo Hutchings Simon Hutchings Richard Jeffcoat Maureen Jepson Annette Jerram Irene Jerram Vin Jerram Dave Jordan Kayla Justice Lindsay Keen Julie Kent Lorraine Kimber Chris Kingsman Robert Lawton Ann Lee David Lee Nick Leigh Nicky Leigh Pat Leigh Diana Lester Connie Liddiard Di Loadman Daphne Loch John Loch Daphne Ludlow Peter Ludlow Nina McKeon Mary McKrill Duncan McPhedran Pat McPhedran Gill Mann Chris Martin Di May John May John Miles Pauline Mills Bill Moir Janet Money Monica Moreton Shane Moreton Ian Nash Cecil Newton Geoff Newton Carol Northam Ivor Noyce Mary O'Malley Olive Orchard Ruth Pakenham Graham Palmer Jane Palmer Wally Palmer Bridget Partridge Anne Payne Eddie Payne Albert Pennington Cheryl Phelps Tom Port Ruth Powell Adam Power Alison Power Joan Price Linda Pryce Pam Puttick Peter Rapson Jonathan Rayner Gillian Reeve Jenny Rendell Chris Roberts Anne Robertson David Robertson Marcus Rouse Madelaine Rubach Trish Rushen Valerie Sanderson Alan Scutt Andrew Sewell Ishbel Sewell Bob Shepherd Harry Sheppard Florence Sherman Malcolm Shuttleworth Geoff Slater Peggy Slater Lesley Smith Margaret Stedham Michael Stedham Richard Stevens Ann Sullivan Bryony Sutton Deborah Tarry Sally Thomas Jean Thomson Trevor Tiplady Bruce Titcombe Janet Todd Robert Todd Eileen Turpie Dorothy Walls Sam Walls Lestor Walshe Maryanne Ward Jean Warrington Alan Watson Ian Watson Val Watson Molly Watts Don Webb Elizabeth Webb Guy Wentworth Andrea West Frank West Peter West Fred Westall Nancy Whittington Dorothy Wilkins Daphne Williams Jo Williams Paul Williams Rob Williams Sam Willmott Jean Wootton Lou Wright

Aldbourne Housing Group Environment Agency Hastoe Housing Association Kennet District Council Kennet Housing Society KFC (Fine Art) Ltd Sarsen Housing Association Southern Electricity Thames Water The Strict Baptist Historical Society Transco Wiltshire Constabulary Wiltshire Fire Brigade

FOREWORD

Aldbourne, Our Aldbourne

Our village is portrayed in this book by nearly two hundred contributors. This has been co-ordinated by a Working Party for whose time and effort Aldbourne must be very grateful. However, two persons stand out as deserving special mention.

Ralph Emerson wrote 'talent cannot make a writer, there must be a man behind the book'. This man is David Lee whose enthusiasm has been infectious. Many of us have been caught up in his eagerness to succeed. He has not bullied but has cajoled and encouraged the artists, the writers and the helpers to produce outstanding contributions for such a special book.

Malcolm Shuttleworth with technology at his fingertips has designed the book page-by-page incorporating this mass of material into the complete volume now in your hands.

Jesse Jackson, the American politician, said that when people come together flowers always flourish. The people of Aldbourne have come together and the book will flourish, thanks primarily to David and Malcolm.

David Robertson
Chairman, Aldbourne Civic Society

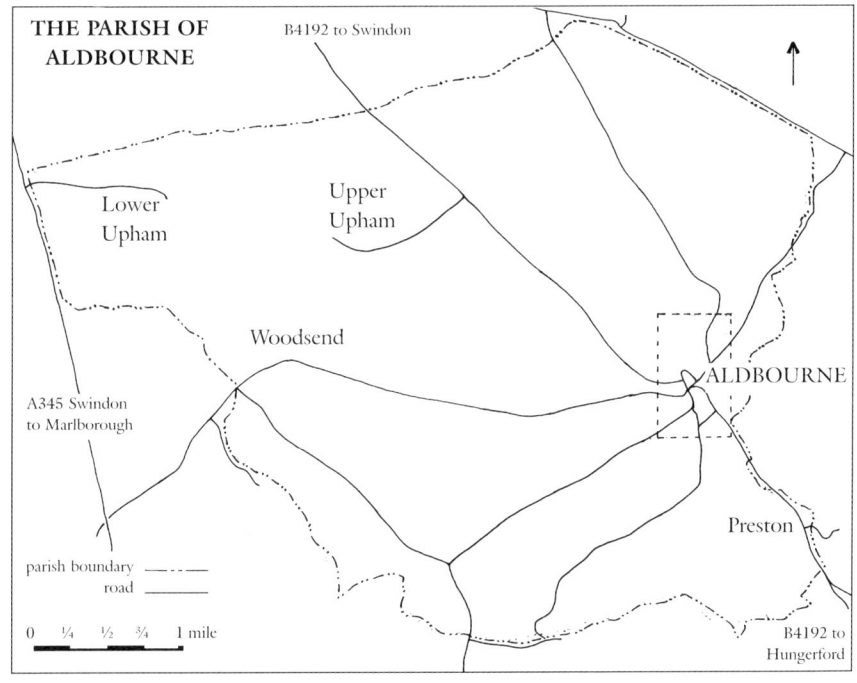

INTRODUCTION

We have reached the year 2000.

Some would have us believe that the new millennium actually begins next year. Yet Christians in our community rejoice that the occasion marks two thousand years of Christianity and additionally one thousand years of Christian worship here in Aldbourne.

Meanwhile many of us are also content to note that it is a year with several zeroes at the end of it – the opportunity for a celebration which reflects the past and embraces the future.

In 1997 the Memorial Hall Committee approached the Parish Council with a proposal to organize another Festival. This was agreed and the Aldbourne Millennium Festival Committee was formed. Ideas were sought from people in the parish as to how the millennium might be celebrated; one of the suggestions was to have a sort of Domesday Book. This project was offered to the Aldbourne Civic Society who formed a working party to take the idea further and then make it happen.

The book is by design a snapshot of the parish at the turn of the millennium. The words and pictures were compiled and collected during 1998 and 1999. We have checked and double-checked but nevertheless accept responsibility for any errors we have not spotted and trust we will be forgiven. Eventually the inevitable deadline arrived and we had to stop amending and start printing.

For convenience, we have divided the book into geographic areas which follow a clockwise sequence. The house drawings appear in a natural left-to-right sequence as they will be found in the roads and lanes of Aldbourne. The brief items in tinted boxes are scattered randomly throughout the book and can be located using the index. The boxes hold snippets of information gathered from many sources. Those items in quotation marks are taken verbatim from recently recorded reminiscences. A fuller account of this fascinating oral history and also a more complete buildings history are to be found in the archive of the Civic Society.

Over forty artists have produced drawings, over sixty writers have written articles and many others have helped with research, photography, proofreading and other areas of expertise. With regard to all contributions, the editors tried their best to change as little as possible. We are sure that those whose items may have been amended will understand.

Whilst we are particularly grateful to the publishing professionals who have been generous in their support, to our Working Party for their patience and hard work and to the Millennium Festival Committee and the Civic Society for their encouragement, it is the list of contributors which tells the real story.

In the last twenty-five years our numbers have grown by 25 per cent to about 1900 today. No doubt the population will continue to increase. We hope our evolving village will retain the character and spirit so vividly illustrated in these pages.

For the Millennium Book of Aldbourne is testament to a huge and immensely gratifying community effort. This truly is a book about the people of Aldbourne by the people of Aldbourne.

We trust you will enjoy it; we hope you will treasure it.

David Lee & Malcolm Shuttleworth
January 2000

Chapter One

The Square & The Green

The Square

Paul and Mary Swadling live at No 1, *Horbrook House*, with their three children Tamsin, Tory (Victoria) and Tom. Paul runs a business at Membury airfield, manufacturing and distributing specialized furniture. Mary works at Marlborough Medical Practice. They came to Aldbourne by accident; they were living in the Middle East and Paul's employers relocated their head office to Swindon.

Michael and Rosemary Cummings (and border collie rescue dog, Bess) rented their flat at No 2 *Smithfield* four years ago when a house sale fell through, and have never moved. They enjoy the view of the Square and love the beautiful countryside drives and walks with Bess.

After a long career in Southern Electric, Michael has come full circle – he was born on a farm in Berkshire and now shows prize-winning Sussex bulls all over the country.

Peter Thurston and Rachel Koktava are relative newcomers to the village, having moved into No 3 *Smithfield* during May 1999 with their cats Moo and Uemi. They both work in information technology for Lucent. Rachel has lived in the area for five years; she is originally from Northamptonshire. Peter is from Essex, although his parents are from Swindon, and legend has it that his great-great-grandfather was landlord of *The Crown*.

Margaret Wilson at No 4 *Smithfield* has lived in the village for over twenty years since she and her husband, a teacher, came to live at

Horbrook House *(1) Oxford Street*

> ### Stepping Stones
>
> "It used to be a natural pond fed by springs and it was much bigger than it is now. It extended right up to *Pond House*, across the car park and as far as the bus shelter.
>
> There were stepping stones across it near *Pond House* and across the open brook where the railings are now. Below this it flowed off down South Street. The cows drank from the pond so it used to get churned up. On VE night there was a big bonfire by the pond."

Chapter One

Glebe House. She has many friends in the village who share her enjoyment of the Church, Mothers' Union and trips to the theatre.

The Jarvis family moved to *The Old Manor* from London in March 1996. The family consists of parents Sally and John, two grown-up children, Samantha (twenty-six) and Jamie (twenty-four), and a late addition Daisy Tabitha aged six. Oh, and Rosie the family spaniel! Samantha (in fashion PR) married Mr Julian Birch (an IT specialist) in St Michael's Church, followed by festivities at *The Old Manor*, on 21 August 1999. They live in London, as does Jamie (in sports management and a keen sportsman himself). They all return to *The Old Manor* most weekends. A lively household! John and Sally are hopeful that the house will now stay in the family. Sally, a Londoner, is a retired publisher and a governor of St Michael's School. She is involved in many aspects of the community. John originated from Yorkshire and is a CBE and chairman of Jarvis Hotels plc. He is also chairman of The Prince's Trust – Action, an organization he has been involved with for twenty years. John is a director of United Racecourses and owns several horses himself. He also sits on the British Tourist Authority Board.

Linda Pryce has been running an accountancy practice at No 9 for over ten years, employing four people. Their local clients include farmers, professionals, solicitors and horse-racing people.

Jonathan and Suzanne Hill moved to *Toad Hall* in May 1997 at the time of their marriage. Jonathan came from Kent originally; he works at Harwell as a computer specialist. He is also seen in ALEC's dramatic productions. Suzanne was born in Nigeria and has lived in many places including Kuwait and the Isle of

2 & 3 Smithfield *The Square*

4 Smithfield *The Square*

> ### The Old Manor
>
> The Old Manor, formerly 'The Old Rectory' is one of two buildings in Aldbourne mentioned by Pevsner. It was owned for many years by the Neate family who leased the rectorial rights from the Dean and Chapter of Winchester. They were thus called the rectors, but the vicar was the parson and lived elsewhere. It has nine bays, of which the central five date from about 1740, the ones on the left probably from the early 19th century and the ones on the right from about 1900.
>
> A 20th century conservatory extends along much of the rear elevation. Ida Gandy said there were racing stables here in the early 1900s.

The Square & The Green

The Square

The pond once filled most of the Square; the road and bridge over the brook ran between the present *Ivy House* and *Bay House*. *Ivy House* dates back to the 18th century with later additions.

No 1, *Horbrook House*, was a bakery earlier in this century, later an electrician's. *The Crown Hotel* has been here since the early 18th century.

The premises occupied by the offices of Barnes Coaches, next door to the Post Office, was *The Bell Inn* until 1958, and a mounting block still stands on the pavement.

No 12 was once an iron foundry and agricultural engineering business owned by W T Loveday; the cast iron railings of No 3 are said to have been made by them. The premises subsequently became a petrol filling station and hardware store, but is now a private dwelling.

Pond House, formerly 'Smith's Forge', covered the whole block. At one time it belonged to James Wells, of the bell-foundry family, who had two furnaces for casting bells and other work. Part was pulled down for road widening in 1960.

The Old Manor *The Square*

CHAPTER ONE

9 & Toad Hall *(10) The Square*

> ### THE POST OFFICE
>
> The Post Office transferred to its present location at 13 The Square in 1986. It is classed as a sub-Post Office and is part of the general stores owned by Beverley and Ges Dolman. It covers a wide range of services: banking for Girobank, the Co-op, Lloyds TSB and the National Savings Bank; all Royal Mail and Parcelforce services; paying pensions and allowances; selling stamps, postal orders, Premium Bonds, TV, fishing and game licences and, more recently, foreign currency and insurance.
>
> Our Post Office continues to serve as community centre, meeting place for friends, ticket agency for village events, home to lost property and noticeboard. Bev and Ges find themselves acting as direction finders, announcers of local news and keepers of the village diary.

Yew Tree Cottage *(11) The Square*

12 The Square

— 10 —

> ### Barnes Coaches
>
> The company started in 1920 when the population of Aldbourne was 980. It was the latest in a long line of carriers run by men bearing familiar village names. Tommy and Ada Barnes began then with two carts and six horses on the site where the Barnes garage now stands.
>
> Barnes currently has twenty-three coaches operating including one used by Swindon Town Football Club. These are modern vehicles and well maintained. No longer do passengers have to be asked to get out and walk up steep hills, as happened in the early days of under-powered charabancs. Many of the memories of the locals include comments about the Barnes company which are always interesting, often funny and show the regard in which the company is held. This reputation is jealously guarded and is being maintained by the latest successors of Tommy and Ada Barnes headed by direct descendants of the founders.
>
> The backbone of the business remains private and contract hire but Barnes also offer package holiday coach tours with itineraries throughout the British Isles and on the continent, and regular trips to theatres and to shopping malls within 150 miles.
>
> A history of the company was produced in 1995 entitled 'From a Packet of Pins'.

13 & 14 The Square

Wight; she works for Lloyds TSB in Bristol. They share the house with a small tabby cat called Tigger.

Yew Tree Cottage has been the home of Andrew and Jill Hunter since 1994; they had already made many friends here through a crib team at *The Crown*. Andrew drives a car transporter, having previously spent many years in sales, and Jill is a lecturer in hairdressing and beauty at Swindon College. Andrew is also secretary of the Golf Society. They share their home with Rufus, who is a large friendly airedale, and a tabby cat called Oscar.

Daniel Lewis has lived at No 12 since May 1999 (along with a cat called Squiggles), although the house is owned by his parents, Peter and Daisy, who live in America. Daniel previously lived in Oxford, and his family are Welsh. He works in Hungerford for a contract car hire firm.

Ges and Bev Dolman took over the Post Office and Stores in April 1997 after Ges had spent many years in business, first in engineering in Leicester then with a hotel on Exmoor. They have been married for twenty-five years and have two children; Jackie is at Manchester University and Chris has just left school. They have liked the atmosphere of the village ever since they first arrived, and Ges is enjoying his role as a parish councillor.

Barnes Coaches next door have been running excursions and providing transport from their offices in the Square for most of the century.

Chapter One

15 The Square

16 The Square

Café in The Square

This was originally a grocery shop owned and managed by Mrs Louise Stacey who started the business in 1910. In 1943 her daughter, Mrs Alice Hale, took over and when she died suddenly in 1958 her son Richard carried on the business. In the 1980s there were further changes, Joan and Richard Hale opened a craft and gift shop in one section of the premises and in 1989 Terry and Beryl Gilligan started a health-food store with a tearoom. They also sold greengrocery and a range of specialist groceries. The shop closed in 1996, Joan expanded the craft shop and Rosemary Buckler took over the café. She had started a catering business (Bucklers Banquets) for weddings, parties and receptions and ran the two in tandem until 1998. She continues to run her catering business in a more modest way from her home in Cook Road.

Michael and Sue Palmer then moved the café into the front room and extended their opening hours. They offered a more comprehensive menu and took on the fish-and-chip business from West Street.

For a short time in 1998–9 Nicky Leigh ran a gallery in the old craft shop.

Stable House *The Square*

3 The Square

6 The Square

Butcher's Shop *(6a) The Square*

During 1998 and 1999 Mick and Sue Palmer ran 'Palmer's', the teashop, which also served all-day breakfasts and fish and chips. They are both long time residents of the village.

Paula Mander-Jones and her son Tom have lived in *Stable House* for over ten years. They came most recently from East Woodhay, near Newbury, although Paula spent some years in Costa Rica, where Tom was born. Tom was in the sixth form of Kingswood School, Bath. Their move to Aldbourne was a decision made when they happened to be visiting and found the house for sale.

The owners of No 3, James and Karen Oliver, work in London but spend as much time as they can in the village.

MEAT

In the 1930s the Humphries family ran the butcher's shop virtually from the present site when the building was a substantial house as well as a shop. This was demolished in the 1950s in a road widening scheme. *Smithfield House* in the Square then became the butcher's shop – a house with a slaughterhouse behind. It had been a butcher's for several generations, recently owned by Mr Arthur Liddiard, Mr Mayo and Mr Gilbert. Mr Bill Humphries bought the business and continued there until 1987 when *Smithfield House* was demolished.

The site was developed into a shop with a flat over and two houses: all are rented. Initially the shop became 'The Painted Thimble' selling fancy goods, embroidered fashions and haberdashery. It then became 'Hair in the Square', a hairdresser's. It is currently used as an office.

The present butcher's shop was re-erected on its original site. Mr May had been manager for several years at both premises and he bought the business in 1992, renting the property from the Humphries family.

Chapter One

Pond House *(4) The Square*

The Crown Hotel *The Square*

Shops in The Square

No 11 was a grocer's shop owned by Mrs Stacey. No 13 was originally owned by Charlie Barnes then by Joe Wilkins, Howard Gibbs, Terence Dyer and, now, Ges Dolman. The Post Office has now been subsumed into this business.

Other grocers were:– Mrs Wilson where 'Hair by Maxine' is now; at Stable House fronting onto the Square was Mrs Margery Barrett who also sold petrol; and Richard Hale where the café is now.

'Raffles' was previously a corn and seed shop, also selling animal feeds. Mrs Liddiard then made part of the premises into a knitting wool shop and haberdashery. Liddiards had the property as a DIY shop.

Pond House was a newsagent's also selling sweets and tobacco and was owned successively by Mr and Mrs Walls, Clive Hewlett, John Proctor, Kevin and Liz Brown, and is now 'Locketts' millinery.

Withy Barn *The Green*

Tony and Ann Swinmurn gave up their careers in Swindon to run *The Crown* with their two sons Mark and Paul (not to mention dogs Cassie and Scruffy and black cat Gizzie). It is a flourishing pub and two-star hotel. Tony coaches a boys' football team in the village.

Nicola Mann and Michael Landless moved to No 5 in June 1999; Nicola comes from Newbury and Michael has spent much of his life in Marlborough. They both work for Kerridge Computers in Newbury making systems for car dealerships. They enjoy the quiet atmosphere of the village and they fell in love with their house as soon as they saw it. They are planning to spend the millennium itself in Zimbabwe.

'Raffles' & Red Cottage *(2) The Green*

Jasmine Cottage *(3) & 4 The Green*

'Locketts' couture millinery was established at No 5a during 1999 offering sale and hire of hats and a 'hat hospital'.

Claire Stenhouse at No 5b moved into the village from Taunton in May 1999. She has been working as head gardener for the Ramsbury Estates in Axford for a year.

'Humphries', the butcher's shop at No 6a, is run by Francis May, who originates from Ramsbury. Janet his wife was born and brought up in Aldbourne. They lived in Lottage Road for over thirty years but have now moved to Stratton St Margaret. Francis originally worked in the old butcher's shop in the Square. Francis and Janet have two married children, Jerry and Katrina, and a grandson called Samuel.

The Green

How many are we and where?

Fifty-nine of us live in the twenty-seven houses on the Green. To be more precise fifty-nine of us have The Green as part of our address, which is not quite the same thing. Of the twenty-seven houses with this address only nineteen actually look out on the Green and their occupants alone have both this amenity and the address. Five others line the approach roads from the Square and three lie hidden from view in the lane which runs between *Vine Cottage* and *Wall Cottage*, so that unless you are persistent and curious you might easily

CHAPTER ONE

Bell Court (5) *The Green*   7 *The Green*

THE GREEN

The Green was given to the parish by the Brown family in 1892. In the 18th and early 19th centuries the whole area was known as High Town and that is now the name of the house in the south-east corner. There was once a regular market here and there may have been permanent houses. A market cross has stood here for centuries. The present No 11, now called *The Market House*, was apparently used as a market in 1700; with its neighbours it dates back in part to the 16th century. Most of today's buildings date from the late 18th or early 19th century; many have undergone several changes of use. 'Raffles' restaurant was previously a shop; Robert Wells started a bell foundry at *Bell Court* in 1760 and there was one at *Hightown* between about 1830 and 1858. The authors Gerald Brenan and Anne Duffield lived in *Bell Court* and No 10 respectively. *Wall Cottage*, first mentioned in 1703, was part of *Southby Farm*, which included *Hightown* and extended to the present Goddards Lane and the other side of Lottage Road. In 1860, when it was sold to a willow weaver, there was a shop, slaughterhouse, stable, and so on. In 1892 there was a reading room. In 1932 the house and the plot behind were bought by Dr Francis Camps, the famous forensic pathologist; part of the house was still a shop. The barns and stables of *Hightown* house were burnt down in 1921, when the fire engines Adam and Eve made their last appearance. The stables were rebuilt and J B Powell ran a very successful racing stable there until the 1970s. Two cottages on the south side, Nos 23 and 24, were an inn during the 18th century and were the Post Office for many years.

---

never discover the whereabouts of numbers 17, 18 and 18a.

Considering we live in the age of the computer we are not really very well organized. The house numbers run from 1 to 25, but this is not much of a guide. No 6 and No 13 have been absorbed and no longer exist; *Sarsen House*, one of the most recent additions to the buildings, has no number at all; *The Old Post Office*, meanwhile, has been sub-divided into 24a and 24b; and several others have been remodelled. Until recently there were no numbers, every house having a personal name which each new postman and commercial supplier was expected to master.

On the Green proper we have *The Market House*, *Bell Court*, *Vine House*, and so on, but surprisingly no 'Rose Cottage'. We must be one of the very few village centres not to have one. As compensation *The Market House* has a splendid display of the roses 'Danse de Feu' and 'Jacob's Coat'.

Housing Costs

A few of the deals in which Peter Ludlow was involved:

St Michael's Close was built on Hales Farm in West Street and the site was sold at auction to Messrs Leafields for £20,000.

The Police House at 25 Lottage Road sold for £750 in the early 1950s and recently went for a figure in excess of £125,000.

14 The Green was bought for £350. The old Fire Station was sold for £420 and is now the garage attached to No 15.

A syndicate sold land in Grasshills to Cowleys for the Cook Road development. They built sixty-eight houses which were priced from £2,750.

Farm land was purchased at Woodsend in 1937 for approximately £10 an acre. Currently the value is somewhere in the region of £3,000 an acre.

8 The Green

9 & 10 The Green

The Market House *(11)*, Chantry Cottage *(12)* & Corner Cottage *(14)* The Green

CHAPTER ONE

The Church Today

St Michael's Anglican Church, on the Green where it has stood for about 800 years, and the Methodist Church, situated more conveniently since 1985 in Lottage Road, are, at the turn of the millennium, memorials to the parish's 1,000 years of Christian history and centres of its Christian faith for the future, surviving because they are supported by the community and maintained for the benefit of all.

St Michael's, whose picturesque setting and architectural beauty attract attention, is primarily a place of Christian worship open all day and much visited. With neighbouring parishes it is part of the Whitton Benefice sharing a vicar with Baydon. Church affairs are run by the Parochial Church Council which annually finds over £40,000 to cover all expenses including a share of the vicar's stipend and maintenance of the fabric of the church. There are two services every Sunday, a communion service or matins, usually following the Book of Common Prayer, and at 11.00am the main service with a more contemporary liturgy. The congregations for both services average in all about 100 though festivals, weddings and funerals fill the church.

There is a peal of eight bells, rung by an enthusiastic team that welcomes youngsters; their practises on Friday evenings herald the weekend while the peal before the 11 o'clock service is the traditional call to worship. Church activity extends to midweek home groups, a youthful band and much pastoral work.

St Michael's Church *The Green*

Older residents, not surprisingly, feel that the village has lost some of its former social intimacy with people less inclined to greet each other than previously. On the other hand, newer arrivals find that it contrasts favourably in this respect in comparison with villages nearer London. At least one household stresses the fact that it is rare, perhaps unique, in having a village green through which there is not a main road with a constant stream of traffic.

We have not enquired too closely into the precise ages of the residents but it is clear that we include representatives from the whole of the normal human life span.

How many Dabchicks?

Being born in Aldbourne is a distinction. To most recent immigrants it seems self-evident that being a Dabchick means being old, or at least not young. This is a misconception; we have Dabchicks of many ages. Of the fifty-nine of us, eight only were born in the village. (Or were born to parents who lived in the village at the time. The actual birth may have taken place in a nearby hospital.) Philip Ludlow is one of the Dabchicks as is his sister Jackie Weedon. The others are Philip and Thea's children, Peter and Elizabeth; Harry and Maura Sheppard, and the two children of more recent arrivals, both still at school – Hannah and Lydia de Blangy.

Where else do we come from?

Other than the Dabchicks, our geographical origins are diverse.

John Loch was born in Paris and Chanterelle Jamieson in South Africa; but mostly we were born in other parts of Britain. Earlier

15 The Green

Buildings on the Site of the Church

There was probably a wooden church here before the Norman Conquest. The oldest parts of the present one date back to the 12th century, though most are from the 13th with many 15th century additions. It was dedicated to St Mary Magdalene – later changed to St Michael. It was heavily restored in the 1860s by the famous architect William Butterfield and has been refurbished more recently. Its history is recorded in a book by the late Frank West, Bishop of Taunton, who retired to Castle Street. There are several interesting memorials, to the Goddard and Walrond families among others. The pipe organ was taken down in 1995 and given to the cathedral in Lusaka, and a new electronic organ was installed in 1999 after extensive fundraising. Three of the eight fine bells were cast in the village.

generations of the de Blangy family were royalists who became émigrés around 1790 and never returned to France. Judy Hill, who comes from Weymouth, traces her ancestry back to Sir Francis Drake.

No fewer than eight of us – Marion Deuchar, Mary Bailey, John and Daphne Loch, Philip and Ann Duncan and John and Jean Coker have spent considerable periods of their working lives abroad.

Residence permits

The Green is essentially an area of recent settlement and of considerable movement. Each household occupies a separate dwelling. Not one has been in the same continuous occupation for the full lifetime of the existing householders. Philip Ludlow comes closest having been born in the village and not moved outside it, but he has lived in other houses.

Other Dabchicks, like Harry and Maura Sheppard, have moved away from the village at some time and then returned. Only one non-Dabchick arrived prior to the end of World War II – Nina McKeon who came in 1918. The next longest established residents are Marion Deuchar (1955), Susan Bailey and June Rawlings (both 1966), Terry and Judy Hill (1972) and John and Daphne Loch (1974).

> CHANTRY
>
> In the Middle Ages there was a chantry in the village charged with praying for the souls of the dead. There have been claims the priest lived variously on the site of the present *Chantry Cottage* or where *Hightown* is. The prayers were said in the Lady Chapel, added in the 15th century.
>
> There is a brass representation on the chancel floor commemorating the life of Henry Frekylton, chantry chaplain, who died in 1508.

16 The Green

Wall Cottage *The Green*

A further five families came during the 1980s and no fewer than twelve during the 1990s.

This preponderance of newcomers is not all that recent. Gerald Brenan, the writer and expert on Spanish politics, returned from supporting the government side in the Spanish Civil War and bought *Bell Court*. In his autobiography, 'Personal Record 1920–72', he writes, not very flatteringly, of neighbouring properties being

> cottages rebuilt in brick on a larger scale .... providing convenient homes for retired gentry, most of whom were either widows or spinsters.

Important people we have met

We are not conspicuous for our contacts with famous people.

However, Barbara Baker at No 8 has the rare distinction of having witnessed at first hand, while working in Berlin, the meeting of Hitler and Mussolini.

A distant echo of this event took place just before the start of World War II when Oswald Mosley who lived near Ramsbury sent his Blackshirts round the neighbouring villages. They were not on a threatening mission but delivering water to villagers, including those in Aldbourne, who were suffering from a desperate water shortage.

17, 18 & 18a The Green

19 The Green

Cycle Co

12 The Square was originally Aldbourne and District Cycle Co owned by Charles Alsop. He sold petrol and paraffin, ironmongery, hardware, DIY, cartridges, rabbit wires, cigarettes and condoms – strictly under the counter – as well as bicycles. He charged accumulators for the wireless and did cycle repairs. His motto which he proudly displayed for all to see was 'no repair too large, too small or impossible'.

Harold Herring worked there for forty years.

Chapter One

The Blue Boar *The Green*

Sarsen House *The Green*

> ### Books for Children
>
> In 1976 five friends got together to found the Aldbourne Children's Book Group – a member of a national charity. The Federation of Children's Book Groups is dedicated to bringing books and children together. Now the largest book group in the Federation with over a hundred members, the ACBG has brought many authors and illustrators to local schools as well as running a variety of book-related events for children and interested adults. The ACBG has long been a testing group for the Children's Book Award, one of the Federation's major projects. Over the years thousands of books have been donated to the local surgery, churches, the Women's Refuge in Swindon, Homestart, childminders and especially to local schools.

More user-friendly celebrities have visited the village in person. Evelyn Glennie gave a percussion recital and master class in the church in June 1991, and many sporting personalities have lunched at 'Raffles', including Glenn Hoddle, Steve Cauthen and the TV presenter David Vine. Johnny Morris, the radio and television personality, lived in The Square and there were frequent visits to 'Raffles' from his many acquaintances. Gerald Brenan lived in *Bell Court* for fifteen years from 1953. His many friends from the Bloomsbury Group visited the house and, among others, Dylan Thomas was a frequent visitor to *The Crown*. Diana Dors, who was originally from Swindon, and Hammond Innes also figure among the celebrity list.

The Blue Boar has had its own share of visiting celebrities including the actress Dame Judy Dench and the actor Nigel Havers.

Tinker, tailor, soldier, sailor .....

Our skills, occupations and interests vary a great deal. Most of us are busy but not all our work is paid. Of the total residents, twenty-seven still work full-time, two undertake serious and time-consuming voluntary work, twenty-one are non-active or retired and nine

Hightown *The Green*

21a The Green

are still at school. Non-active does not mean, of course, that they are not busy, merely that they receive no remuneration.

Harry Sheppard is a farmer working land near Marlborough. Philip Ludlow is a stocktaker, valuer and auditor for licensed premises and clubs.

Gill Reeve is a designer and artist. Peter de Blangy runs an interior design company operating mainly in Goring.

Beth Liptrot is a dentist working in Swindon. Mark Jamieson is an estate agent working in Pangbourne. Terry Hill is an electrician working in Swindon and Judy his wife also works in Swindon.

> ### Boar Trap
>
> There has been an inn since the 15th century where *The Blue Boar* now stands. You can still see an old manger with the original water trough for the horses which were once stabled there.
>
> A slightly macabre feature is a 'coffin trap'. At one time *The Blue Boar* was a lodging-house with elderly residents. A trapdoor was constructed so that coffins containing the deceased could be lowered from the first floor instead of having to negotiate the narrow staircase.

Chapter One

Beating the Bounds

At 8.00am on the first Monday in May a determined group gathers at the Cross on the Green. In the 1990s there were usually over 100 people representing a wide cross-section of the village plus a scattering of visitors. At the stroke of the clock and to the sound of the horn, the group commence a walk of some eighteen miles 'beating the bounds' of the parish of Aldbourne.

Doctor Trevor Tiplady and Commander Davies restarted this tradition in the 1960s and for many years Don Barnes led the walk. Permission is obtained from local landowners to traverse the sections of the route which do not lie on rights of way.

There is a lunch stop beyond Woodsend. The group usually meets those beating the bounds of Ramsbury Parish near Loves Lane and the journey ends on the Green at around 5.00pm. Those participants successfully completing the walk are given a ribbon – a much-prized possession.

23 & 24a The Green

James Hannan is chef-proprietor of 'Raffles' assisted by his wife Mary.

Until recently Bob and Jackie Weedon helped by their son Mark ran *The Blue Boar*. Now Mick and Jan Pattemore from Crewkerne have taken over and love the village.

Recent arrivals at *Hightown* are Tanya and Geoff Eccleston. Geoff is managing director of an electronics firm in Swindon.

Peter Liddiard, with his sons David and Patrick, designs and markets a variety of building components including an under-floor heating system. His wife Jennifer has a flower business supplying receptions and weddings.

David Carkett works in Bagshot for a property management company.

Hugh Thomas operates his own property development company in Pangbourne while his wife Sally runs an interior design company from her home. Philip Duncan runs a fine art publishing company in Cornwall.

Of course there is also unpaid work. There are two voluntary workers. Thea Ludlow puts in many hours a week for a Swindon women's help line and Willows Counselling Service. Anne Duncan sits as a magistrate on the Swindon Bench and is also a debt counsellor for Swindon Citizens' Advice Bureau.

John Loch is still chairman of the Aldbourne Housing Group which he helped to set up to provide housing at affordable rents.

Kenneth Baker is the secretary of Brendon Care.

John Coker is secretary of the Kennet National Association of Decorative and Fine Arts Societies (Kennet DFAS) and until recently

Schools

There were small schools in the village including one above the church porch.

However, the present church school was founded with a gift from the Brown family in 1857 and a subsequent government grant, and was built by Butterfield. An infants' school was added in 1873. Butterfield's building was replaced in 1966 and a new wing added in 1972. The original infants' school has recently been restored by members of the parish as the *Old Schoolroom*.

22 The Green

24a & **The Old Post Office** *(24b) The Green*

Dawn Cottage *(25) The Green*

was president of the Swindon Anglo-French Club.

What we did before we retired

Our former occupations are also varied. Susan Bailey taught in the village school for twenty-five years and consequently knows the virtues and failings of most people in the village. She also served as a parish councillor for twenty-five years. Her sister Mary was a teacher too, but also worked in the Allied Control Commission in Germany for seven years from 1966.

With her husband, Nina McKeon established Aldbourne Engineering which offered motor and agricultural machinery service and repairs for many years. It closed in 1996. John Loch was in the Colonial Service and he and Daphne spent ten years in Malaya during the emergency. He also served on the Parish Council for seven years. John has written his autobiography, 'My First Alphabet', a copy of which is in the village library.

Marion Deuchar's husband David, who died in 1998, was a Royal Marine Commando. They lived in Malaya and Malta where he was on service. He was briefly, despite a modest rank, the senior allied officer overseeing the Japanese surrender in Japan in 1945. The Duncans also spent ten years in the Far East, in Singapore and Hong Kong, during which time Philip was managing director of Castrol Far East. Kenneth Baker was managing director of a steel products company.

Chapter One

Martin Smith worked in the research department of British Coal as a physical chemist. John Gasking worked as an electronic engineer and information technology expert and Fiona was in a solicitor's office.

June Rawlings was a nursery teacher. John and Jean Coker spent twenty years in Brussels after an initial two-year secondment by ICI. After leaving ICI John was on the staff of the European Commission for eleven years.

Where do we think we are?

With the wider ownership of cars the village has attracted many people who travel into Marlborough, Hungerford and Swindon each day to work. The building of the M4 motorway has occasioned a major extension of this working area.

Of the residents who work, most drive into these towns or operate from the village as a

---

THE COURT HOUSE

In about 1365 John of Gaunt hunted in Aldbourne Chase and is said to have come down to *The Court House* for his bath, as there was good sweet well water. In the 16th century it was occupied by tenants of the demesne farm. Thomas Bond bought the house when he acquired the manor of Aldbourne in 1631. In 1694 William and Robert Corr started the manufacture of bells and wooden buttons here, the beginning of an industry associated with Aldbourne for nearly three centuries. John Starrs and Edward Read took it over in 1713 until Read went bankrupt in 1762. It was the vicarage between 1806 and 1956.

The central part of the house dates back to the 16th century. It has thick walls of flint and chalkstone with stone mullioned windows. Additions in diaper brick were made on the east side in the 18th century, and the east façade was made approximately symmetrical and rendered in stucco. Further extensions were made on the west side during the 19th century, and the north side was rendered. The roofs are tiled. The carriage house and stables are 18th century, built of sarsen and chalkstone with a clock tower, although the roof is a 20th century replacement.

The Court House *Crooked Corner*

1 Grasshills

2 Grasshills

> ### BLACK MARKET
>
> "Petrol was rationed but my father had an extra allowance because he worked at an armaments factory in Swindon. There was a black market in petrol – some of it obtained from the Americans. A friend of my mother had some in her garage but heard the local police were checking. 'Bring it up here' said my mum, 'we'll put it in the kitchen and cover it with a carpet'. Later that evening three US officers arrived to visit one of mummy's evacuees. They sat on the carpet covering the petrol cans and I can remember mummy saying after they had gone that they had no idea what they were sitting on. I asked what would have happened if someone had smelt gasoline?"

base for the local area. It is a comment on the supremacy of the car in the year 2000 that four breadwinners travel to Pangbourne, Goring, Bagshot and Liskeard and still consider Aldbourne 'convenient'.

What we do in our spare time

As a member of the MCC Kenneth Baker naturally follows cricket enthusiastically and enjoys the not-too-frequent England successes. Most of us have gardens and tend them with greater or lesser enthusiasm and expertise. The Gaskings play golf, as do Philip Duncan and John Coker who also paints. The Lochs, Bakers and the Cokers are members of the Kennet DFAS. Gill Reeve plays the classical guitar and Philip Duncan plays jazz on the banjo.

Grasshills & Crooked Corner

This group includes a wide variety of buildings ranging in age from over six hundred years (*The Court House*) to less than twenty. The family backgrounds, occupations and interests of the people who live here are equally varied thus contributing to the lively atmosphere of the village. There are roughly equal numbers of Dabchicks and incomer families.

The Court House is now the home of the Fitch family. Janet is a writer, journalist, jewellery retailer, prison visitor and a board member of the Crafts Council and the Royal Academy. Rodney Fitch CBE is a designer, a trustee of the Victoria and Albert Museum, deputy chairman of the London Institute and a Swindon Town FC season ticket holder. They have five children – a psychologist, a fashion

Chapter One

3 Grasshills

4 Grasshills

stylist, a sculptor, a jewellery designer and a student of medieval history.

Grasshills

Cecil and Joy Newton have spent over forty years at No 1 which has superb views in all directions. The top end of their garden is now a mature woodland which they planted years ago and contains at least ten different species of trees mostly native to Britain. A retired quantity surveyor, Cecil paints, plays the piano and cycles. He instigated the Aldbourne Civic Society in 1970. Joy is a retired nurse. Botany is her main hobby; she is a founder of the Wiltshire Botanical Society and contributed to the book 'Wiltshire Flora' published in 1993. She is one of four founder members of the Aldbourne Children's Book Group.

At No 2 Marion Bradley, née Jerram, has lived in Aldbourne all her life. She worked for the village postmistress throughout World War II and then with her husband Tom ran the Post Office, then at 24 The Green, for twenty-four years. She has a wealth of memories of the village, its inhabitants and events including parties on the Green, and how, when she was a small girl, her school class sang while the pink chestnut tree was planted by the Pond.

Robert and Janet Todd live at No 3 with an anti-social cat, Weasel. They have used a lot of energy adapting the house and garden to suit their needs. Robert's job as a fishing vessel inspector has taken him all over the world including the Falkland Islands, South America and China. His main interest is motor racing, particularly TVR sports cars. Janet was a conveyancing and building society clerk; she is a member of the WI and enjoys swimming,

Five Gables *(5) Grasshills*

6 Grasshills

walking and reading. Their three children and four grandchildren are frequent visitors.

Until recently Peter and Anne Sullivan lived at No 4. He is an accountant and has audited the accounts of many local organizations as well as helping with the Carnival. Anne spent many years as a warden on the Wiltshire section of the Ridgeway National Trail and also worked on the WI village map located in the Memorial Hall. They have two sons and two daughters.

The Wyatt family live at *Five Gables*. James, Christopher and Claire all attend St Michael's School and are variously involved in Scouts, Cubs, Brownies, football and rugby.

Michael, a civil engineer, and Katherine Ward lived at No 6 until recently with their daughters Laura, Elizabeth, Grace and Maryanne. Having returned from a contract in India, Michael worked on a project to develop Bournemouth pier. Katherine ran the 'Mini Mart' in West Street selling fruit and vegetables, hardware, and so on. She had previously been the organizer of the Drop-in Centre and then the resident warden of the Priory sheltered accommodation centre, both in Marlborough. Daughter Maryanne was Aldbourne Carnival Queen in 1998 and Elizabeth and Grace have

MONUMENTS AND TREES

Cecil Newton surveyed the archaeological monuments in the parish and prepared a report for the Department of the Environment and the County Council to create a permanent record.

Eleven survivors of the original twenty-two barrows are now protected and farmers are paid a recompense for not ploughing them up.

Cecil also completed a land usage map and carried out a tree survey.

Willowbank *(7) Grasshills*

Chapter One

Hillside *(8) Grasshills*

Rivendell *(9) Grasshills*

Crooked Corner

In 1631 Thomas Bond bought the Manor of Aldbourne, which included *The Court House* and some neighbouring cottages on the north east corner of the Green. In 1773 a cottage, a barn, a stable, a garden and a close of land here were sold to Richard Crook of Aldbourne.

At present a row of six cottages stand here. No 2 is mostly 18th century, the rest are 19th, but all have 20th century alterations and additions. They are built of sarsen and brick with tiled roofs. Some modern buildings stand behind. In 1617 there is reference to a 'Grazells Inn' being hereabouts although no supporting evidence has been found. It is thought it may have been associated with the malthouse that was at *Beech Knoll House*.

Beech Cottage *Crooked Corner*

Beech Knoll Cottage *Grasshills*

Beech Knoll House *Grasshills*

> ### Beech Knoll House
>
> A malt-house is known to have been here in 1820. The present house was apparently built between about 1820 and 1840, of diaper brick with wide eaves and a hipped slate roof. An extension meets the 19th century coach house, which is also built of brick with a slate roof, a clock tower and weather vane, and has been converted as a dwelling. A conservatory was added at the back in 1998. There is a swimming pool and the wall along the roadside is listed as of interest.
>
> The land originally extended down to Lottage Road. It was scheduled for redevelopment by the County Council in 1961 and has been built on since to form The Knoll.

been Carnival Princesses. Their hobbies include pigeon shooting (Michael), Guides and Brownies and coping with two dogs, two birds and three cats.

Hugh and Sue Humphreys, who in 1999 took over ownership of *The Masons Arms*, have lived at No 7 since 1992 with children Stephen and Laura. Hugh works for Vodaphone in Newbury and Sue for Thames Water in Swindon. Stephen is studying maths at Cardiff University and Laura hopes to do a college course in sports studies.

At No 8 are Alan and Ann Scutt who enjoy photography, painting, reading, swimming and walking. Their sheltie enjoys some of these activities. Alan is a retired civil engineer who spent most of his career on marine projects and a lot of time overseas. He is a former chairman of the Civic Society and helped in a land-use survey for Wiltshire County Council. Ann was secretary to a regional general manager of Barclays Bank before moving to Aldbourne. She is now a member of the WI and a fundraiser for Prospect Hospice.

CHAPTER ONE

Deacons Knoll *Crooked Corner*

Haydon Way *(7) Crooked Corner*

Graham and Karen Cook live at No 9. He is a civil engineer and his work has occasionally taken the family abroad. Karen has raised a great deal of money from jumble sales over the years for local organizations. They have one son, Nathan, and two daughters, Natalie and Tabitha who is the youngest and still at school, plus two dogs and a cat. The family's main hobby is bell-ringing but golf and ALEC are also on the agenda.

Paul and Kim Niblock moved to the village to *Beech Cottage* in 1997. Their two daughters Rosie and Grace attend the village school. Paul is a copywriter and Kim an osteopath. They are keen gardeners. Some years ago they spent twelve months going round the world. *Beech Knoll Cottage* is occupied by a teacher, Sheila Evans, and 'Benjamin Bunny'.

Joan and Richard Price live at *Beech Knoll House*. They first lived at *Duck Cottage* (1964–86) and brought their parents to the village. The Silks came in 1968 to Hungerford Road and the Prices arrived in 1973 to live at *Chalice Lodge*. Their son has a diploma in music recording and technology and is an information technology consultant; their daughter, who has learning difficulties, now lives with the Home Farm Trust, a sheltered community. Joan is a graduate of the Royal College of Art, Fashion School and became merchandise manager of Peter Jones and Liberty's, then bought for Harrods and is now retired. Richard is a television producer and distributor. He is a

---

ZEPPELINS OVERHEAD

"During World War I there were no air raids in Aldbourne and people continued to live a normal life, buying eggs, milk, butter, and so on. It was a tremendous treat to escape from London and the German 'stink bombs' the smell from which permeated through the chimneys to the open fireplaces until the dampers were shut off.

I remember my mother wrapping us children in blankets and taking us outside to see the Zeppelins going over."

Candlemas Cottage *(6) Crooked Corner*

Fellow of the Royal Television Society (RTS) and former chairman of the British Academy of Film and Television Arts (BAFTA). He has twice run for parliament, is vice-chairman of the Home Farm Trust, a board member of the Watermill Theatre at Newbury and a trustee of the Aldbourne Band.

Crooked Corner

Olive Deacon lives at No 8; her late husband, a Dabchick, was a builder. She attends the Methodist Church, loves gardening and enjoys the church fête, the carnival and the band events.

Richard and Claire Thorne live at No 7 with baby daughter Molly and a retriever. Richard is a scientist specializing in water research and river pollution; Claire is a medical researcher at the Institute of Child Health. Hobbies include world travel and cycling.

Dennis Hunt and his wife Janet live at No 5 and have two Dabchick daughters, Nicola and Joanna. Dennis made the weathercock on the church to replace the one rumoured to have been used by the Americans for target practice during World War II. Jan has worked for many years as an assistant at St Michael's School and as a collector for Christian Aid and other charities.

Next door to Dennis at No 4 are his brother David, and Mary; they also have two Dabchick daughters, Louise and Lorraine. They have many memories of sheep and cattle being driven past the house and of village events including the filming of an episode of the TV series 'Dr Who'.

Mark and Yvette Hennessy moved to No 2 in 1991. They walked the few yards to St Michael's Church for their wedding. They have three toddlers, Hannah, Kate and Harry, and a cat. The house has views over the Green and a lovely homely feel. Mark is a marketing manager with an airline ticket company.

Philip and Tracey Braney live at No 1 which they have extended since moving here in 1994. They have two children of school age, Natalie and Greg.

5, 4, 3 & 2 Crooked Corner

1 Crooked Corner

Chapter One

The Churchyard

The immediate surroundings of St Michael's Church are part of the parish's greatly appreciated heritage. The church, standing above the Green and surrounded by verdancy is admired, painted, photographed and visited. Burials continue in the churchyard, ashes are deposited and several generations of graves are tended. Parishioners use the path for a shortcut between Crooked Corner and Back Lane, people sit on the benches enjoying the views and tranquillity, and children play there after school. The constant to-ing and fro-ing of people and the fresh flowers on the graves give life and beauty to the place and, of course, solace to the bereaved.

The churchyard is cared for by those tending graves and also by volunteers, not all members of the congregation, who mow, weed, cut hedges and clear up. The immediate surroundings are short mown but the rest is mown once or twice a year allowing nature to flourish. Under the benevolent, conserving and perceptive influence of Susan Bailey the churchyard has become a wildlife area. Apart from a few bulbs and some seeds of local downland yellow rattle no seeds or plants have been introduced; all were lying dormant under frequent mowing, but now, and gradually, different species have appeared.

In spring primroses, preceded by snowdrops, are followed by buttercups, mainly creeping or meadow, but for the first time Goldilocks buttercup has established itself. In early summer ladies smock and several patches of meadow saxifrage and bugle are seen. In mid- and late summer mainly downland flowers, for example, lady's bedstraw, knapweed, moon-daisies, self heal, mouse-eared and ordinary hawkweed, appear followed by patches of harebells.

Hedgehogs are increasing and there are voles and bats, frogs and slow-worms. There are lots of butterflies – gatekeepers, meadow browns, tortoiseshells, and a few holly blues, small blues, brimstones and red admirals.

Table Tennis

When Roy and Gwen Hazell, both experienced players, came to Aldbourne from Swindon, they were contacted by Richard Palmer who wanted to establish table tennis in the village.

In August 1987 the Club was founded and Roy was elected chairman. The clubhouse was a wooden building and used for coaching and practise. The two teams entered in the Thamesdown League played matches in the Methodist Hall. In this first season the 'A' Team comprising Roy, Richard and Richard Eldridge won Division Four, and Richard and Karenza Palmer and Philip Comley all won titles. The next season John Proctor, Richard Palmer and Karenza all won titles and Richard Eldridge was a finalist.

In 1989 an all-ladies team entered the League and have continued to date. The junior members increased to thirteen and, as Thamesdown had started an official Junior League, three teams were entered to play. Steven Littler won the Under-twelve title in this first season and Nicholas Butler won the title the next year.

In 1994–5 the 'B' Team of Don Webb, Richard and Richard won their division and are now playing in Division Two. Several of the juniors have stayed and are playing in the senior teams and membership remains at about twenty.

The aims set out in 1987 have been achieved: to establish and maintain a Table Tennis Club for the enjoyment of its members, to enter teams in the league, and to ensure that the game is played in the right spirit of friendship and sportsmanship.

Chapter Two

Up & Down Lottage Road

Methodist Church *Lottage Road*

Methodist Church

As an integral part of the Newbury and Hungerford Circuit of Methodist Churches, we currently benefit from the leadership of a lay worker who is a member of staff. Annual expenses of £17,000 represent our share in work locally and nationally.

There are two services on Sundays, with a total average congregation of fifty. Other services and meetings are held throughout the week for young people as well as others. Indeed the new premises were built with the community in mind and are heavily used by people of various age groups and organizations, as well as for civic needs, for example as a polling station.

Members of the churches in the village are working together increasingly in church affairs and in the community at large – as expressed in our covenant of January 1999.

Chapter Two

1 Lottage Road

Shane's View

"A quiet village environment is not one that the younger generation is likely to appreciate. We look to towns and cities for opportunity and enjoyment and the standard response when talking to a teenager about the village is 'its boring'. We tend to overlook the beauty and tranquillity because we are eager to get out and experience life. As one person said; 'it's great for families with young children and older people but there isn't a lot for you'. And I'm nineteen years old.

It's nice however to walk down the road and be recognized and greeted; the community spirit is appreciated and you feel welcome. No one is interested in who you are in a city.

Long term I don't think many of us can remain here. There is too much to see and do in the world but I also think that because our friends and childhood memories are here at some stage we will return – to visit or settle as our parents have.

In the future I think it's important that the village remains for the most part unchanged. It would be devastating to return in twenty years and find the bus shelter gone or the football field covered in houses. I'm not averse to technology, mobile phone towers for example, but I think that Aldbourne should remain a quiet village community so that future generations will have somewhere to be 'bored' and remember the place in which they grew up."

3, Spragnells (5), 7, 9 & Ill Quattus Dar (11) Lottage Road

Lottage Road

To The Knoll

No 1 Lottage Road was home to Simon and Sandra who moved to Aldbourne from Windsor in 1997. Simon, formerly from Zimbabwe, is an airline pilot whose interests include cycling and fishing. Sandra was born in Assam, India and is an airline stewardess and likes walking. Both Simon and Sandra are avid readers. Baby daughter Devon Acacia was born in July 1998. They left in 1999.

Michael Clifford Nicholls, better known to all as 'Nicky James', and Martine moved from London in 1973 into No 3 where Fred Teagle used to make coconut matting and baskets. Nick and Martine have two children, Samantha, twenty-five, and Louis, eleven. Nick's interests are, of course, musical and he has converted part of the property into a studio where he does his writing.

Kirstie and Chris Rodgers have lived in *Spragnells* since 1997. They came to Aldbourne from Winkfield Row near Ascot. Chris is from Wootton Bassett and works as a forecaster for the National Grid. His interest is sailing. Kirstie is a teacher and former editor of the BBC's *Home & Antiques* magazine.

No 7 has been home to Bill and Olive Stacey for forty-eight years. Bill is a local man having spent all of his life in the village – with the exception of five years as a 'Bevin Boy' in the mines during the war years. A bricklayer by trade and an Aldbourne footballer for many years, Bill can be seen at the local games every Saturday. Olive is from Chilton Foliat and was a 'lollipop lady'. She enjoys her weekly visits to the club to play bingo. They have three children; Tony lives in Swindon, Susan is also in Swindon and Andrew lives next door.

Andrew played football for Aldbourne for many years and married Louise, formerly from Cirencester, in 1990. She is a community care worker. Andrew is in the building trade. They have spent the last few years doing much renovation work on their home, No 11.

No 21 is home to Neil, Monica and Shane Moreton. Neil moved to Aldbourne in 1962 and is a director of Continental Polymers,

ALDBOURNE DYNASTIES

Village families who were here prior to 1830, an arbitrary date, we can describe as the Aldbourne dynasties – outstanding and influential citizens of ancient local lineage.

The most ancient line with continual presence in the parish is the Wentworth family of Ewin's Hill. Guy Wentworth and his son Jonathan (born 1991) are direct descendants of Peter Wentworth who came to Aldbourne in the 1640s.

William Brown of *The Manor House* and his elder son William Henry, born 1991, are direct descendants of the first recorded William Brown (1767–1833). Incidentally, in all that time their doctors have been several generations of the Maurice family of Marlborough.

Daniel Cook's family have lived here since the early 19th century and his descendant Terry Gilligan and his son Richard (born 1976) still live in Cook Road.

William Read lived at *Warren Farm* (died 1801) with his wife Grace (née Bunce). Their great grandson Richard Read was connected with the chair making industry set up in the village. Their direct descendant is Graham Mildenhall (born 1965) of Southward Lane Farm.

A member of another old village family is Harry Sheppard and his son James, born 1962, direct descendants of Henry Brind (born 1742).

There are also a number of other dynasties who have been almost as long established: for instance the Barnes, Liddiard, Palmer and Jerram families, to name but a few.

And finally those great 15th century benefactors of the church, the Goddards of Upham, have direct descendants living in the village – Mrs Camilla Sheppard (née Goddard) and her children, James Stuart (born 1988) and his sister Elizabeth May.

Long may these ancient dynasties continue to live and flourish among us.

travelling world-wide. He is a keen motorcyclist and a founder member of the Honda Owners Club. Monica moved here in 1954, working for Allied Dunbar for twenty-six years. She runs Aldbourne Guides having joined the movement at the age of thirteen, and has been a stalwart of the Carnival committee for ten years. Shane, their daughter, was born at Savernake Hospital in 1979 and is studying for a degree in packaging design. Her four grandparents live in the village – their total age 331!

Peter and Maggie Grant moved to Goddards Lane in 1991 and to No 23 in January 1998. Peter was born in Chippenham but lived at Russley Park where his great-grandfather Sonny Hall trained racehorses. He works for Siebel Systems. Maggie is from Swindon, although born in Australia, and worked for Nationwide for eight years. They have two children, William, seven, and Josephine, five. Maggie is interested in tennis and Peter plays cricket and rugby and he is a founder member of both village clubs.

John and Felicity Fraser have lived in Aldbourne since 1993. Their daughter Annabelle is at university and their son James is training to be a chartered accountant. Family interests include horse racing, classic cars, art, cinema, history and travel. They live at No 25.

David and Victoria Parmiter moved to No 27 from London in 1996. They have two children, Amelia, four years, and Molly, a genuine Dabchick, born in Aldbourne in May 1998.

RECORD BREAKERS

Back in January 1978 the Aldbourne Band undertook a marathon 'blow-in'; one purpose was to become record breakers and the other was to raise £1,000 to help buy new uniforms.

The players were to perform in shifts; each brought with them their favourite breakfast ingredients which were stored in separate named bags. A small group of ladies volunteered to stay all night to make drinks and then to cook the breakfasts as each group completed their shift. From about 6.00am we proceeded to cook bacon, eggs, sausages, tomatoes, bread and some also had beans. We had several frying pans on the go and were sometimes worried that we might mix up some of the meals but all went well.

Those of us who had cooked early went home to snatch a little sleep and were replaced by a fresh group of helpers who supplied cups of tea and sandwiches during the day.

Eventually in the early evening the 'blow-in' was completed with a rousing rendition of the Floral Dance. The Band had created a new record with thirty hours of continuous playing.

21 Lottage Road

23 Lottage Road

Victoria enjoys walking and horse riding while David, who is a photographer, enjoys cycling and is interested in old cars and music..

No 29, the home of Peter Boaden and Kerstin Schiff, was a dairy and hayloft before conversion. It was known as 'Stone Cottage' but is now *Kays Cottage*. Peter, who is in engineering sales, came to Aldbourne from Pewsey in 1984 and moved into No 29 in 1986. His interests are walking, music, art and architecture and he is the chairman of the Carnival committee with six years service. Kerstin is from Detmold, Germany, and came to Aldbourne in May 1997; she likes the village and the way things are done here very much. Kerstin is a sales co-ordinator for Raychem and is interested in travel and dancing.

25 Lottage Road

27 Lottage Road

Kays Cottage *(29) Lottage Road*

LUTWYK?

The name 'Lottage' is said to be a corruption of 'Lutwyk' and was in use by the mid-13th century. No 1, formerly a pair, is 17th to 18th century with later additions. The Methodist Church and Hall were built in 1986 to replace an earlier chapel. Nos 7, 9 and 11 also date from the 17th to 18th century. *Kays Cottage*, formerly a farmhouse, is thought to have originated as a single storey house in the 17th century, being raised to two storeys in the 18th century. No 39, *Foundry Cottage*, is part late 17th century. The former council cottages were built in the 1950s.

The first two cottages on the east of the road, formerly *Chadwell Cottages*, were once three – with a well. They were owned for many years by Miss Palmer, 'Aunt Nell', who died at a great age and is still remembered.

Chapter Two

Redston is the home of Trish and Dave Rushen. They came to Aldbourne in 1979 to 25 Lottage Road and built their present house in 1987–8 with materials, including a complete staircase, from Ramsbury School. Dave originates from Ramsbury and Trish from Middlesex. Their daughter Susan lives in Devizes and has two children, James and Stephanie. Dave's interests are horse racing, cricket and football (at Ramsbury though). Trish is the local librarian and is a well-known member of both the WI and ALEC with many fine acting performances to her credit.

The four semi-detached three-bedroom houses 31–37 Lottage Road were built in 1935 by Richard Stacey on farmland that he owned. They stand where the barn and stables once were. Water was pumped from a well into a tank in the scullery and then piped to taps over the sink and bath – an innovation in those days.

No 31 is the home of Kevin Whittle and Fiona Greaves. Kevin, who is commercial director of Rutpen Ltd at Membury with responsibility for specialist fuels, was born in Reading and moved to Aldbourne in 1984. His hobbies are model making and creating multi-user games for the Internet. Fiona was born in New Zealand and settled in Aldbourne in 1974. She has a degree in Law and in 1993 set up a safety management consultancy. Both do voluntary work for NCH Action for Children and are practising Christians.

Ron and Marion Hacker moved into No 33 in 1975 after a spell in Australia. Ron is a Dabchick, born in Lottage Road, and Marion is from Liddington. They met in 1958 and married in 1960; they have three daughters Susan, Diane and Anne, and three granddaughters Ellen, Vikki and Natalie. Both Ron and Marion enjoy walking and skiing. Marion is a member of the WI and also reads a lot.

No 35 is the home of Graham and Rachel Browning and their family. Graham, who worked as an HGV mechanic, is from Ramsbury and is an Assistant Scout Leader. Rachel is a part-time mature student, Rainbow Guider and member of the Methodist Church. Mickey is a Lackham College student working towards a career in agriculture. Stephanie, who plays the piano, enjoys drama and has been Carnival Queen attendant. Justine enjoys Brownies and drama.

Next door at No 37 are Rachel's parents, Jim and Molly Cullis. Jim was a London wartime evacuee to Swindon. Having retired from teaching Jim's hobbies include walking, gardening and DIY. Molly was born locally, working for some years with a Ramsbury solicitor. She enjoys cooking, knitting, reading, crosswords and nomograms and is a member of several village societies. Jim and Molly have three daughters: Lindsay who has a City and Guilds librarian qualification, Rachel who is a part-time mature student and Helen who, at the age of twelve, was seventh in the National Age Groups Swimming Championships and now teaches swimming. They have seven grandchildren.

Farming in Aldbourne Parish

The parish consists of 8,502 acres of predominantly chalk-based average quality (grades 3 and 4) soil. Fourteen or so farms make up the whole parish with an average size of 560 acres. Only one farm is tenanted, the rest are owner-occupied or farmed in various forms of joint ventures; five farms account for the lion's share of the parish. As the labour force has declined their houses have become available to others and now form a large part of the rented housing stock. The capital cost of farming is now very large, arable land being about £2,000 an acre, and a large combine harvester will set the owner back about £200,000 while a small 80hp tractor costs £20,000.

Very little of the food produced in the parish is actually consumed here. Co-operative marketing of grain, milk, and livestock is strong in the area and is the first part of the chain that goes on to the six multiple retailers who sell 80 per cent of our food.

Businesses in Lottage Road Today

The whole site is owned by Pat Matthews, a builder and construction engineer, who uses the site for storing building materials. Three other companies are based there.

QED is a picture framer's dealing mainly with commercial framing. It is owned and managed by Nick Leigh who lives in West Street, and Andy Halsey from near Pewsey. They have eleven employees.

NDS (Neil and Debbie Services) is a motor repair centre owned and managed by Neil O'Riordan and employs four people.

Gilomatics supplies and manages entertainment machines for clubs and pubs. It was founded by Tony Gilligan and continues to be managed by his son Sean. There are seven employees.

Redston *Lottage Road*

31, 33, 35 & 37 Lottage Road

CHAPTER TWO

BOMBS

"We heard a German plane go over and then we felt a terrible shaking and we learnt that seven bombs had been dropped on Russley.

My mother used to do the washing for the American soldiers and after the war she had lovely letters from their mothers thanking her for looking after their sons. We didn't keep the letters.

The Americans were very generous with sweets for the children."

From The Knoll to Alma Road

The four semi-detached three-bedroom houses at 47–53 Lottage Road were built in 1947 by Charlie Stacey on land which was previously part of Lottage Farm and were acquired by Marlborough and Ramsbury RDC as council houses. They were offered for private sale in the mid-1980s. Each has a very long garden both front and back.

No 47 is the home of Neilson and Rosie Pearse. Neilson is a Dabchick whose father moved to Aldbourne from Bishopstone with Major Powell's racing establishment. Neilson worked as a carpenter for a local builder before setting up in partnership with Ron Hacker in the early 1970s. Rosie is from Ramsbury and works in the local grocery store. They have two children, John who also lives in Lottage Road, and Beverley who lives in Swindon, and three grandchildren.

Raymond Edwards and his parents came to No 49 in 1948 having moved from London to Woodsend in 1941 to escape the bombing. Raymond's father Percy worked as a shoe-repairer in the village. Raymond himself began work by delivering milk for Chris Hawkins and then worked for almost fifty years for three generations of the Hale family at Baydon Hill Farm. He enjoys spending

Foundry Cottage *(39) Lottage Road*

43 Lottage Road

evenings at the Sports and Social Club. Raymond's aunt, Edith Taylor, now keeps house for him.

Yusaf and Sally Saeedich came to Wiltshire from Northamptonshire moving to No 51 in 1993. They have two sons, the elder moved to Bristol to work after graduating from university, the younger is in his second year at university. In the back garden is a very large conifer planted as a Christmas tree in the early 1950s.

Alan and Madeline Gansert moved from Croxley Green to No 53 in 1989 in search of a more rural way of life. Alan worked in the ambulance service for nineteen years and has just finished four years training in homeopathic medicine. His main interests are railways, dowsing and occasional bell-ringing. Madeline works as a catering assistant in Stones Vegetarian Restaurant at Avebury and is also a qualified reflexologist. Her interests are dowsing and wildlife. Both Alan and Madeline are spiritually aware and are healers. They have two children, Carolyn and James. Carolyn works for W Liddiard Ltd at Baydon, is interested in horse-riding, badminton and socializing and is involved with the Youth Club and Beavers. James is still at school where he plays football for the school team and also enjoys computer games.

Sarsen Rise *(45) Lottage Road*

47 & 49 Lottage Road

> ### THE FOUNDRY SITE
>
> The site was previously a foundry owned by Mr Loveday and some of his castings (manhole covers, railings, and so on) can be seen in the village today. The unoccupied house on the site burned down in 1966. Mr W E Stock continued the business and developed it into an agricultural engineers. Donald McKeon had worked for Mr Stock and took over in 1943. He changed the business to Aldbourne Engineering Co doing motor repairs and selling petrol. The business was moved to West Street which was at the rear of his house on The Green and adjoined *Oak House* and a shop owned by his wife.

51 & 53 Lottage Road

Chapter Two

55 & **Ringside** *(57) Lottage Road*

Meadowcroft *(59) Lottage Road*

> ### Mail
>
> The Royal Mail make two collections a day, mid-morning and mid-afternoon from five postboxes at the Post Office, Farm Lane, Lottage Road, Upper Upham and Woodsend.
>
> On Sundays they collect only from the box at the Post Office. Collections for Parcelforce are made from the Post Office twice a day.
>
> Household deliveries are made once a day by van. We have two regular postmen serving the parish and sorting is done in Marlborough.
>
> Those who run our postal services become familiar and friendly figures who dispense good cheer as well as the mail.

At No 55 are Greg and Liz Nice who moved to Aldbourne in 1994 and were married in the village. Both Emily and Molly, who likes ballet, were born and christened in the village and the family increased in 1999 when Katie was born. Liz had an office in The Square. Greg, a corporate account manager, works in Weybridge. They both have a keen interest in village affairs. The house has been extended.

John and Jill Regan came to Aldbourne in 1983 to live in No 57. John, a retired army sergeant and fireman, helps Jill with her home improvement business, 'Interiors', and her horses. Both are pet lovers. Previous owners have considerably extended the house from the adjacent granny flat and the revision is now complete.

No 59 is home to Miss J Rothwell, who moved from Liverpool in 1996 to help set up Thorn UK in Swindon and train staff. She chose to live in Aldbourne because it feels safe and everyone is so friendly. She found that the village had a comfortable and relaxing environment and she was quickly accepted. 'The pubs are good, there is a lot on and it is possible to shop late.'

Charles Stacey built numbers 61 to 83 in 1929; he was a local builder and used local labour. Each pair of houses shared a well (now filled in), they had a privy in the garden and used open fires for cooking. By 1940 the houses had electricity, an inside tap, a coal shed with copper and a toilet complete with 'bucket and chuck it system' outside the back door. In 1958 they were connected to the mains sewer. The Bourne was enclosed in the late 1970s. In 1991 the final modernization was carried out with bathrooms moved upstairs and hot water and central heating systems installed with tenants being offered the choice of solid fuel or gas.

George and Hilda Chamberlain and their three children moved into No 61 in 1960. Both George and Hilda are from local families

61 & 63 Lottage Road

and have worked locally. They bought the house from the council in 1987 and have had a kitchen and bathroom built on. George is still a keen gardener. Hilda died in the late 1990s.

No 63 has been home to Russell, Jenny, Keith and Richard Mrowczynski since 1992. Jenny works for an electronics company in Wootton Bassett while Russell, Keith and Richard have all worked for Barnes Coaches. Keith is now a Somerfield manager in Hungerford. Drummer Richard is the Aldbourne Band's property manager and is also a keen darts player and captain of the local team. They are keen gardeners.

Denis Fryer and Josephine Woolford have lived at No 65, which they now own, since 1978. Denis is a project manager for a building company and Josephine worked at Crowcastle. Denis is chairman of Aldbourne Football Club. They both love cats and gardening.

Christopher and Teresa Flett have worked hard on No 71 and its garden since they moved in 1998. The previous owner turned around the staircase. Teresa is a personal assistant to an agricultural surveyor in Swindon and helps the Regans with their horses. Christopher is an accountant and is captain of the local rugby team. Both are dog lovers.

Roy, Alison and Lucy Keen took over No 73 in 1995 and since then they have single-handedly added to the house a large living room, utility room, second bathroom and another bedroom. Roy is a motorbike mech-anic and is North Gloucestershire Motorbike Champion. Alison works at Nationwide and loves horses and other pets. Both Roy and Alison have parents living locally, as do their neighbours on each side.

65, 67, 69 & 71 Lottage Road

Chapter Two

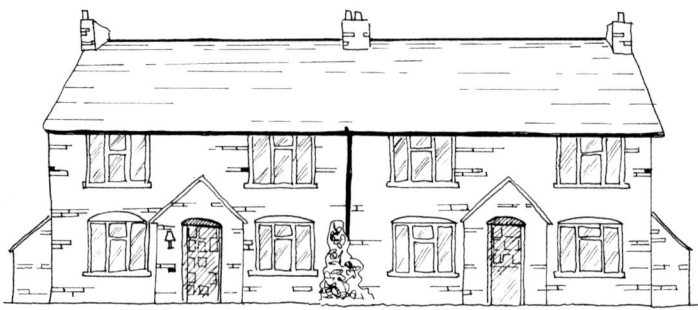

73 & 75 Lottage Road

Francis, Julie, Jenna and Ian Wright have lived in No 75 since 1982. Francis is a self-employed builder and has extended the house. He is keen on speedway and cribbage. Julie works as a data processor for Securicor and likes gardening. Both Francis and Julie enjoy darts and are dog lovers.

No 77 is home to Paul Newman and Elaine Mould. Paul, Elaine, Clare and Fern moved in in 1995. Elaine works in a local shop. Paul keeps the grass mown in the village and has contracts in many surrounding villages too. He is also involved in the entertainments scene; he runs discos and helps with the lighting at village events and beyond. Paul's family has been in the village for several generations and his grandfather is buried in the churchyard.

Ray and Carol John live at No 79. Carol has lived in the village all her life and works at Thames Valley Eggs. She is devoted to her three cats, feeds three more and collects cat plates and rugs. Ray married Carol in 1988 and loves the village. He is a fork-lift truck engineer covering Wiltshire, Oxfordshire and Gloucestershire and enjoys line dancing. Both are keen walkers.

Bert and Joan Steggles who moved to No 81 from Froxfield in 1975 celebrate their Golden Wedding in the year 2000. They take great pleasure in their garden and are active members of the Silver Threads. Joan knits and goes to bingo while Bert enjoys bowls in Ramsbury, and a pint. Their sons live and work locally.

Lottage Road in the 1920s – 1

"Down Lottage Road was a foundry owned by Mr Loveday. Just before it there was a footpath from Lottage Road to Grasshills called Lovedays Lane. The foundry – what a wonderful place! Many times I have watched them preparing the moulds – then casting day came!

To see the furnace in action and the molten metal being poured into the moulds, it was a wonderful sight. Next day the castings would be taken out of the moulds and all the flashes broken off. The castings were all for agricultural machinery.

Past the foundry on the left was a large house with a meadow behind and a barn lower down with a grain-store house on staddle stones in which a Mr Eddles lived. After Mr Stacey's barn were two cottages, then came Kandahar House owned by Mr Wakefield. Behind this house was a sloping meadow where we used to toboggan when there was snow.

Next to this house was another barn where the Jerram brothers – Fred, Wilfred and Frank – carried on their carpentry business. They made anything anyone wanted, house furniture, farm vehicles, including the wheels. Some of these were six feet in diameter and were trundled to Noah Liddiard's blacksmith's shop to have metal tyres fitted."

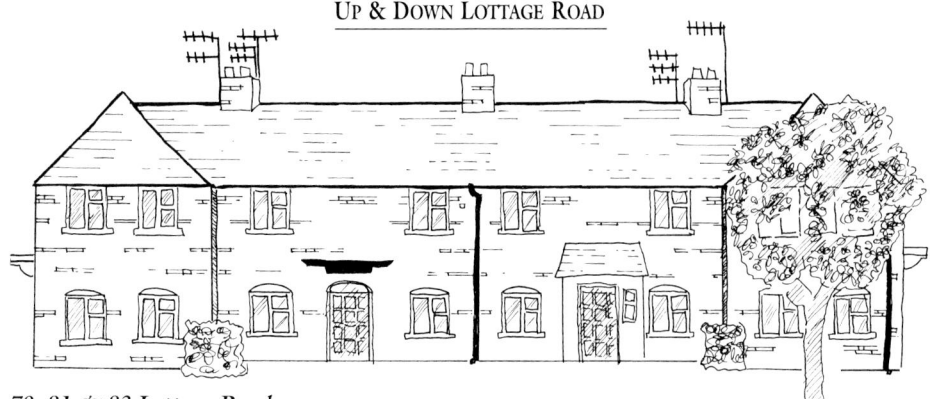

77, 79, 81 & 83 Lottage Road

Adrian and Pat Keen took over No 83 in the late 1970s. Adrian is our local garden handyman. Pat is an excellent darts player and has won many trophies. They are both from local families and have five children.

Beyond Alma Road

Odette and Arun Shenoy were married in Aldbourne church in July 1997, and in January 1998 they moved to No 85. For Odette, a Dabchick, it was a homecoming. For Arun, who is of Indo-German descent, it was a welcome move to a beautiful part of the English countryside. They both enjoy supporting the National Trust and are looking forward to starting a family soon, cricket and golf allowing!

Deborah, Neil and Alistair moved to No 87 in 1997 from another part of the village. Neil is a mechanic and Deborah was a freelance hairdresser, whilst Alistair attends the local school. They started their own garage business in 1994, which unfortunately leaves little time for hobbies. Any spare time is spent decorating or carrying out repairs to the house.

Sally and Bob Shepherd came here to No 91 from the Midlands in 1976. Now enjoying (early) retirement, Bob still does some freelance proof-reading. They have shared interests in gardening, walking, bird-watching and family history. Sally listens to children reading at the village school, enjoys sewing, embroidery, learning piano and belongs to the ALEC. Bob reckons he has enough DIY jobs to last a lifetime!

85 Lottage Road

87 Lottage Road

Chapter Two

89 Lottage Road

91 Lottage Road

Kate, John, Sally and Roger moved to Aldbourne in 1986, and to No 93 in 1997. John is a keen supporter of Swindon Town FC. He comes from Chilton Foliat, where he still runs the garage business begun by his father. Kate, from Bakewell, Derbyshire, has worked in Sixpenny Nursery for the last ten years and enjoys both gardening and walking. Roger and Sally both attend St John's School. Roger enjoys sport whilst Sally loves music.

Charles and Fenella Elms with Mungo and Hebe bought *Alma Cottage* on 5 November 1996; coincidentally the weathered date on the barn is 1605 – the year of the Gunpowder Plot. The premises were run as a farm by the previous family who had been associated with the house for at least five generations. 'We continue to spend much of our spare time on renovation work and on laying down roots in Aldbourne. For the millennium we are planting trees in the paddock, including an elm.

Audrey and Don Greaves built the bungalow *Windley Ridge* in 1975, having moved from Baydon, although originally they were from Birmingham. Both now retired, they are very involved in the University of the Third Age and the Methodist Church, as well as being very active in the Camping and Caravanning Club (Folk Section). They have two daughters, Penny and Fiona, and one grandson, Robert. Penny is a chartered surveyor and Fiona is a registered Health and Safety consultant.

School Memories

"Mr. Strickland had high standards. There were 150 pupils in school and five teachers. The new school was already built but there were too many children so the old building had to be used again. Infants had to go to the new school for the toilets.

There was no running water and two old stoves for heating. The school had a good reputation and pupils came from a wide area to the school."

93 Lottage Road

Alma Cottage *Lottage Road*

LOTTAGE ROAD IN THE 1920s – II

"After Jerram's barn there were fields as far as *Alma Cottage* where Mr and Mrs Wallington lived. He worked over at Russley Park in the stables and I have a feeling that he usually walked there and back. Farther along we came to Eastleaze Road where Mr Wentworth farmed. Past the crossroads with Peaks Road and Grasshills and after about half a mile is North Field. When the brook was in flood, a lake appeared on the left before North Field and after a further half a mile one came to *North Farm*, belonging to Mr Chandler, which had its own windmill for providing water."

Windley Ridge *Lottage Road*

Chapter Two

Coronel Cottage *Lottage Road*

> **HOME WORKING**
>
> According to the 1999 Parish Appraisal about 40 per cent of Aldbourne's working population work within the parish and over half of them are based at home.
>
> This is clearly substantially higher than the estimated national figure (also 1999) of 4 per cent.

North Farm *Lottage Road*

North Farm Cottage *Lottage Road*

Beyond the speed restriction

North Farm is now the working centre for about 2,500 acres of Lawton Farms and consists of a dairy unit, young stock and beef, and storage for about 2,000 tonnes of grain. Seed potato production is a recent introduction.

The Lawton family has occupied the Farmhouse since 1969 when they bought the farm. Robert and his wife Mary have four children. James, the eldest, is married and works on the farm. Kathryn is married and a helicopter pilot. Emily, who is married to Chris Lovell, is a three-day event rider living at *Hellscombe Cottage*. Ben, single, is working in advertising near Oxford.

Robert Lawton CBE runs the family farm from an office in the farmyard. He is active in many farming and environmental issues. He has been an adviser to eight Ministers of

Hellscombe Cottage *Lottage Road*

Northfield Cottage *Lottage Road*

Chapter Two

72 & 70 Lottage Road

68 & 66 Lottage Road

64 & 62 Lottage Road

Agriculture and one Minister of the Environment, is a director of the Silo Research Institute, Kingshay Farming Trust, Yattendon Estates, Royal Agricultural Society and a governor of the Royal Agricultural College. The farm was awarded LEAF status in 1991.

North Farm Cottage is the home of the dairy manager Richard Millington and his wife Pamela. Previously for many years it was the home of Brian and Rosemary Buckler.

Denis and Pam Paget live at 1 Northfield Cottages, they moved in 1963 and have brought up three children here – Suzanne, Linda and Christopher who all now live in Aldbourne with their families. Denis will take away any old scrap and is also a champion vintage ploughman. Pam works in 'Alldays' part time and in her garden the rest of the day.

Paul and Annette Jerram moved to No 2 in 1970; their three children were born here. Carla still lives with them while Cleo and Cassie live in Swindon. Paul had his own driving school for thirty years but is now more interested in Blues music and motorbikes. Annette helps run pre-school and works part-time in the Post Office.

Returning to Chandlers Lane

Kelvin and Helen live at No 70 with two children; Jordan who is four, and Jade who is two; they also have two pet chipmunks. They have lived here since the houses were built in 1994. The house has two bedrooms, and a lovely big garden. Kelvin is a hod carrier and Helen a housewife. Jordan attends pre-school and started school in September 1999. Jade started pre-school at Easter 1999. Their interests are gardening, music, DIY cars(!) and motocross.

Julie, Lewis and Rebecca Newport moved to No 68 in December 1994. 'We enjoy living here with fields behind and a nice-sized house and garden.' Lewis and Becky go to St Michael's School and Julie helps with swimming there. Lewis is into football, rugby and swimming. Becky enjoys swimming, rugby and art. Julie likes music, swimming, crafts and walking; she works in the village. The nearby farm is a constant source of entertainment.

Until recently Sarah Jennings lived at No 66 having moved here in 1995. She spent four happy years in the village. Her spare time activities included looking after her two dogs, three cats and four chickens. She also spent a lot of time walking and gardening and loved living in the country.

Now living at No 64, John Pearse has been in Aldbourne all his life. Sarah moved here from Harbury, near Leamington Spa, Warwickshire in September 1994. John is a keen Dabchick rugby player. Their shared interests include walking their black labrador cross, Mylow. Sarah works as a receptionist at

CHERRYWOOD CHAIRS

"I had just decided to get married and one day near the old Post Office I met Thomas Orchard and stopped for a word.

'Planning to get married ee be', he said.

'How do ee know?'

'Ah ha' he said 'Udn't 'ad stopped me if you 'adn't bin'.

'I want half a dozen kitchen chairs and an armchair for meself.'

'Alright' he says 'but before I takes your order I want you to go down to the chair shop and see one of the older men 'cos somewhere down there is some cherrywood your grandfather put by to make chairs for his first grandchild's marriage and that's you.'

I wanted six matching chairs.

Mr Orchard said: 'No. Young folk gets married and after about a year they gets a baby. When mother sits in an ordinary chair the baby rolls off her lap. So we makes a chair with shorter legs so when she sits down the baby stays on her knee.'

And what's more he always made a gift of a footstool.

In 1909 my chairs were going to cost 10/6d (52p) each. But on 11/- (55p) a week I had to save up."

Lottage Farm *Lottage Road*

56 & 54 Lottage Road

Chapter Two

52 & 50 Lottage Road

48 Lottage Road

46 Lottage Road

Ramsbury surgery. They have a five-month-old daughter, Lilli.

In 1994 Denise and John Welch, with children Samantha and Troy, moved to No 62 from No 50 when they were made redundant from their jobs as steward and stewardess of the Sports and Social Club in which they were very happy. Denise now works in 'Alldays' doing the baking and on the till. John works for Swindon Contractors, Artexing and painting. They now have a lovely grandson, Jordan Welch, born in 1993.

Mr and Mrs Sansom and family moved into No 54 in the late 1980s. Teresa Ward and Colin Stroud moved into No 50 from Hungerford

---

LOTTAGE ROAD IN THE 1920S - III

"On the right-hand side going down Lottage Road were *Chadwell Cottages*; I grew up in the centre one.

Next door were four cottages and, when the brook was in spate, water used to come out of the two centre ones, just under the front doors. It also came out under Aunt Nell's which was the last *Chadwell Cottage*.

Further down was a large barn belonging to a Mr Arthur Stacey who also had a farm in West Street."

44 Lottage Road

in December 1996. They have an eighteen-month-old daughter, Megan. Bernard and Edna Simpson have lived happily at No 46 since 1956, moving from Ashbury, and their daughter Monica still lives here.

Geraldine and Phillip Bradley live at *The Beeches* (42) Lottage Road. Geraldine was born in Aldbourne and attended St Michael's School, became a member of the Girl Guides and later became a Guider, enjoying many a memorable summer camp! She met Phillip, who lived in Baydon, and they married at St Michael's Church on 1 May 1971. Phillip played for the Aldbourne Football Club and later became a referee. He also joined the

The Beeches (42) Lottage Road

LAW AND ORDER

Aldbourne is within the Marlborough sub-division of the Wiltshire Constabulary, and is served twenty-four hours a day from the police station at Marlborough. The division has nine operational officers assisted by the Kennet traffic and dog units and reinforced when necessary by police from other divisions and from specialist units employing modern techniques of investigation, surveillance and protection.

Fortunately the parish, though spirited, is reasonably law-abiding and suffers little from major crime. Often burglary and car related offences are committed by those who target rural areas by using the M4 motorway.

Though the local village bobby has gone, his replacement, the Community Area Officer, soon becomes a familiar figure. The stern look, the friendly smile and the admonition backed by authority still works well to discourage anti-social behaviour while the sympathetic help that uniformed officers give in times of trouble are noticeable evidence of a necessary police force.

Much of the work of the Community Area Officer is preventative and is backed with twelve Neighbourhood Watch schemes, advice from a Crimes Prevention Officer and the increasing installation of burglar alarms. The police aim to be here within twenty minutes of receiving a 999 call. A recent development has been the use of the Ambulance/Police helicopter that can quickly arrive on the scene of serious accident or other incident.

We are, by and large, a decent law-abiding lot and this must partly be due to the influence of our families, good-humoured community leaders, good publicans and neighbourhood care. However not least is the way that an efficient, courageous and reliable police force applies itself to its duties in the community.

Chapter Two

40 & 38 Lottage Road

Scouts as a Leader. They have three children Da, Odette and Marianne. In 1978 they moved away, returning in 1994. Geraldine's mother and grandparents lived in Aldbourne. Her grandparents, Edith and William Tucker, lived at *Rectory Lodge* where William was head gardener to *Rectory House*. They had six children, two of whom died shortly after birth. Their remaining daughters were named Violet, Frances, Lillian and Cynthia. Geraldine and her three sisters are distantly related to several village families. Geraldine and Phillip enjoy gardening and walking their two dogs. They also keep various rare breed bantams as a hobby.

Half-way back

In January 1921, Mr Charles Stacey divided a field running alongside Lottage Road into twenty-eight allotment strips. The strips were worked for a number of years and eventually the strips numbered 20–24 were brought together and Mr William Deacon built a house on them for his own occupation. He named it *Green Gables*. Later it was bought by Mr Stanley Mildenhall who allowed his brother, Frederick, to build a bungalow on the land alongside. This became 40 Lottage Road and was named *Hawthorns*. At that time, a large

*36 & **Greta Bank** (34) Lottage Road*

mixed hedgerow, mainly hawthorn, ran along the roadside verge.

In 1970, Alan and Valerie Watson bought No 38 which has been extended over the years. The garden no longer has chickens, nor the pig which once occupied a large shed at the top. In 1985 Valerie's mother, Mrs Ruby Smith, moved into the bungalow at No 40.

Dr Mark Davies and his wife Dr Sandy Muirhead have lived at No 34 since 1991. They have two children, Natalie, born in 1994 and Carys, born in 1998. Mark and Sandy are both environmental consultants. Mark is chairman of ALEC and has appeared in many of their productions. Sandy is on the Parish Council and, for a time, ran the Aldbourne Conservation Volunteers.

Mrs Pat Hayward, a retired medical secretary, lived at No 32 from 1983 to 1999. She was a keen bridge player. Her daughter Patricia lives in Oxford Street and her son Colin works abroad in Sweden in telecommunications.

Mr and Mrs Jack Watts moved into No 30 in about 1978. Jack died in 1995. He was chairman of Aldbourne Parish Council for many years. Molly was a teacher in Swindon until she retired in 1983. She was well-known as the producer of the WI pantomime. Daughter Annette lives with her family in *Northfield Cottages*.

32 Lottage Road

NORTH FARM

Some land and buildings known as *Northfield Farm* belonged to Southby Farm, now *Hightown*. The houses in Chandlers Lane were built in about 1994. A new housing estate was built at the same time by Hastoe Housing Association on land belonging to Lottage Farm. In 1910 a Captain Barnett had a racing stable there. *Alma Cottage* was a farmhouse in the late 18th to early 19th century. North Field Barn to the east of the Wanborough Road was built in the late 19th century and the house to the west in the early 20th. *North Farm* has been farmed continuously for about 4,000 years and there have certainly been settlements here since Roman times. Elizabeth Bond sold land in 1694 to form *North Farm*, which was inherited by Robert Wells in 1760. The rear of the house is the oldest part, possibly 17th century on an earlier site. The front, including a cellar, was added after 1828. The farm buildings were modernized in 1865 and again after World War II.

The present owners, Robert and Mary Lawton, bought it in 1968 and have made many improvements. The water supply is still from the well which was originally dug in Roman times, although it was deepened in 1921.

CHAPTER TWO

CHANGING TASTES

A survey by the Aldbourne WI has shown that tastes in food are changing quite rapidly.

While meat, particularly as a roast dinner, is enjoyed by all age groups, 12 per cent of those surveyed were vegetarians and food scares reported in the press will probably increase this number.

Fish and chips and chicken are also favourites and, for the under 40s, pasta, particularly lasagne and spaghetti, is much eaten. Also gaining favour are other imported tastes – Chinese, Indian and Mexican. 'Fast food' such as pizzas, fish fingers and burgers are popular too.

Few eat a cooked breakfast. For most of us this meal consists mainly of cereals and/or toast.

The main meal is usually meat or fish and two vegetables. Puddings and cheese are mostly eaten by the older age groups. In place of pudding the majority of others eat fruit, yoghurt or ice cream. On most days vegetables, salads and fruit are also on the menu.

The majority of people eat their main meal in the evening and those with children tend to sit down as a family group once a day.

In the younger age group some only eat together once a week and a few never.

30 Lottage Road

28 Lottage Road

26 Lottage Road

No 28 started life as a pavilion in Swindon but has been extended and is now a splendid bungalow. Owners Guy and Shireen Waterer have lived there since December 1995. Guy works for Thames Water in Reading and Shireen for Blick in Swindon.

No 26 has been the home of Mr and Mrs John Fisher since 1954. John had lived next door at No 28 since 1937. He was born in Punta Arenas, Chile, while Mrs Fisher comes from Hungerford. Their children, Clive, Anita and Sally-Ann are grown up and have left home. John has been player, secretary, treasurer and is now vice-president of Ald-bourne Football Club. He is also vice-president of Swindon and District Football League.

Rob Williams moved to No 24 in October 1996 after previously living in the Square. He works in Camberley as a computer consultant. He is a keen bandsman and plays the tuba in Aldbourne Silver Band. He claims to have done the 'Full Monty' on stage in 1998 whilst performing in the revue 'Rick, Wyn and Friends' to raise funds for the millennium projects.

Terry and Pauline Harland, together with their children Katie and Robert, have lived at No 22 since May 1995. The previous owner was Mr George Wilkins. Terry is treasurer of the Sports and Social Club. Pauline used to work at Crowcastle. They are both DIY enthusiasts.

24 Lottage Road

22 Lottage Road

FUNERALS

A V Jerram Bros, one of the village builders, were funeral directors and closed their business in 1990 after over seventy years of helping and guiding parishioners through the difficult procedures connected with death. They made many friends and were trusted counsellors.

The cost of funerals has greatly increased. The firm's records show that in 1929 a funeral cost £6. 5s (£6.25) which included making the coffin, polishing it, lining it with pitch, adding white linings with mauve frills, solid brass furniture and inscription painted on brass breastplate, taking coffin to small cottage, removing bedroom window completely to allow access, leaving deceased in coffin until day of funeral, replacing window temporarily, removing again to get coffin out and replacing permanently later in the day, hiring bier from Church Council, digging and filling in grave, paying church fees, pall-bearers and undertaker.

Most people are cremated, though many are still buried in the churchyard, and ashes are deposited there and gravestones erected. The churchyard with its flowers is a quiet and beautiful place to honour and mourn the dead.

Chapter Two

Mayfield *(18)* & **Bedlam Cottage** *(16)* *Lottage Road*

> ### Lottage Road in the 1920s – IV
>
> "On the left after the Wesleyan Chapel were four or five stables or garages. Next was a workshop where a man made doormats to the size you required from coconut fibre. Still on the left past three or four cottages, Goddards Lane to the back of Hightown, and three more cottages was Charlie Stacey's builders' yard.
>
> Next on the left came Mr Blanchard's farm, where we got our milk, butter, and such like and, on Sunday mornings, buttermilk for the Yorkshire pudding.
>
> Also on the left side was a single cottage with the best red apples I have ever tasted."

Inglenook *(14)* *Lottage Road*

Two Beeches *Lottage Road*

And back to the start

Inglenook is the home of Ann Barkworth and Ruth Powell. The house was built in 1950 by Charles Stacey and was named after its inglenook fireplace. The lounge is wood-panelled with oak ceiling and floorboards. In the garden are scale models of St Michael's Church, the Memorial Hall and the Old Wesleyan Chapel, all built by Mr Stacey who was born in 1884 and was father to Ruth and grandfather to Ann.

The three terraced cottages (Nos 2–6) are thought to be some three hundred years old. The foundations are large sarsen boulders and the walls are two feet thick at the base. Miss Palmer, who died aged 101, bought the three cottages in 1920. She had stable lads as lodgers before the war and soldiers during the war. A deep well in the garden of No 6 always provided water in the driest summers when others in the neighbourhood had gone dry. Dennis Keen lived with his aunt, Miss Palmer, at No 6 from 1934 until he converted his workshop into the bungalow where he now lives. Recently retired, Dennis had his own car repair business. His hobbies are football, motorcycle road-racing and table tennis. Dennis and his wife Doreen had four children, Denise, Helen, Royston and Marion; the last three still live in the village.

Matthew Whittle moved into *Chadwell Cottage* (No 6) in 1994 and has done extensive refurbishment. Due to an accident on his thirteenth birthday, Matthew has speech and movement difficulties. He works at Rutpen Ltd at Membury with his brother Kevin and has travelled extensively, including trips to Lourdes. His hobbies include playing saxophone, drums and other instruments; he has accumulated a large collection of bottles and is supporter of the Dabchicks Rugby Club.

Medicine Now

That medical care and treatment will be forthcoming and on demand we take almost for granted. It is when a crisis occurs that we appreciate those who apply their skills and care with sympathy and often humour.

Dr Jonathan Rayner, a parishioner and a partner in the Ramsbury surgery, says that medicine and general practice has changed enormously since the days of the surgery at Neals. Now there is greater emphasis on 'preventative medicine' (well-person checks, immunizations, cancer screening, and so on) and more support from nurses, health visitors, physiotherapists and counsellors.

The Lambourn surgery looks after 10 per cent of the village and the Ramsbury surgery about 90 per cent, with a very small number going to other surgeries. Each year the residents of the parish make around 8,500 visits to their doctor and the doctors make around 1,000 home visits a year.

Aldbourne has its share of the major diseases such as heart disease, strokes, cancers, diabetes and arthritis. The last thirty years have seen a huge fall in the incidence of many potentially fatal childhood infections (such as measles, whooping cough, diphtheria and scarlet fever) but has seen a rise in various allergic conditions, particularly asthma. Asthma seems to be prevalent in Aldbourne perhaps because of its low-lying position.

District nurses act as linchpins providing care in rural practice. Their work has increased enormously over the years, not only because of the rising proportion of us living into our ninth and tenth decades, but also because more and more of the work previously done in hospital is now carried out at home. The nurses make approximately 1,900 visits a year.

One of the more recent additions to the village has been the Nursing Home. This has meant that many who can no longer be nursed at home can continue to stay in the village, and this has been a great asset.

Chapter Two

12, 10 & 8 Lottage Road

Chadwell Cottage *(6), 4 & 2 Lottage Road*

No 4 is the home of Pat and Fiona Cheney. Pat came originally from Surrey and is a self-employed builder. He collects coins and stamps. Fiona, who came from Axford, is a part-time chef and deeply involved in the 1st Aldbourne Guides. Since moving to No 4 in 1981 Pat and Fiona have made several improvements. During the work a large open fireplace was discovered which they have kept as a feature. They have two children, Mark, eleven, and Abby, seven.

Ena Gibson moved to Aldbourne after the death of her husband in 1970 to live at No 2 and served on many village committees. Her sister Audrey Gilligan lives in the village.

Theatre Club

The club was founded some thirty years ago by our Hon Life President, Mrs Dot Walls. There are some 120 members who go on trips by coach to the theatre every month or so. In addition to fairly local theatres such as Salisbury, Bristol, Bath, Oxford and Newbury where we go to evening performances, the club goes to summer matinees at Stratford and Chichester. The annual subscription is £5.

Members live mainly in Aldbourne, Baydon, Ramsbury and Hungerford.

Chapter Three

The Roads off Lottage Road

Goddards Lane

Off Lottage Road is Goddards Lane, a cul-de-sac as far as traffic is concerned though a footpath leads up Goddards Lane to Crooked Corner and Grasshills. The small development of eight houses which dominates the lane is built on what was a builders' yard, owned in turn by Mr Charles Stacy, Mr Mantle, Philimore Construction and W Liddiard Ltd until sold for this development.

Alexander and Phyllis Campbell and Phyllis' sister Madge Beau moved from Surrey to Aldbourne in 1978. They moved to No 2, which was then a new house in a small development on the site of an old racing stable owned by Mrs Fortune Powell. They are retired and their main interests are the arts, crosswords and gardening. Colin and Sybil Welch came here in 1980 to live in No 4, although for the first few years they were in London for some part of each week. Colin was deputy editor of *The Daily Telegraph* for fifteen years and after his retirement wrote book reviews for *The Times*. Sadly, after being unconscious for nearly two years, Colin died in January 1997. Sybil

1 Goddards Lane

> ### Sliding in the Dark
>
> "The village pond was connected to the brook. When it was frozen in the winter – and it did freeze in those days – we used to slide on it and when it was dark – no street lamps then – we used to put candles on Mr Everett's wall so that we could carry on sliding. The pond went right up to the wall in those days."

CHAPTER THREE

2 Goddards Lane

is a founder member of the ALEC and still performs in some of their productions. She has five grandchildren.

5 Goddards Lane was originally two houses in a row of workmen's cottages built around 1580 – a date given credibility when the remains of ornate cotton reels were found under the floorboards. The Lawlers learned that a family of tailors had lived in the house for two hundred years. Peter Lawler says: 'I came with my parents to live at 25 Oxford Street in 1969. On my first night in the village at a disco I met my future wife Rona. We married in 1978 and lived briefly in a cottage at Snap Farm

4 & 5 Goddards Lane

6 & 7 Goddards Lane

8 & 9 Goddards Lane

where I worked as a stockman. We have two children, Matthew born in 1985 and Christopher born in 1990. I work from home running my agricultural sales business whilst Rona works part time as a clerical assistant at St John's School in Marlborough.'

No 9 is the home of Jean Thompson, a district nurse in Swindon, she arrived in 1989. She is a keen gardener and is developing the garden in front of all the houses. Goddards Lane opens up into a courtyard and tucked in the corner is No 10; Arlette and Guy have lived here since February 1998. 'For us the area is perfect as we are both originally from villages. The house is one of eight and although small is ideal for us.' Mark and Karen Houghton moved into No 12 in June 1997. Karen (née Newman) originates from Baydon and Mark from Warrington, Cheshire. He now works in Swindon for a firm that deals with telecommunications research and development. They married in September 1996 at Baydon Church and held their reception in the Memorial Hall. Most of their spare time is spent walking their German shepherd, Maxi.

At No 13 are Wally and Sheila Palmer, formerly proprietors of the shop in Oxford Street. They bought the house in 1989 and moved in

10 & 11 Goddards Lane

12 & 13 Goddards Lane

14 Goddards Lane

GODDARDS LANE HISTORY

Goddards Lane is named after an old Aldbourne family. Nos 4 and 5 date back to about 1580. They were part of the *Hightown/Southby Farm* complex originally in a longer row and were each a pair. Derelict in the 1970s, No 5 stood to be condemned within six months. A family of tailors lived there for over 200 years. Many ornamental cotton reels were found under the floorboards.

No 1, *Myrtle Cottage*, has the brook flowing through its garden. No 2 was built in the 1970s with The Paddocks where *Hightown* stables and paddocks stood.

Chapter Three

October House *(1) The Knoll*

2 The Knoll

Threeway *(3) The Knoll*

Millennium Celebrations

The residents of Aldbourne and their friends filled The Green as the clock ticked over from the 1900s to 2000. There was a wonderful atmosphere and over 1,000 people of all ages enjoyed each other's company at the historic moment. It was an event which many will remember.

Two days later on Sunday 2 January 2000 at St Michael's Church the Aldbourne Churches Together held a United Covenant Service conducted by the Anglican and Methodist ministers. In a congregation of about 120 people, over a hundred took Communion.

Next the parish will celebrate Festival 2000 starting on 26 May 2000 and lasting ten days. The theme will be 'Saxon times to the present day'. We hope to attract everyone to the wide range of exciting and entertaining activities which we have organized.

The Memorial Hall has been chosen as our millennium project; all money raised will be used to renovate the hall which was given to and used by the parish in memory of those who died in two World Wars.

We will revitalize a proud building that will be equipped to honour those who died for us – a fitting way to commemorate the new millennium.

4 The Knoll

in 1993 on their retirement. Wally was born on the premises at the shop and Sheila came to Aldbourne from Hungerford when they married in 1954. They have two daughters, Jane and Ruth.

The Knoll

The Knoll is just beyond *Foundry Cottage* and is approached via a private road. There are four detached four- or five-bedroom houses built in 1987 on land which was originally part of the gardens of *Beech Knoll House*.

Tony and Rosemary Alexander come originally from the Midlands and have lived at No 1 for three years. Tony is an accountant with the Nationwide Building Society and is a member of Ogbourne Downs Golf Club. Rosemary is also an accountant and works for Linda Pryce and Co. They have two daughters, Laura, five, and Katie, two.

At No 3 is Joan Phizacklea who was brought up in Aldbourne by her foster mother, Lucy Slade. She married Eric Phizacklea at the age of twenty and set up home in Essex, later moving to Hampshire. On Eric's death in 1994 Joan moved back to the village. Of their three children, a son and daughter are still living and Joan has five grandchildren and two great grandchildren. One grandson, Tristan Webber, is making a name for himself in the couture fashion world. Her garden abuts onto that of her twin sister, Molly Cullis.

Tony and Janet Spath, originally from Surrey, moved into No 4 in 1995. Tony works and travels abroad extensively for Dolby Laboratories. He is a governor of St Michael's School and occasionally plays the organ at the Methodist Church. Janet works in the office at St John's School in Marlborough. All three of Tony and Janet's children are piano players. In addition, Christopher plays the saxophone and guitar, Nicholas plays the violin while Freya hopes to learn the flute.

FOUR BROTHERS

Jerram Bros was started by four brothers after World War I. They built a few houses but their main business was alterations and repairs. They were also the village undertakers. On one occasion Fred sat on a board suspended by a rope from the top of the church tower in order to paint the clock face. They made toboggans and other toys for the children, only charging a few pence. Carnival was very important to them and they produced some exceptional entries. All four were devout churchmen, singing in the choir and ringing the bells twice every Sunday. The business was continued by Fred's son, Vincent, and Frank's son, Gerald.

Chapter Three

1, 2, 3 & 4 Chandlers Lane

5 Chandlers Lane

Chandlers Lane

Ewan Hayward and his partner Suzie Wheelwright met on a train in Vietnam. Suzie moved from Brisbane, Australia in July 1997 to join Ewan who had moved to No 1 in 1995 and now plays second row for the Dabchicks Rugby Club.

Helen and Peter Chambers came from Swindon to No 2 in April 1994 when the house was first built. Helen originally hails from Haverfordwest, Pembrokeshire and Peter came from Chard, Somerset. Helen is the deputy headteacher at Preshute CE Primary School, Manton and Peter is the head teacher

ALL SHOOK UP

Did you spot several 'trashy women' and a couple of 'reggae cowboys' on Wednesday evenings in the Methodist Hall as they 'fly like a bird' until they're 'all shook up'?

What is going on? It's American line dancing, currently one of the most popular pastimes in Britain. Although generally based on country music, line dances are now choreographed to a wide variety of music including disco and Irish.

Our group, the Silver Liners, has about fifteen members who have been meeting for over three years. It is a very enjoyable way to exercise and suitable for all ages and abilities. The social aspect is all important – after all, 'life's a dance'!

6 Chandlers Lane

The Roads off Lottage Road

7 Chandlers Lane

8 Chandlers Lane

at St Nicholas CE Primary School, Baydon. Heather White has lived in the Aldbourne area for a total of twenty-three years and recently moved to No 3. She is a PE teacher at a comprehensive school in Newbury and is particularly fond of horse riding in the wonderful Wiltshire countryside. Mary and Gerald O'Malley moved to Aldbourne in 1994 when No 4 was newly built. Gerry retired from his work as an accountant in 1990 and now enjoys golf and gardening. They have one son Timothy who gained BA(Hons) and PhD at Durham University. (They left in 1999.)

At No 5 are Steve and Vivien Mason who moved to the village in 1994 from Basingstoke. They have two children, Shara-Grace, born in 1991, and Alexander, born in 1993; they both attend school in Baydon. Steve is a company secretary working in Newbury. Vivien works locally as both a care assistant and a catering assistant. Steve enjoys sport and plays cricket for the village. Vivien's interests are musical; she plays the piano at two local schools and the organ at a church in Marlborough. Through their children and interests they have made a number of friends in the village.

The owners of No 6, Ronald and Jane Wallis, moved to Aldbourne in April 1994 from Ninfield in East Sussex. Ronald works for the Ministry of Defence as an IT project

---

Snow and Newspapers

Dot and Sam came to the village from Bradford in 1960. They took over the newspaper shop next to *Pond House*.

Dot was instantly struck by the natural curiosity of the villagers who always said 'good morning', and the warm welcome they were given. They were also intrigued to find that many families had lived in the village for a long time and had to be mindful of the many inter-relationships. Their daughter attended the village school and they were again surprised how softly spoken and uncompetitive the children were at that time.

They remember the village being snowed up in 1963 and all the extra jigsaws, cigarettes, paperback books they sold then.

In order to get the papers Chris Humphries drove Sam in his four-wheel drive to collect them from Liddington. And the paper boys had to come back in the afternoon to deliver them.

Dot changed the suppliers from Reading to Swindon so that the villagers had their regional news, especially for the sports news.

The winter weather never stopped the papers being sold: only the union going on strike managed to do that.

Chapter Three

> ### Lottage Way and Kandahar
>
> Lottage Way was a smallholding paddock of about four acres.
>
> Kandahar, a group of houses built in the 1960s and 70s, was also meadow with a barn, a stable and other buildings. Nos 38 and 40 were built in the 1930s on the sites of three allotments set up for returners from World War I.

9 & 10 Chandlers Lane

11 Chandlers Lane

12 Chandlers Lane

manager and Jane for W H Smith Ltd as a business analyst. They had their first child in 1998.

Brian and Liz Fielder who live at No 7 tend to turn to verse to express their feelings about living in Aldbourne – the church choir and the band, wildlife and sweet country air, friends and a bottle of good wine.

Richard and Alex Womersley, who are originally from Yorkshire and Germany respectively, married in 1992 and settled in Swindon. They moved to No 8 when it was built. Their daughter, Rebecca, was born in 1997. They enjoy walking and cycling, and life in Aldbourne.

Ian and Kim Waud bought No 9 within fifteen minutes of seeing a site plan during a drive through the village. They first lived in Aldbourne, after their marriage in 1987, in a house at The Knoll. They have a business in Newbury.

No 10 is where Martin and Jane Manion moved in 1997 having previously lived in Hong Kong, Bournemouth and London. Martin is a chartered civil engineer (marine specialist), originally from Dublin, and a former international runner. Jane is a Registered General Nurse. They have two young daughters. Paul and Karen Blatchford moved into their new house at No 11 in 1994. 'It was our third relocation. We sat at the top of the churchyard on a hot July day and knew the village was a star find. Like our home, we

1 Kandahar

2 Kandahar

> **SECRET SOCIETY**
>
> On a Wednesday evening in the winter months as you wander round the village, you may hear distant cries of 'fifteen two!', 'Morgan's orchard!' and 'one for his knob!'.
>
> You could be forgiven for making the assumption that coded messages are being bandied about relating some secret society or ancient ritual.
>
> Well, this is true to some extent. It is the Ridgeway Crib League. This consists of groups of dedicated card players who play in teams representing their local hostelries.
>
> They sometimes demonstrate a competitive spirit by actually trying to win a game but usually it only really becomes serious on the so-called 'beer leg' which decides who buys the drinks at the end of the match.

only have a short history here, but are hoping our roots will grow deeper – especially in the garden.'

Kandahar

Pat Batterson came to Aldbourne in 1983 from West London after her early retirement from the nursing profession and lives at No 1. Pat had worked at the Hammersmith Hospital where she had been the nurse in charge of the theatre. She is a steward at the Methodist Church and in her spare time enjoys gardening, home decorating, drawing, découpage and knitting, and is also a member of the WI Choir. Pat has been a member of the Institute of Advanced Motorists since 1969. 2 Kandahar is home to Olive and Mervyn Orchard. Olive has lived in Aldbourne all her life, Mervyn came from Ramsbury and they were married in 1952. Before moving to Kandahar they lived on the Green in *Beaconsfield Cottage*. They have three sons, five grandchildren and a great-granddaughter. During his working life Mervyn was a carpenter for Chivers of Aldermaston. Now that he has retired, he and Olive enjoy walking.

No 21 has been home to Nigel and Amanda since 1996. Amanda is presently absorbed in studying for a degree in psychology in High

Chapter Three

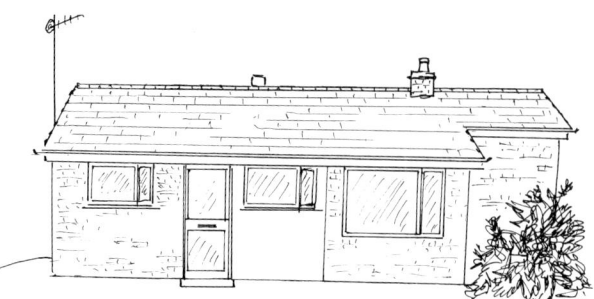

4 Kandahar

3 Kandahar

21 & 20 Kandahar

The Romans

The parish is in what was a thriving area of Roman Britain, with a flourishing economy of small farms, yet the only surviving remains are pottery sherds, probably distributed in dunging, and the odd coin on the upland arable.

Ermin Street running through Baydon and what is now the Ogbourne to Swindon road define sections of the parish boundary. *North Farm* and Wanborough Plain just to the north were part of a 'ribbon development' for traders using the route to Cirencester. Here there are signs of iron working and pottery including imported Samian ware.

In 1980 the Aldbourne Hoard of some 5,000 Roman coins (now in Devizes Museum) was found near Ewin's Hill. The Hoard was possibly the savings from the small villa farmstead on the Ramsbury boundary beside the track from Peaks to Hilldrop. This was probably an outlier from the Littlecote settlement with its substantial and impressive remains.

Romano-British sherds in the *Manor Farm* area are signs of casual habitation. However, the village site was still largely marshy and overgrown until the Saxon period brought an increased population and demand for more and better farming land.

19 & 18 Kandahar

> ### SYMINGTONS SOUP
>
> "When I was a little girl my grandmother would call me across the road to run an errand. It often involved fetching Symington soup tablets from the shop. As I couldn't pronounce 'mulligatawny' I had to ask for 'the soup with the long name'. The ladies in the shop knew just what Gran wanted."

Wycombe and Nigel travels the world to train people in marketing. When they are at home they like to relax although Nigel plays second row for the Dabchicks Rugby Club and Amanda is learning to play the saxophone (quietly!).

No 20 is home to Michael and Cheryl Hills and their two sons, Luke and Christopher, who both attend St Michael's School. Michael is a heating engineer and Cheryl works with people with learning difficulties. Michael is a keen Reading football supporter and has been an Assistant Scout Leader for the last two years. As a family they all enjoy the freedom of living in a village and walking their dog. Their house is 'upside-down' with bedrooms downstairs and lounge and kitchen above.

Tim and Wendy Beattie live at No 19 with their two children Laura and Joe. Aldbourne has been Tim's home since 1973 and Wendy's since 1969, although she was born at Woodsend. Tim has worked at West Street Motors since leaving school. Hobbies include motorbiking, cooking and guiding. Laura and Joe both attended St Michael's School and Laura is now at St John's.

Ros and Chris Oswald have lived in No 17 since the mid-1980s and used to live in No 16. They have two daughters, Elly and Nicola, and two cats and a pony. They enjoy amateur

17 & 16 Kandahar

Chapter Three

15 & 14 Kandahar

13 & 12 Kandahar

11 & 10 Kandahar

> **MEN'S LUNCHEON CLUB**
>
> It was back in August 1984 that Mr Peter Norman (now sadly deceased) proposed the formation of the club. Its purpose would be to encourage friends and neighbours to get together over lunch in congenial circumstances. The first lunch was held in October 1984 at 'Raffles' and was attended by thirteen people, only few of whom are still with us.
>
> Today the membership stands at thirty-four and we meet on the last Friday of each month, in turn at 'Raffles', *The Crown* and *The Blue Boar*. The original purpose of the club is still retained but the total membership is necessarily restricted due to the seating capacities of the venues. Our ladies are invited to join us at one of the summer meetings and again for Christmas lunch to which the widows of former members are also invited as guests of the club.

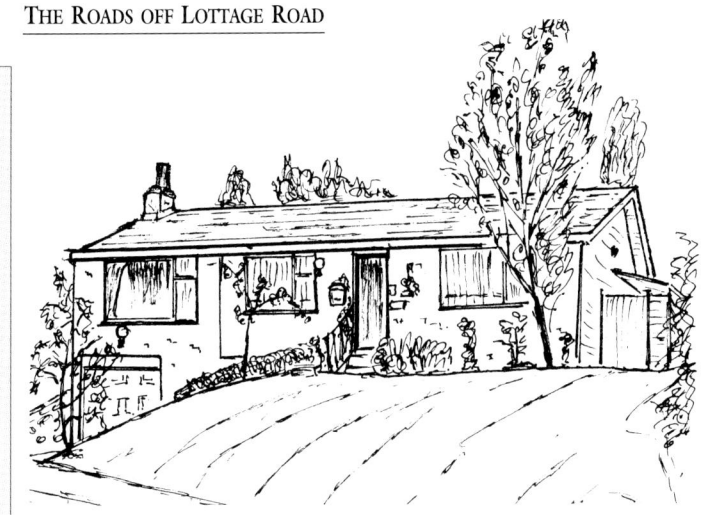

9 Kandahar

8 Kandahar

dramatics and music and have spent five years running 'The Elastic Band' for young people. Ros is a lawyer and Chris a mediator and locum advocate. No 13 is home to Bob and Monica Turner. In 1952 Bob worked for Major Powell in Aldbourne and then for thirty-two years for Major Hern at Ilsley as travelling head lad; all his working life was with horses. He and Monica married in 1963 and have two daughters and two grandchildren. Bob retired in 1996 and his hobbies are gardening, fishing and canaries.

Roger Hak has lived in Aldbourne since 1995 after moving from London. He is a self-employed computer network designer currently working for Sun Microsystems. Roger enjoys walking, cycling and travelling with his girlfriend, Venty. He is slowly renovating the house (No 12) and fighting his way through the wilderness of his rather steep garden. Roger intends to live in the village for many years and has no plans to return to living in London.

Steve and Sue Cox have lived at No 9 since the mid-1980s. They both work at Nationwide's headquarters in Swindon (Sue part-time) and when at home enjoy walking their dog, cycling, motorcycling and DIY. Sue is a

Chapter Three

Toddlers

Aldbourne Toddler Group opens its doors at the Methodist Hall at 10.00am each Thursday morning during term time. For an hour and a half, the children, aged from birth to three, enjoy a variety of toys and creative pastimes. The toddlers learn to play together and practise social skills to take them through their school days. They can also participate in activities such as painting and colouring, which in some cases they are unable to enjoy at home.

The babies have their own little club within Toddlers run by the health visitor. Mums, many of whom are first timers, can discuss any problems they may be experiencing. The health visitor discusses various stages of child care as well as weighing and measuring the babies.

Mums/carers also gain a great deal from the group. Some of them may be new to the village and can make friends. Others enjoy a change of scenery from their homes and the chance to have a cup of coffee and a chat with others in the same situation. Throughout the year fundraising activities are arranged to provide enough income to pay for the hall, replace any damaged or worn-out toys and provide paint, paper and so on.

7 Kandahar

6 Kandahar

5 Kandahar

member of WI and sings in the WI Choir. They both enjoy cooking and love their very steep garden which, although hard work, has the most wonderful views.

Lindsay and David Keen have made their home at No 8. Lindsay was born in the village but Dave came here at the age of six months from Stitchcombe. He is a builder who enjoys angling and Lindsay is an office administrator for Barnes Coaches and enjoys walking and swimming. They have two children, Sarah who lives in Swindon and Simon, also a builder, who plays football for the village reserve team. Mike Allen and Mandi Iles live at No 6. 'Since moving here in June 1995, when not working, we have both enjoyed redesigning and renovating the house and garden and aim to have finished by the year 2000! We also enjoy walking our dogs, vegetable gardening and music, including performing as a duo in pubs, clubs and even locals' gardens!'

No 5 is home to Philip and Susan Weeks and their two sons, Elliott and Michael. Philip is Allied Dunbar's recruitment manager whilst Sue provides childcare facilities for eight families in Aldbourne. Elliott attends St Michael's School and Michael commenced pre-school in September 1998.

THE HEAVENS

For the past millennium, as for countless ages before that, the sky has played out its eternal dance: Orion the Hunter announcing the coming winter; Cygnus the Swan dominating the summer sky; the planets wandering the heavens. What have the generations of peasants, yeomen and craftsmen of our village thought of these wonders above them? Did one of our Saxon forbears look skywards and marvel at the new star which appeared above Orion in 1054? We know the Chinese saw it, and Native Americans in Arizona, but nothing tells us what the sons of Ealda might have made of it. Twelve years later did they watch mighty Halley's comet as we all watched Hale-Bopp a couple of years ago? And did the news from Hastings a few weeks later strengthen their belief in the comet as a bad omen? But such things are global phenomena, and our interest is in Aldbourne. Nature reserves her greatest spectacle – a total solar eclipse – for very specific tracks across the face of the globe. We all know that, as the millennium ended, such a wonder occurred in the south-west. In Aldbourne the sun dimmed as the moon covered all but a tiny fraction of it; but it was nothing like as spectacular as 80 miles south of us in the track of totality.

Let us look back over the past 1,000 years to see whether our ancestors would ever have stopped in their fields and gazed in awe at the rushing shadow of the moon, the sudden darkness and the flashing glow of the sun's corona. Solar eclipses are not as rare as many think – August's eclipse was the 369th visible in Aldbourne since 1000AD, fifty-eight of which covered more than 80 per cent of the sun's face. But how many of us noticed almost half the sun disappear one October lunchtime three years ago? Our forefathers in the fields would have noticed. There have been just three total eclipses in 1,000 years. For the first, Aldbourne was just on the edge of the moon's shadow and the peasants serving on the King's Warren would have gazed in wonder as the sun blinked out for a few seconds on the afternoon of 9 March 1140. More than five hundred years passed before Dabchicks witnessed such a spectacle again – and then they saw two within a decade. Work in the fields and the foundries would have stopped on the morning of 22 April 1715 and again nine years later on 11 May 1724 when Aldbourne was in the centre of the shadow and the darkness would have lasted several minutes. Or perhaps the weather intervened and they cowered under darkening skies without marvelling at the glory above the clouds.

And the next? A few of our toddlers might still be here to see the great spectacle again in the early evening of 23 September 2090.

CHAPTER THREE

2 Lottage Way

Lottage Way

Peter and Daphne Ludlow live at 3 Lottage Way which Peter built in 1968–9 on what was Don Powell's paddock. Daphne was born at 15 The Green as was her daughter, Jacqueline. The Ludlow boys, Philip and Nigel, were born at 34 Oxford Street. Peter, originally from Ramsbury, served from 1943 as a glider pilot and then as a para with the 6th Airborne Group. He made his career in the field of auctioneering with Dennis Pocock whom he joined in 1948. Both Daphne and Peter have been centrally involved in village life. Daphne with Peggy Bendle started the first playgroup in the Memorial Hall with four children. She taught in the Sunday School for eighteen years and has been closely associated with the Scout and Guide movement. She and Peter were founder members of the Scout and Guide supporters, which is responsible for providing the excellent hut which is used, free of charge, by Scouts, Cubs, Beavers, Guides, Brownies and Rainbows. Both Peter and Daphne were involved in pantomimes in the village, Peter as a memorable 'dame' and Daphne as choreographer for the children's dancing. Peter keeps his hand in on the auctioneering front by regularly helping to raise funds within the village for a variety of good causes.

3 Lottage Way

Chapter Four

The Cook Road Estate

Alma Road

Simon and Joanne Hutchings live at No 7 which was built between 1962 and 1964. It has been increased in size twice with a kitchen extension and a loft conversion. Simon and Joanne are the second occupiers having moved in March 1993. Simon was brought up in the village, living at *Greenacres*, Southward Lane from 1965 to 1987, and prior to that, in London. He attended St Michael's School and became a Cub Scout. He moved on to Marlborough Grammar School which later became St John's, travelling daily on Barnes Coaches. Simon is an active member of the Tennis Club, has been a member since his schooldays and regularly plays in the club's

1 Alma Road

> **Livestock**
>
> Grazing livestock numbers are in decline reflecting national trends, particularly after the BSE scare of the last ten years. Sheep have been and still are traditional and predominant, followed by beef, dairy cows and horses.
>
> Horse numbers have in fact shown a resurgence at the end of the century and are now a significant feature in the parish, particularly eventers, race horses and hacks.
>
> There are only three dairy herds left in the parish whereas at the turn of the century there were about twelve; herd numbers are static or falling as the industry is governed by a very strict quota system imposed by the Common Agricultural Policy.
>
> Interestingly there is a flock of sheep milked for cheese production.
>
> Pig and poultry continue mainly in specialist units. Stock is still driven on public roads outside the village although seldom as they used to be through the village being watered at the pond on their way to the grazing.
>
> Field sports are actively pursued including hunting, beagling, pheasant and partridge shooting (family shoots) and roe deer stalking, as well as ferreting and rabbiting.

Chapter Four

> ### Dowsing
>
> Dowsing is a mysterious and a practical occupation (says Major General Bill Cooper, an active dowser, a teacher and, until January 2000, president of the British Society of Dowsers). It is practical for those looking for oil or water, public utility cables or pipes, or those looking for something lost. Healers and many others use it yet no one really knows how it works. Our house, *Neals*, used to be the local surgery and it is fitting that I carry out healing here and use dowsing as a diagnostic tool.
>
> The simplest dowsing is performed by holding a twig or piece of metal in the hands and noting its movement but many use complex electrical equipment.
>
> Nevertheless, no one has been able to explain distant or map dowsing where the experienced dowser is situated miles from the site and pin-points the target from a map or plan.
>
> What is absolutely necessary is that the dowser asks the correct and very detailed question of his or her subconscious.
>
> Earth energies and geopathic stress, both connected with dowsing, cannot be proved but I believe they do exist as do Peggy Delmé-Radcliffe and Marcus Rouse, both good dowsers.

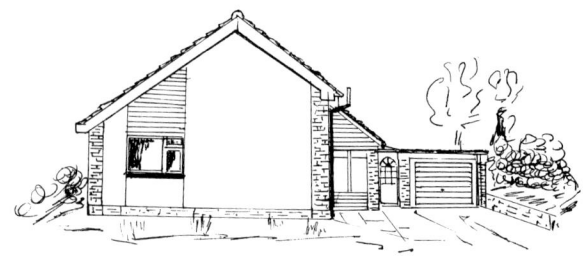

3 Alma Road

5 Alma Road

7 Alma Road

9 Alma Road

The Cook Road Estate

24 Alma Road

league sides. Joanne was brought up in London and Wootton Bassett. She met Simon at Supermarine Bowmen Archery Club in Swindon and they were married in 1991. They have two children, Samuel and Catherine.

No 9 is the home of Tony and Ivy Gray to which they moved in 1964. Tony's memories of the village have been recorded as part of the oral history of the village.

No 24 is where Anne and Eddie Payne and their son, Martin, have lived since it was built in 1964. Anne belongs to a village family; her father's grandparents moved here. Martin is very much into motorbikes. Eddie is a blacksmith. They enjoy their garden which is much admired. Lestor Walshe has lived at No 22 for fourteen years. He is a retired builder and enjoys the odd game of golf.

At No 20 are Don and Rosemary Wilmot, both retired. Don was a heating engineer and Rosemary a teacher. They have two children, Melanie has a BSc(Hons) in occupational therapy. Mark was a Queen's Scout. They have lived in the village for twenty-one years, four of them in Alma Road.

> ### Birds and Butterflies
>
> Swifts in summer scream around the church where they nest and swallows and house martins breed, but all in reduced numbers. All migrant warblers seemed scarce in 1998. The west side of the churchyard is managed for wildlife, contributing to the number of meadow and downland flowers and making a splash of colour that encourages butterflies – browns, skippers, small tortoiseshells, blues, marbled whites, painted ladies and others.
>
> Many garden birds live here too – blackbirds in plenty, a few song thrushes, robins, wrens, goldcrests, blue-, great-, coal- and long-tailed tits. Though linnets are rare, greenfinches, chaffinches, and goldfinches can be heard and seen. The latter are very striking in winter at bird tables, as are the great spotted woodpeckers and pied wagtails on the ground.
>
> Rooks, jackdaws and collared doves are increasing, but there are fewer starlings and house sparrows. Those with goldfish ponds get occasional visits from herons! However, in the hedgerows and open fields we still have quite a number of larks, yellowhammers, corn buntings and occasional quails. Sadly we are following the national trend in the loss of lapwings.
>
> There has been some success locally in encouraging barn owls, but in general owls are scarce.

22 Alma Road

20 Alma Road

Chapter Four

Chris and Sue Tucker have been at No 18 Alma Road for four years also and have two small boys. Sue was born at Witcha. 'Someone enjoys a game of golf.'

The Stevens family live at No 14, the household consisting of three adults and one child. They have lived here for thirty years and their three children were born in the village. Their hobby is dog agility training. No 12 is a household of three adults and a child. They have lived here for seven years and their hobbies include theatre, racing, art and gardening.

Mrs Pringuer and her son David, who has been awarded the MBE, have made their home at No 10. David spends six months of the year in Papua New Guinea where he owns a group of security companies.

No 8 has been the home of Mrs Beacham and her dog for five years. She can be seen walking her dog most days. She previously lived at 3 Cook Road. Mrs Waite lives at No 6 with her dog. She has been in the village for thirty-seven years.

Mr and Mrs Painter have lived at *Hillsview* for twenty-eight years. They enjoy gardening and are both members of the Methodist Church. Ken Towsey, who enjoys golf and DIY, has lived at No 2 for twelve years.

Corner Fields *(18) Alma Road*

16 Alma Road

14 & 12 Alma Road

The Cook Road Estate

> ### A Royal Wave
>
> In the early 1940s Margaret and her sister-in-law walked to Littlecote in the pouring rain as they had heard that the King, who was very ill at the time, was arriving to review the troops staying there.
>
> As they walked along the track, two motorcyclists overtook them, followed by the King in his car. He was wearing uniform and as he passed they were delighted when he raised his stick to wave at them.

10 & 8 Alma Road

6 Alma Road

Hillsview (4) Alma Road

2 Alma Road

1 Cook Road

Chapter Four

Cook Road

To Cook Close

When the bungalows were built in 1965 Michael and May Nolan bought No 1. Their daughter Jacqueline was born in 1967. Mike, who died in 1986, was well-known because he was chairman of Carnival Committee for many years. May who suffered with arthritis, died in 1998 just before she was to move in with her family in Ramsbury.

Mr and Mrs Elliot came to live at No 2 in 1965. Mr Elliot has been a widower since 1983 and retired from Vickers in 1985. Both he and his wife received clocks for completing thirty years service at Vickers. Mr Elliot has an immaculate garden but claims he tends it purely for the exercise.

Geoffrey and Linda Maslin moved to No 3 in 1994; son Thomas was born in 1996. Linda is the daughter of Mr and Mrs D Paget of *Northfield Cottages*. Geoffrey is a collector of old farming equipment, mostly tractors and ploughs. He competes, sometimes successfully, in ploughing matches.

Richard and Kate Digman have rented No 4 from the Rev Viv Brookes since August 1997. They both work in Newbury, having moved from Hull, and would very much like

> ### NOTHING FANCY
>
> Aldbourne Luncheon Club has been running for over twenty years, providing luncheons on the first and third Thursdays of each month in the Memorial Hall. Twenty-four people, chosen from among residents of the parish who live on their own, attend and are asked to pay £1.50.
>
> The meals – 'nothing fancy' – are cooked and served by teams of volunteers. Each diner gets a free raffle ticket, the prize being one of the flower arrangements that always grace the tables. A car service picks up those who are unable to walk to the hall. The luncheon ensures that elderly people living alone have an adequate diet but it also provides the opportunity to meet others in similar positions and the occasion is enjoyed as much by the helpers as by their guests.

2 Cook Road

3 Cook Road

to buy a property in Aldbourne. They are keen motorcyclists, owning a 900cc Triumph. Richard is an expert woodworker and they also make wine.

Dave and Jacqui Henshaw, with children Daniel and Carly, arrived at No 5 in June 1997 from Warrington. Dave works as a toy salesman and Jacqui helps to cook dinners at St Michael's School. Dave is a keen footballer and manages the senior team at Ramsbury. Daniel plays for Ramsbury Under-fourteens. Carly enjoys being a member of the Brownies.

Adrian and Susie Wilmot have lived at No 6 for two years. Adrian's family also live in Aldbourne and he belongs to the Dabchicks Rugby Club as well as enjoying other sports. Susie is a lawyer at Burmah Castrol and Adrian works as accounts manager for Britvic.

No 7 is owned by Emi and Tony Smith who lived there for fourteen years with their children Joanna, Heloise, Max and Charlotte until moving to a viable cider orchard near Malmsbury in 1998. The property is now let. Tony directed a business locally and was a governor of St Michael's School.

Brian and Daphne Hale and family have lived at No 8 since 1970. Sons Matthew and Francis (Frank), and daughter Rachel have now left home. Brian is a retired college lecturer with a keen interest in photography.

4 & 5 Cook Road

6 & 7 Cook Road

> ### The Cook Estate
>
> Cook Road and Close were named after the Cook family who lived in the village for some 200 years and owned the adjoining land.
>
> When Mary Cook, who became Mrs Paddy Gilligan, sold the land just before she died it was meadow with allotments on the east side.

Chapter Four

8 & 9 Cook Road

Beryl and Terry Gilligan have two children who both gained university degrees. They have lived in No 9 for twenty years. In fact, the Cook Road estate was built on land originally owned by Terry's ancestors called Cook. The Gilligans and the Cooks go back many generations in Aldbourne. Beryl started Aldbourne Tearoom in 1989. Terry enjoys bell-ringing and was previously captain of Aldbourne Cricket Club and Scout Leader.

Madeleine and Martin Rubach moved to No 10 with Emma and Megan in 1983. Madeleine teaches English to foreign students and Martin is a film and TV producer as well as yachtsman. The girls attended St Michael's and St John's Schools and Madeleine was clerk to the governors at the former and a governor of the latter. The family has supported a variety of local organizations.

Gillian and David Mann have lived in No 11 since it was built in July 1965. They have three daughters, Julie, Kathryn and Teresa, all of whom are married, and two of whom now live with their husbands in the village. Gillian belongs to the WI Choir, the Ladies' Group and ALEC and also paints, knits, sews and

10 & 11 Cook Road

The Cook Road Estate

Corinium House *(3) Cook Close*

2 Cook Close

gardens. David occupies his retirement with fishing, shooting and woodworking.

Cook Close

When Nora and Eric Attoch moved to Ramsbury in 1982, Ann and David Lee, now both retired teachers, took over No 3. They love travelling and are both active members of village societies – WI, Theatre Club, Civic Society, as well as the Millennium Committee. David is not only co-editor of the Millennium Book of Aldbourne but also editor of *The Dabchick*. Ann and David are enthusiastic orienteers and were two of the team of three which won the British Orienteering Relay Championship in 1993. They have two adult sons who enjoy their visits to the village.

The Warren family moved into No 2 thirty years ago and have two sons, one a horticulturist, the other a civil servant, living with them. There is another son in the village and also an uncle of the three boys. Ivy's main interests are cooking and gardening.

No 1 is occupied by a retired electronic engineer, Charles Gape, who moved into the house thirty-three years ago. His two daughters, Fiona and Helen, went to the local schools but now live out of the village, although in

1 Cook Close

> ### Celebrating
>
> "In 1990 I celebrated my fiftieth birthday with family and friends at *The Crown* and in the year 2000 – no prizes for guessing in which village I plan to celebrate the big six-0.
>
> It's so great having a place where you have many childhood memories and which is always there for you to return to. Aren't we Dabchicks lucky?"

Chapter Four

12 & 13 Cook Road

Grave Digging

"Grave digging requires great skill. It is not just digging a hole and filling it in after the funeral.

Expertise is needed if accidents are to be avoided. The digger needs to know the exact measurements of the coffin and also how much extra to allow for handles and the green grave linings. Depth is another factor if more coffins are to be buried in that grave at a later date. Minimum depth is 4 feet 6 inches and there should be at least three feet of soil above the coffin lid.

The sides and ends must be kept truly perpendicular so a plumb bob is part of the grave digger's tools. A short ladder is always at hand for a quick exit if, as sometimes happens, a side starts falling in. A gravedigger must not suffer from claustrophobia because at six foot down the grave gets quite tight.

The weather also plays an important part as very wet weather can cause the earth so laboriously thrown out to a distance of eight to ten feet to get wet suddenly causing the side of the grave to give way."

So writes Vin Jerram who has dug many graves.

the area. Charles is treasurer of the Memorial Hall Committee and involved with the Civic Society and Cricket Club. He enjoys walking and gardening and is a volunteer driver for Medicar and Prospect.

From Cook Close to Grasshills

Chris and Lance Kingsman, Nathan, Clare and Stacey bought No 13 from the Barnes family ten years ago. Lance is a postman and Chris an accounts clerk who also types for *The Dabchick*. She is a member of the WI and her mother and one sister both live in the village. Stacey and Clare are at St John's School and Nathan is an apprentice electrician. No 14 has been the family home of June and Peter Pickford since 1971. Their sons Andrew (a bricklayer), Gary (a farrier) and David (a carpenter) grew up in this house and are all now married. Andrew still lives in the village with his family and June lists her grandchildren as one of her hobbies together with hairdressing and gardening, the WI and Sports and Social Club. Peter used to be a steeplechase jockey.

The Reverend Charles and Mrs Pauline Pakenham have occupied No 15 since 1976. Charles still works as an assistant priest (Church of England) in the Inkpen area and enjoys fishing and the Gentlemen's Luncheon Club. Pauline is a retired teacher and a keen member of the WI and Mothers' Union. Her interests include spinning and handicrafts. Charles' sister Ruth also lives in the village.

Mrs Bunker moved into No 16 in 1997 and has a daughter living in the village. She is an active member of the Methodist Church.

No 17 is the home of Vic and Margaret Hanks who have lived there since it was built in November 1964. They are retired from being a motor mechanic and an office secretary. A notable feature of their property is the rose garden enjoyed by all that pass by. Vic spends much time on maintaining the house and garden. Margaret is a skilled craftswoman, particularly with her knitting, crochet and embroidery, and helped make the kneelers in

> ### HISTORICAL RESEARCH
>
> One of the sources for information for producing this book has been research organized by the Civic Society with supporting funding from Kennet District Council. A lot of information was gathered by the researchers into the building history and oral history of the village.
>
> The Civic Society plans to produce pamphlets which will be available to all from the secretary covering each of these subjects. They will contain much additional material which is fascinating in its own right but is not covered in this book.

14 & 15 Cook Road

16 & 17 Cook Road

CHAPTER FOUR

St Michael's Church. They both enjoy walking the dog, reading and listening to music. 'We have found Aldbourne to be a very friendly village, particularly Cook Road and Cook Close which have an exceedingly good community spirit. We have never regretted leaving Swindon to come to live in the country.'

Michael, Lesley, Nadia and Callum Murray live at No 18. Lesley, who was raised in Chiseldon, moved here 1988. Aldbourne was Lesley's grandfather's favourite village and she used to come here as a child. Michael was born in Bulawayo and came to England in 1989. They met when Michael was working on Ramsbury Farms. He now works at Honda while Lesley is a mobile hairdresser. Nadia was born in 1991. She goes to school in Baydon and enjoys horse riding. Callum came along in 1994 and has a turn on the pony. Mum and Dad can be seen supervising the ride that enables Michael to get in his walks.

Ron and Eileen Wordley moved into the bungalow, No 21, in 1993. Mr and Mrs John Oliver previously owned it. Ron is self-employed in the building trade and Eileen is a housewife. They enjoy gardening, golf, eating out and reading. Eileen has long connections with the village – her grandparents, Mr and Mrs William Tucker, lived at 9 The Square and her mother, Mrs Lillian Jones, was born in the village. Her sister, Geraldine Bradley, lives in Lottage Road.

18 & **The Three Graces** *(19) Cook Road*

MY FIFTH BIRTHDAY

"I was born at *The Crown* in April 1940 – the oldest of six children, of Dick and Denise Holland. Our early life, as with most people during that time, was necessarily frugal. As the war progressed I imagine food became more scarce. It was therefore with some delight that I heard my Mum say I could have a party on my fifth birthday. By that time I had two sisters of one and three years old, but the great thing was that Mum and Gran said I could invite some friends from school. I remember we had a table put up in the pub lounge and I was promised jelly and blancmange.

At the appointed time, a couple of children were brought to the door by parents and we went to play in the lounge. More children arrived, then more and more, until poor Mum said: 'Meg, how many "friends" have you invited?'. I guess a large proportion of the children of the village turned up. I have often wondered how we managed to feed all my guests that day, even whether they all had 'birthday fayre' – there wouldn't have been any 'extra rations' in the freezer waiting to be defrosted! Jelly and blancmange take time to set.

I remember the games were great."

The Cook Road Estate

20 Cook Road

21 Cook Road

22 Cook Road

23 Cook Road

The Liddiard Family

"Our name dates back to the 1600s. When we were children they used to say if you stood in the Square and called Barnes, Palmer, Stacey and Liddiard then you would get almost the entire village turning out.

My mother's parents, the Orchards, were another old village family. Grandfather Thomas Orchard had the chair factory. Recently I found some chair seats in the loft. There was also a bench where grandfather used to do the paperwork and the accident book for 1904 with an entry for Barrett who had cut his thumb.

I was born just outside the village and my sister Kate was born on the Green opposite *Ivy House*. We lived at the house on the Green facing the church nearest to High Town which was a stables.

My grandmother and mother were both postmistresses. At the beginning of the war I spent my time pedalling my bicycle around the area delivering telegrams. I cycled as far as Preston, Lambourn and Russley. I used to deliver a lot of telegrams to *Upham House* where you might have expected there to be a phone. While I was waiting for Lady Currie they took me to the pantry for a glass of cider. This was a big deal as I was only fourteen or fifteen."

Chapter Four

Ann and Bernard McEntee moved to No 22 in the hot summer of 1976 when Bernard relocated to work in Swindon and felt that Aldbourne had everything to give them and their son and daughter: they were right.

Until recently Edith Tweddell lived at No 23. She moved there from London in 1964 when the bungalow was new, adding a conservatory. Edith was the Mothers' Union enrolling member for ten years and a PCC member. In 1974 she was a committee member for planning and working the church kneelers – 75 per cent of which are her designs.

Betty and Derek Smith moved to No 24 in 1984, the property's fourth owners. The location of Aldbourne on the Downs, midway between the Berkshire homes of daughters, Janet and Carole, was perfect. The view from the lounge window settled the matter beyond doubt.

Bridget and Roy Partridge came to No 25 as agricultural lecturers. Roy joined Bartrops and is still in the trade, Bridget did social work. Best known for sailing around the English Channel, Roy also restores Bentleys. Both are pet lovers. Their two children went through to university degrees and good careers. The house has been extended three times.

Robert and Diana Loadman moved to No 26 from London in 1964 for Robert to work as a manufacturing engineer in Swindon. The

24 Cook Road

25 Cook Road

> ### Memories of 1945
>
> "I was from Blackpool, Fred from Aldbourne. We became squatters.
>
> We wanted a home and there were none so Fred and I decided we would move into the deserted army camp in Farm Lane. Peggy and Ron Dew agreed to join us. So we picked a hut each and then got to work.
>
> Water was laid on and electricity was available in each hut. We put partitions in to make our different rooms. We got a range from Charley Stacey the builder and installed it.
>
> I also got a large fire guard to go round the back of the range to keep my little girl away from the heat. We had to get beds, table and chairs from Swindon with our precious dockets.
>
> Then more people joined us – Ethel and Charlie Underwood; Rose Crook with her twins; Les Miles, a groom from Major Powell's yard, and his wife and little boy.
>
> I had to get a paraffin stove and oven which I had never seen before!
>
> This was the start of our first home and the start of our life together, as Fred had been in the RAF. We had great fun and it was great to be together in our own place."

house was new. They have had three children since coming here and their house too has been extended. Their village activities include scouting and guiding, stage lighting and the Luncheon Club.

Fred (known as Mac) and Mary MacKrill moved into No 27 when it was new. Mary is a Dabchick and Mac was born locally.

Bob and Margaret Preston moved to No 28 on Election Day, 9 June 1983, with daughters Lara and Joanna. They are the seventh occupants and the longest residents. Margaret is a head occupational therapist and Bob a fisheries officer with the Environment Agency. Bob's hobbies include game fishing at which he has represented England.

26 Cook Road

> ### Fire Service
>
> Adam and Eve are retired and fire cover is the responsibility of the Wiltshire Fire Brigade with immediate cover from Ramsbury, a retained station where all firemen receive retainers and are rostered to stay within bleeper call and two minutes reach of the station. If there is a fire call from Aldbourne the controller bleeps the firemen, briefs them and within 2–4 minutes they are on their way reaching the village within about eight minutes of the alarm being received. Two engines will come from Ramsbury, a water carrier and a pumping appliance. A house fire would need another from Marlborough.
>
> Anyone who has been present as a fire starts will have experienced the short, anxious time waiting for the fire engines. The firemen's well-practised skills are honed during the weekly two-hour drill and backed by experience.
>
> The crisis over, a helmet is removed, a brow wiped and a familiar and friendly face recognized (it could be the painter, bricklayer, mechanic or curate). The response to the fire has been made by members of our larger community living in Ramsbury providing a service for which Aldbourne is truly grateful.

27 Cook Road

28 Cook Road

Chapter Four

29 Cook Road

30 Cook Road

31 Cook Road

Local Government

Three elected councils apply their care to the Parish; the Parish, District and County Councils and, in 2000, the chairman of the Parish Council, Chris Humphries, is also its elected District and County Councillor.

There are fifteen parish councillors who are elected for four years. The council has few powers but a degree of influence which depends largely upon the councillors and the acumen of the parish clerk, all of whom serve the parish well.

The powers of the Parish Council include raising a precept or tax which is added to the District Council Tax Bill. In 1999–2000 it was £13,500. This is used to pay, for example, for street lighting, grass cutting and the salary of the parish clerk.

There are nine committees that cover local matters. All planning applications are considered by the Planning Committee and sometimes by the full council. With a councillor for about every 100 electors the Parish Council is, of all elected authorities, the closest to its electorate. The council has influence when it expresses the views of the parish; the more it applies this lively influence the more influential it becomes.

The District and County Councils are more remote but their decisions greatly affect the common good of the parish and the private circumstances of parishioners.

The District Council's planning decisions are particularly important as they affect the neighbourhood. Also important are the council's decisions on housing developments, industrial sites, waste disposal, and so on.

The County Council has most impact on education and highways.

Though none of the councils can claim the close interest of most parishioners they are generally well-regarded by the parish which depends on the services they provide.

The Cook Road Estate

32 Cook Road

Ian, Ingrid and Oliver Nash moved into No 29 in May 1996, Rebekah was born in 1997. Ingrid and Ian met at City University and both have honours degrees in science. They like Aldbourne because of the countryside, the sense of community and the people – 'a wonderful place to raise a family'.

John and Diana May moved into No 30 in August 1964 with Peter and Joanne. Philip was born at home in 1966. In the large garden they planted silver birch, horse chestnut and walnut trees which thrive. House extensions include an entrance hall and large dining room (1971), a bay window (1997) and, in 1999, a conservatory.

The bungalow at No 31 is where Wendy Home moved to in November 1996, being the second owner since it was built. Wendy, her husband, mother, brother, sister and grandmother were all born in Aldbourne. Her father-in-law owned land in Alma Road and farmed all the land occupied by Cook Road until Cowley Brothers of Wroughton built the estate.

Prehistory

Beyond a few earthworks and flint tools turned up on the arable there is in the parish little to remind us of our earliest ancestors. A Palaeolithic (c.10,000BC) flint scraper found near Woodsend from the period just after the last Ice Age and quite a number of Mesolithic (c.7–4,000BC) axes remind us that 'hunter-gatherers' were followed by the first Neolithic (c.4–2,000BC) farmers. Other survivals from the Neolithic period include a probable sewing kit and two flint knives with ground edges for left- and right-hand use reminding us that these people were like ourselves.

The Bronze Age burial mounds, such as Four Barrows, date from about 2,700–800BC. Notably, a small pottery incense cup, 'The Aldbourne Cup', excavated from a barrow near the Swindon road is displayed in the British Museum and designates a particular cultural period of about 1,400BC. Many of the barrows were excavated in the early 19th century and the finds are recorded in the Devizes Museum.

The early Iron Age (1,000BC–500AD) continued the farming pattern exploiting the chalk uplands after they had been cleared by slashing and burning. At a distance we can see the hill forts, such as Liddington Castle, which were the predominant physical and political features of the area before the Roman invasion.

Chapter Four

Aldbourne Band

The Aldbourne Band was formed in the middle of the 19th century by the village church organist, Richard Brown-Bunce. Originally made up from a variety of instrument types, including clarinet and flute, the band gradually evolved, as most English bands did around the turn of the century, into the familiar format based around 3-valved brass, trombone and percussion.

A busy schedule of concerts and events in and around the Wiltshire area, often in conjunction with choirs or other musical groups, is maintained. Aldbourne Band has a reputation of playing very lyrically, selecting popular programme items, and it never fails to entertain the audience. The Band has played one particular concert, Upham Road Church in Swindon, each January for thirty-seven years and always plays to a full house. Traditional brass band music can often be something of an acquired taste for the die-hard listener so theme concerts are also presented based on the Broadway shows or from films. Concerts also provide an opportunity to play outside the immediate area reaching new audiences, playing different music and promote the village of Aldbourne – something the Band wishes to develop further in the coming years.

Close ties to Aldbourne village are maintained, with many of the Band members living in the village. The Band is very appreciative of the strong local support it receives from the village residents, and plays at local events including the carnival, fête, carol concert, Remembrance Sunday, and often at private weddings, parties and celebrations.

The first contest the Band entered was before World War I, and during the 1920s and the 1930s it achieved great acclaim performing at the Crystal Palace, London. A consistently high standard is maintained, competing locally and nationally, and regularly winning prizes. In 1963 the Band was promoted to the championship section of the national organization. In the early 1980s the band was at the height of its fame when it was placed first in the West of England Championship Section and consequently qualified to perform in the national finals at the Albert Hall.

In 1999 the Band holds a ranking of sixth place in the West of England Championship Section, draws in players from the North Wiltshire and Berkshire areas, remains a formidable force in the contesting arena and now has its sights firmly set on national contests. It hopes to maintain its prowess as a contesting band, to continue to provide entertaining music for the diverse range of public performances, to encourage the teaching of music, to set up a local training band and to simply enjoy the strong spirit that exists in the brass band world.

Vicarages

There have been various parsonage houses. The earliest known is the *Old Priest's House*, the residence of the vicar, John Stone, who died in 1524. His memorial is in the church. In 1805 a vicarage stood on a plot behind the present St Michael's Close but under the Enclosure Act of 1806 *The Court House* was awarded to the vicar and became the vicarage. It remained so until 1956, when 11 The Green was given to the Crown Commissioners by Miss Eve. In about 1973 the present vicarage was built to the east of the church. The property in the Square currently called *The Old Manor*, previously 'The Old Vicarage', was marked on the enclosure map as 'Parsonage' but this related to the rectorial rights owned by the Dean and Chapter of Winchester.

A Bird's Eye View – Then and Now

(above) An aerial view of the village believed to have been taken in 1926.
(left) A similar view taken in April 1996.

(below) Where we were and are!

Some Members of the Farming Community

(from the top, left to right) Andrew Puttick, William Brown and Bernard Price (whose family has worked for the Brown family for over 125 years); John Lee and Hugh Bland; Jonathan Mildenhall and Betty Gentry; Ray Edwards and Michael Hale; Joy Hobby and helper; Adrian and Gordon Hale; Graham Mildenhall; John Hill; Betty Pound.

(left) Guy Wentworth; Robert Lawton.

YOUNG PEOPLE AND SOME OF THOSE WHO HELP

(top left) Guides: Laura Beattie, Monica Moreton and Catherine Startin with Laura Hutchin in front.
(top right) Toddler Group: Liz Cullen with Daniel, Sharon Lappin, Alex Womersley with Rebecca and Billy Paget, Claire Shaw with Tilly, Vicky Davies with Aaron Lappin, Lyn Clough with Lauren and Linda Maslin with young Jack.
(above) Scouts: at the back – Peter Dinwiddie, Paul Williams, Nathan Williams, Billy Grimm and Mary Grimm; in front – Scott Marsh and Joe Beattie.
(above right) Brownies: Wendy Beattie, Lisa Williams, Jaqui Henshaw and Laura Beattie stand behind Kirstie Fuller, Freya Spath and Abby Cheney.
(right) Cubs: back row – David Jones, William Hale, Jane Palmer and Nathan Clough; in the front row – Ian Watson, Andrew Hutchin and Bertie Haskins.

(right) Gill Hanlon of the Aldbourne Children's Book Group.
(far right) Hugh Tucker and Jade Watts seen with Annette Jerram at Aldbourne Pre-school.

The Aldbourne Silver Band

(above) A pond concert in the Square in 1999, with David Williams, conductor, and Claire Smith, soloist.
(left) The band under Don Keen's leadership.
(below left) The band in 1911.

(opposite page) Carnival entries over the years.
(opposite page, top right) The 1999 Carnival Queen Shane Moreton with her attendants Lisa Keen and Lisa Marie Hewer, and Carnival Princesses Abby Cheney, Justine Browning and April Matthews.

Carnival Time

CLUBS AND SOCIETIES

(left) Aldbourne Football Club team photo 1999, including Colin Hughes (captain) and Pete Orsi (manager).

(below left) Aldbourne Dab-chicks Rugby Club: standing – John Pearse, Pete Grant, guest, Richard Palmer, Richard Jeffcoat (fixtures secretary), Dave Paulin, Chis Flett (club captain), Ewen Hayward, Mike Stagg, Andy Brown and Mike Mason (chairman); kneeling – Steve Jarrett, Pete Hughes, Phil Comley, Johnny Badger, Paul Beresford, Chris Paget and Anthony Jones (team captain).

(below) Some members of Aldbourne Lawn Tennis Club: Hugh Bland, Anna Bland, Pat McPhedran, Sally Thomas, Kate Harding and Simon Hutchings.
(bottom) Russell and Sandra Barnes of Serendipity Bellringers.

(below) ALEC members on the set of their 1999 production of 'Round and Round the Garden': standing – Jennison Grey, Paul Newman, Brian Buckler, Diane Choules and Malcolm Shuttle-worth; middle row – Mark Davies and Peter Lawler; front row – Jaki Mitchell, Namrita Price-Goodfellow, Trish Rushen and Jonathan Hill.

BUILDING, MAINTENANCE AND ASSOCIATED ACTIVITIES

(left, top to bottom) Richard Kimber; Andy Matthews; Ken Athawes; Doug Hagerty.

(below, from the top, left to right) Anthony Butler; Andy Young; Bruce Titcombe; Donald Barnes; Ron Hacker; Ken Read; Sonia (a garden designer) and Terence Wright; Ron Morley.

COMMITTEES! COMMITTEES! COMMITTEES!

(left, top to bottom) The Parish Council: standing – Ceri Hanlon, Ges Dolman, Harry Sheppard, Keith Evill, Hugh Bland and Peter Lawler; seated – Bill Puttick, Brian Buckler, Margaret Palmer, Chris Humphries, Sandy Muirhead, William Brown and Andy Devey. (Not present – Jane Palmer and Annette Jerram.)
WI committee: standing – Di May, Maureen Jepson, Peta Cook, Ann Lee, Julie Kent and Audrey Barrett; seated – Beryl Phelps, Vi Carr, Ann Hall, Ishbel Sewell, Chris Hill and Geraldine Bradley.
Millennium Festival Committee: at the back – Brian Buckler, Shirley Gibbs, Harry Sheppard, Heather Athawes and John May; in front – Vanessa Butler, Milly Sheppard, Chris Hill and Bob Loadman.
The Working Party for the Millennium Book of Aldbourne: Harry Sheppard, Penny Hagerty, John Loch, Jane Ebbutt, David Lee and Malcolm Shuttleworth.

(below) Not a location shot from 'Last of the Summer Wine' but the officers of the Civic Society – Mike Hillas, David Lee and David Robertson (chairman).
(bottom) Jean Davis, Irene Jerram and Bert Steggles, officers of Silver Threads.

Chapter Five

Oxford Street & up the Hill

Oxford Street

The beginnings

Ken and Joyce Hawkins moved to *The Coppins* in 1987. The site of their house was originally a rubbish dump, possibly for the livery stables nearby. Their bungalow and the one next door were built at the same time. Joyce has been actively involved with the WI, having completed two stints on the committee totalling six years. One of the WI activities that Joyce assisted with was providing a hospital trolley service, selling useful and personal items to patients in the Accident and Emergency department of the Princess Margaret Hospital. Ken and Joyce first met in Bomber Command during World War II; Joyce was a Special Duty Watch Keeper in the WAAF and Ken was a Flight Lieutenant, Air Gunner. He was awarded the OBE and DFC. Joyce was in London during the Blitz. Ken made his career in British Airways and they have lived in many parts of the world including Turkey, the Soviet Union (for six years), Hamburg, Rome and Berlin. They have also met members of the Royal Family, attended a royal garden party and boarded the Royal Yacht. Most recently in 1997 they attended a special service at Salisbury Cathedral followed by tea to mark their fiftieth wedding anniversary in the same year as the Queen and Prince Phillip. One of Ken's outstanding memories was meeting Sir Edmund Hilary. Ken was deputed to look after

Clevedon *(1 New Bungalows) Oxford Street*

> ### Workhouse
>
> "In Hungerford there was a workhouse for tramps, the unemployed and those with a 'low mentality'.
> They came to Aldbourne looking for work and were monitored by the Infirmary."

CHAPTER FIVE

The Coppins *Oxford Street*

him, and he met Sir Edmund at Northolt Airport. He was struck by the sheer size of the man, and also his weatherbeaten face, very wide shoulders and powerful handshake. Ken died suddenly in May 1999. Their son is married with four children between two and ten years old and lives in Kuala Lumpur where his business is based.

Ron and Helen Morley have lived at *Mount Pleasant* for nineteen years. Deeds to the house go back to 1880, and it is known that the house was extended in 1925, 1979 and 1982. The cottage originally consisted of just one room and, indeed, may not have started life as a house at all. Originally it was a low level thatched structure with a wide door, which

Mount Pleasant *(18) Oxford Street*

A HISTORY OF THE CLUB

Aldbourne Sports and Social Club has been in existence for nearly 100 years now. The club is still based on its original site behind the Memorial Hall. The building was originally a Nissen Hut and was provided by Major Bland shortly after World War I to be used as a club for boys and young men. It housed a full size billiards/snooker table and other games such as bagatelle and was open to membership for boys of fourteen years upwards providing a social environment for them to meet in the evenings. Women were only allowed access as honorary members.

Many small extensions were built in the following years providing a bar and cellar area and the club expanded providing teams in various sports including cricket and football. In 1982 an extensive building project was undertaken and the old hut was replaced with new modern premises. In the 1980s the club finally allowed women to be full members with equal voting rights.

suggests it may have been a farm building. In the garden was a well, now filled in, which had a steel rope in it measuring ninety feet in length. There is also a large rounded chimney breast in the bedroom over the inglenook which curves into the room. *Mount Pleasant* has a wonderful view from the back of the house of St Michael's Church and Ogbourne Hill, not to mention the motorway traffic. Ron is a builder mainly working locally in Aldbourne, Ramsbury and Lambourn. He is also a member of 'The Aldbourne Buskers' singing and playing the guitar. His interests include clay pigeon shooting and he is a keen curry cook. Ron helped run the Youth Club and was a member of the Parish Council. He was recently asked to help with a royal visit to the Elm Farm Research Farm in Hampstead Marshall, when Prince Charles visited the organic research centre on an open day. Ron was required to drive his Range Rover as the official car for the Lord High Sheriff of Berkshire to accompany the royal visitor around the farm. During the visit Ron was introduced to Prince Charles. Helen Morley has lived in Aldbourne all her life, with at least four generations of her family living in the village. Ron has lived in Aldbourne for the past twenty-eight years, with three generations of his family living in the village. As a child, Ron's mother lived on Oxford Streeet at 'The Bethal' – now called *Apple Tree Cottage* (No 20). Helen's interests include horse riding; she owns her own horse

Michaelmas Cottage *(16) & 14 Oxford Street*

Bell-Founding

It seems hard to believe, but Aldbourne was once an industrial stronghold. From the 17th until the mid-19th centuries the village was one of England's premier bell-founding sites, and an approaching visitor would have been greeted by the coal stench of the furnaces that produced three types of bells – church bells, hand bells and the Aldbourne speciality, the rumbler.

The rumbler is a bell that is round like a ball and was hung around the necks of livestock or on a harness. Some said that the bells did not ring but 'rumbled', hence the name. They were also known as crotals from the Latin word *crotalus* meaning rattle.

Two families, the Cors and the Wells, dominated the industry and they were an inventive lot.

Aldbourne's Robert Cor was almost certainly responsible for inventing the all-in-one casting method for the rumblers, while another Cor, William, is believed to have been the first founder to make handbells tuned to harmonize.

The last bell-founder in the village was James Wells who specialized in church bells, but he also led the business into bankruptcy in 1825. The foundry's moulds were purchased by the Whitechapel Foundry in London and those same moulds, now returned to the village, are to be seen in the Memorial Hall.

You can tell an Aldbourne bell by the bell-founder's initials that are usually cast into the metal or, in the case of Cor bells, by the outline of a small bird moulded into the bell's inside rim. Local historian, Ida Gandy, once said that the bird was 'unmistakably a dabchick'.

Now there are only two surviving bell-makers in the UK, the Taylor Bellfoundries and the Whitechapel Foundry, but there was a time, and not so long ago, when Aldbourne could claim to be the bell capital of Britain.

CHAPTER FIVE

Orchard Cottage *& 12 Oxford Street*

> **ADULT EDUCATION**
>
> The Memorial Hall has been used for classes for several years.
>
> Currently organized by Swindon College, these include sessions on keep fit, gentle exercise and upholstery. There is a regular clientele for all the classes which are also welcomed as social occasions.

Memorial Hall *Oxford Street*

as well as two sheep which she has had as pets for the past two years, and a dog. Helen is a keen gardener, is a member of the Table Tennis Club and the Tennis Club and has recently started water-colour painting. She was also a member of the Youth Club.

In 1969 both Ron and Helen took part in a fundraising 'bed push' organized by the Youth Club to raise money for a heart machine for the Princess Margaret Hospital in Swindon. The push covered 411 miles around the Cornish coastline and made it into the Guinness Book of Records, though their record has since been broken.

Miss Florence Sherman's family moved to No 14 in 1917 when she was nine years old in order to live with her grandmother. She had two brothers and a sister and her father fought in the Boer War. When she was fifteen she left the village to work in Newbury to help look after the children of Mr Marshall of Charles Lucas and Marshall (Solicitors). Then during World War II she worked at Vickers, only returning to Aldbourne in the 1960s to live with her sister when Vickers shut down in Newbury. Miss Sherman is a member of Silver Threads which she ran with her sister Gertrude for several years. She still knits and donates gifts in support of fundraising. She also attends Methodist Fellowship regularly. Her parents were married in St Michael's Church and originally lived in West Street. Her father used to take the fustian fabric from the factory in Aldbourne to Swindon.

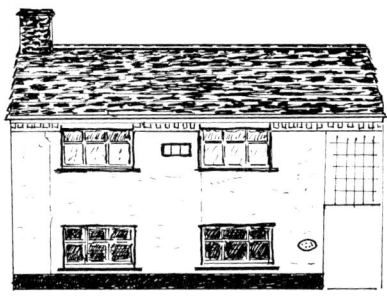

Myrtle Cottage *(10) Oxford Street*

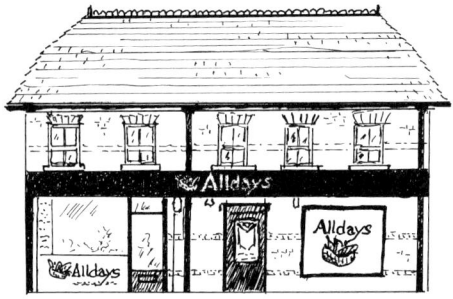

Oxford House *Oxford Street*

Adam, Alison and Cameron Power (aged two) live in *Orchard Cottage*. Adam and Alison moved to Aldbourne in 1995. The house, the barn and the paddock behind were all owned by Mr Tom Wilkins whose family had lived in the house for many years. The land was divided when sold and Adam and Alison renovated and extended the house and landscaped the garden, which was overgrown and sloping. One end of the house was once a separate dwelling with its own front and back door and staircase. This part of the house has the oldest window upstairs and the newest window downstairs, which probably dates the conversion to Victorian times. The house is approximately three hundred years old, dated by the surviving windows, woodwork and building

THE SHOP IN OXFORD STREET

There was a shop on this site in the 1800s which burned down in the 1890s. It was said that the owner who lived in Preston tipped an oil stove over before he left hoping to claim on the insurance. It was rebuilt in 1900 when Miss Thompson had it. Mr Richard Stacey bought the business in 1923 and sold it on to Mr and Mrs A J (Fred) Palmer in 1924.

They built it into a bakery, grocery and drapery business. A new faggot oven had been built in 1900 but it was replaced with a coke-fired steam tube oven, the pony and cart was replaced with a Ford Model T van and a billiard table was installed over the shop – 6d (2½p) a game. Pigs and chickens were kept on land at the rear bought from *Yew Tree Farm*.

There were four children in the Palmer family and each worked in the business. David, the youngest, was in charge of the grocery until in early 1961 when he decided to emigrate to America. Dorothy, the eldest, had been a librarian in Swindon, then a schoolteacher at Chilton Foliat and, on getting married, came into the business and organized the drapery side with her sister, Evelyn. Walter, with his wife Sheila, ran the bakery until 1969. Then the bakery was closed and the grocery enlarged. The drapery was made a separate shop and was known as the Boutique. It was also an agency for the Ramsbury Building Society.

In the early 1990s the business was sold and the new owners enlarged the selling area and changed it from a Spar shop to a Londis. The hours of trading were extended from 5½ days closing at 5.30pm to 7 days closing at 10.00pm.

Kevin and Liz Brown bought the business in 1995 transferring their newsagents from the Square. In 1997 it was sold once more and now trades as 'Alldays'. Extensive alterations have taken place and, ironically, an in-store bakery has been installed.

Chapter Five

Pettywell (4) & 2 Oxford Street

Box Cottage (3) Oxford Street

Mow Cop (5) Oxford Street

Oxford Street Buildings

This was called Baydon Street until the late 19th century and still has many small 18th and 19th century cottages.

No 1 was built in 1960 on part of the High Town estate. Nos 2 and 4 were originally three dwellings; No 2 has been in the Palmer family for many years.

The Memorial Hall, built after World War I, has the names of the fallen of both World Wars on the wall outside and the Remembrance Day Service is held here.

Orchard Cottage, originally a 17th to 18th century farmhouse, was once occupied by Mr Orchard.

No 20 was for many years the home of Maurice Crane, chronicler of Aldbourne.

No 22, a cottage of the 17th to 18th century, was once an inn, 'At the Sign of the Windmill'. Mr and Mrs Walter Barnes brought up a family of twelve here; Mr Barnes was the town crier and postman during the 1930s. Odd nos 23–33 were built in the 1960s on an old chalk pit site. A windmill which was pulled down in 1900 has given its name to *Windmill House*, Windmill Close and *Windmill Cottages*.

Baydon Hill Farm is still a working farm. *White Pond* is a 20th century house which stands beside earlier farm buildings.

> **DANCES**
>
> Olive remembers as a late teenager going to dances in the village hall with friend Lena and at Baydon in a 'hut'. The policeman from Aldbourne walked them back home.
>
> Her father would wait in their garden at bottom of Baydon Hill looking over the hedge for her. It was embarrassing if she was out with a boyfriend.

7 & 9 Oxford Street

11, 13 & 15 Oxford Street

style. In a disused well in the garden a token dated 1666 was found. It was from Edward Witts' fustian factory and indicates inhabitants here since that date. There is also evidence of a considerable fire in the structural woodwork of the house. The paddock behind the garden was used for Church Camp Meetings.

Below that is the Memorial Hall and the general store now called 'Alldays'. They are the latest in a long line of owners on that site.

The name *Pettywell* was added to No 4 after people in the village said that it was the correct name for the house. In the rear garden there is a bottle well, still with water which rises and falls with the water table. There is also a small building with clay tiles and walls the same as the cottage. There was evidence that there had been a boiler in the corner in the past but now this building is furnished as an additional room. It is believed the cottage

Paxton Rise *(19) Oxford Street*

Chapter Five

1 The Paddocks

2 The Paddocks

3 The Paddocks

> ### Mothers' Union
>
> The Mothers' Union was founded in 1876 by Mary Sumner, an Englishwoman. Our aim is the advancement of the Christian faith in the sphere of marriage and family life. One of our members is the MU deanery treasurer and another is the deanery contact.
>
> Besides our regular monthly meetings with various speakers here in Aldbourne we also have a monthly prayer group in which we remember the sick, those in trouble and world-wide tragedies. Two coffee mornings are held each year to raise money to support MU workers overseas and to help provide holidays for disadvantaged families in the MU caravans in Durdle Door.
>
> Sewing machines, materials and haberdashery have been sent to the Sudan so that women can become self-supporting, since many have become widowed and lost everything as a result of the war. In 1998 thick cardigans were needed for the wives of African bishops who had come to the Lambeth Conference and our branch sent six. We also contributed to sending MU pendants to all African members.
>
> At the church fête our branch runs a bric-a-brac stall and at the Christmas fair a rainbow stall.

4 The Paddocks

5 The Paddocks

> ### No Airfield
>
> In the mid-1960s Cecil became a member of the Parish Council.
>
> When the old school, and shortly thereafter Neate's Yard Tythe Barn, were pulled down, he, along with a number of like minded citizens, formed the Civic Society with the object of opposing inappropriate development in Aldbourne.
>
> The Society thrived under Cecil's leadership and it achieved a successful outcome at two separate District Inquiries concerning developments in the village, as well as other matters in the Parish Council. These included a proposal to establish a car park at *The Blue Boar*, which consequently was never carried out.
>
> In addition, a proposal for an airfield at Ewin's Hill was also defeated as a result of the Civic Society's protests.

was once a cobbler's and it is possible that the window could have been the shop front.

The Paddocks

Opposite 'Alldays' is a recent development called The Paddocks. The wall at the entrance is built of traditional materials ensuring the area remains in character.

The Paddocks itself is a short cul-de-sac of five houses developed in 1978 on part of the grounds of the former racing stables. The land is crossed by the bourne with the three houses at the end linked by a narrow bridge. There are many mature trees, the largest of which was unfortunately damaged by the 1990 gale; one group along the bourne is home to a large colony of rooks with some thirteen nests.

Four of the houses are owner-occupied and, except for one toddler, residents are all adult; two houses are still occupied by the original inhabitants.

Gardens, of a good size having regard to the closeness to the village centre, are visited by a variety of birds ranging from the tiny, shy wren to majestic wood pigeons.

Chapter Five

> **BAKERS**
>
> There were five bakers:
>   Charles Barnes employed Joe Wilkins where the Post Office is;
>   Bert Stacey and son Leslie were at 11 The Square;
>   'Hair by Maxine' once housed Frank Wilson;
>   Ern Barrett, renowned for his fancy cakes, was at *Holbrook House*; and
>   Fred Palmer and his son Walter baked at what is now 'Alldays'. They were the last to give up 1969.

21 Oxford Street

The start of the climb

People occupying the houses

Brenda and David Cock; Sarah and Debbie Cock; Anthony and Regina Marreco; David Galbraith and Theresa Robinson; Megan and Francesca Hazel Andrews; Ian Warrington; John and Audrey Nielsen-Hall; Bob Hale; Steve Hatcher; Alwyn and Mary Williams; Evelyn Palmer; John, Margaret and Loretta Hunt; Percy Muckelstone; Rees and Gladys Jenkins; Jose Swash; Ron and Dorothy Wilkins; Lawrence, Gillian and Nicholas Woodward; George and Jenny Rendell; Mark, Eleanor and Alexander Rendell; Andrew Young and Julie Baker; Miriam and Jim Michelmore.

Newcomers, old hands. Why Aldbourne?

People live here for a variety of reasons; some have generations living in the parish. Percy and Rees each married a 'village lass' and started living as 'squatters' in the disused army camp in Westfield Chase. Other people moved to be close to their work but live in a country village. Ian Warrington and the Williams and the Rendell families moved to be near relatives.

The street has seen many changes. John Hunt, Rees Jenkins and Percy Mucklestone extensively modernized their houses in the 1950s when most of the houses were thatched. Many older houses have been renovated since. Ron and Dorothy Wilkins designed their house which was the first one built by Liddiards. Bob Hale, Evelyn Palmer, Gladys Jenkins, Jose Swash, Ron and Dorothy Wilkins were born in Oxford Street and John Hunt was born in Lottage Road. They have relatives going back at least two or three generations in the village.

Schools and various occupations, hobbies and interests

Those born in the village went to the village school, some boarded at the grammar school in Marlborough. John Hunt and Percy Mucklestone worked locally as cowmen and Bob Hale worked as a wheelwright.
 There are many stunning gardens in the summer and Oxford Street can boast more than its fair share of thespians and musicians.
 David Cock worked in Swindon and all over the south for British Rail before retiring. Brenda nursed in several London hospitals before working at the Hungerford Nursing Home. David and Brenda have performed in

23 Oxford Street

25 Oxford Street

Whitehills *(27) Oxford Street*

MEALS-ON-WHEELS

The local meals-on-wheels service started under the County Council scheme some thirty years ago. However, when the county decided in 1992 that the price of meals should be nearly doubled, the village organization became independent.

Meals are delivered to customers in their own homes on Mondays, Wednesdays and Fridays throughout the year, including all public holidays ecept Christmas. The charge is £1 per meal of meat and vegetables followed by a pudding. The number of customers has to be limited to a total of twelve but over the years this has proved quite adequate to meet the demand.

It is the Ramsbury medical practice that decides who requires meals. In general this is determined on the basis of age and disability. Meals are prepared and delivered by teams who undertake all the cooking and delivery arrangements on a monthly basis.

We continue to use the same aluminium dishes that were provided when the national service started during the war. Thanks to this and the willing help of many volunteers the price of each meal has remained unaltered since 1992.

many choral concerts. Debbie is a keen ice skater and has trained with the Swindon Ladies Ice Hockey team. Sarah is now away at university. David has also sailed a yacht from Portsmouth to Lisbon.

Anthony Marreco was educated at Westminster, called to the Bar in 1939 and was a Fleet Air Arm pilot from 1939–45. He was a prosecuting counsel in the Nuremberg war trials, later co-founded Amnesty International and was a director of publishers Weidenfeld and Nicholson. Regina is Brazilian and spent several years working in the Brazilian Foreign Office. Their main interest now is their cottage and garden, both of which have been extensively renovated. David Galbraith is a sports teacher at a specialist deaf school. Theresa was also a specialist deaf teacher who worked in many parts of the country, even spending two years in Canada. She now spends time raising their two daughters. David is captain of the village cricket team.

Hazel Andrews, who originally worked as an engineer in Swindon, now works as an acupuncturist. Her main hobby is gardening and working on her house.

Ian Warrington spent a short time working as the local milkman, when he got to know a lot of the villagers, before working at Membury. He has always been keen on clay pigeon shooting and is now interested in all things computer-based.

29 Oxford Street

Parish Magazines

The Dabchick is the latest in the line of parish magazines. It followed the successful *Parish News* produced by Tony Gilligan which ran to over a hundred issues and only ceased in 1990 when Tony died.

Later that year *The Dabchick* came out and appears every two months. It is financed by advertisements and donations and is distributed free to every house in the parish, with over a hundred more copies sent to readers around the world.

Many articles are submitted by current and former residents and a team of people work to produce and distribute the magazine. It won an award in the Wiltshire Village Ventures Competition, the only village magazine to do so that year.

Its success may be gauged by a statistic revealed in the 1999 Parish Appraisal that almost 90 per cent of villagers read *The Dabchick*.

John Nielsen-Hall works in accountancy and Audrey works as a company secretary. They are practising Buddhists. John has a keen interest in rock and blues music and has trekked across the Karakoram Mountains from Islamabad to China.

Bob Hale worked in the carpentry trade as a foreman for the local health authority. He was treasurer of Aldbourne Football Club and a founder member of the Sports and Social Club in Oxford Street.

Steve Hatcher works in finance for an engineering firm in Oxfordshire. He enjoys riding his horse, which takes up most of his spare time. Alwyn and Mary were respectively a chartered surveyor and a teacher. Both have now retired and are keen travellers. Mary used to make toys by hand.

Evelyn Palmer worked in the family business, 'Palmer's Stores', in the village for many years as did her sister Dorothy Wilkins.

John Hunt has now retired from fork-lift truck driving and Margaret works in the Aldbourne Nursing Home. John and Margaret are keen motor sports and speedway fans, and also enjoy regular trips to the coast. Their daughter Loretta is currently working in Australia.

Percy Mucklestone was in the building trade before retiring. He is a keen gardener and is well known for his gnome collection, built up by collecting while on holiday.

> ## HOUSE PRICES
>
> Aldbourne is a desirable village.
>
> According to Peter Rapson, the local estate agent, demand in the private sector continues to increase, partly because of our position close to Swindon and the M4 motorway.
>
> This and Kennet District Council's strict and limiting planning policies make housing expensive. Large properties sell for £500,000 or more while modern houses with four bedrooms and three reception rooms sell for about £300,000 and period houses more.
>
> Smaller houses, terraced or semi-detached, achieve figures between £100,000–£150,000, in contrast to Swindon where they sell for £80,000–£90,000.
>
> There is also a steady demand for unfurnished accommodation for rent; a large four- or five-bedroom house might be rented at £900 a month and a two-bedroom cottage for £450–£500 a month.
>
> A typical housing association rent for a three-bedroom house with two reception rooms is £67 per week while the rent for a one-bedroom bungalow would be about £61 per week.

31 Oxford Street

33 Oxford Street

Chapter Five

> **Do You Remember?**
> - Lardy cakes and cream horns from the bakery.
> - Litter picking for Mr Strickland for misdemeanours.
> - Nitty Nora, the lice inspector.
> - Carrying water from wells and pumps.
> - Baths in front of the fire.
> - Dances and romances in the Memorial Hall.
> - The World War II Pig Club.

34 Oxford Street

Rees Jenkins worked at Harwell, while Gladys raised the family after leaving the ATS. Rees now spends his time working on the house or doing odd jobs and fixing things!

Jose Swash worked for several companies before settling down to work at Crowcastle in the village. She has always been a keen performer in the WI pantomimes and plays.

Ron Wilkins pursued a scientific career at Harwell, Dorothy worked at the Mechanics Institute library in Swindon. In the early years of television Ron built his own TV set and often carried out repairs on others. Gardening is now Ron and Dorothy's main interest.

George Rendell teaches in Hungerford and Jenny works in medical research. They are actively involved with St Michael's Church and come from a long line of clergy. Mark is studying at university, Eleanor and Alexander are still at home and are both keen musicians playing the piano and the drums.

Lawrence Woodward is director of Elm Farm Research Centre where Gillian also works as a freelance administrator. Lawrence addresses international conferences on organic farming issues. He coaches the Ramsbury Under-twelve football team and Nicholas plays for AFC Newbury.

Andrew Young is an electrician who now owns a health food shop and Julie Baker works as a naturopath in Wootton Bassett. They are renovating their house and have just had a baby boy. Jim Michelmore worked in banking where he met his wife Miriam who had been one of his clients. They both have a keen interest in music.

War time histories

Jose Swash's father would provide a home-cooked meal for solders billeted in the village.

Jim Michelmore was in the Royal Navy and served on the destroyer HMS *Kelly* with Lord Mountbatten.

Bob Hale was in the Black Watch Infantry, even though he wasn't Scottish, and was reviewed by Montgomery before the D-day landings.

Rees, Alwyn and Anthony also saw active service as did Ron, who escaped an Italian POW camp and made it back to safety behind Allied lines.

Gladys Jenkins was in the ATS and Percy Muckleston worked at a tank factory.

Pets and animals

Percy Muckleston used to keep pigs; the sides of bacon were cured by the fire. The Rendell's deeds say they have to let the council water

32, 30 & 28 Oxford Street

Icy Whiskers

"My grandfather, Thomas Brind, was superintendent of the Sunday School for over fifty years.

He lived in Aldbourne and rode to Lambourn to collect the post before delivering it on his way into Swindon.

On his return he sometimes used to sit by the fire in winter to thaw the ice from his beard."

Hope Cottage *(26) & 24 Oxford Street*

Greenhill Bank *(22) &* **Apple Tree Cottage** *(20) Oxford Street*

their cattle on their land! Dogs, cats and rabbits are popular pets. The Michelmores found their cat as a stray kitten just before midnight on Christmas Eve; Hazel Andrews' cat has extra toes, while George and Jenny Rendell's cat has only three legs.

Things missing and found

The Rendell's house is built on the old chalk pit which became a rubbish tip so they have lots of old glass bottles in the garden. David and Theresa recently found a well in their garden but the Williams family cannot find their well. Steve Hatcher believes there may be a cellar under his house. The Marrecos and Ian both found inglenook fireplaces in their houses; the Marrecos also found a bread oven!

Paths that cross and unusual occurrences

Brenda and Hazel went to the same school in Kent and were taught by the same teacher!
Steve Hatcher, Andrew Young and Theresa Robinson have been held at gun point during foreign travels!
Jenny Rendell beat Imran Kahn in a friendly game of hockey.
Miriam Michelmore sang while being conducted by Igor Stravinsky. Jim sat on his great-

> ### THE CLUB TODAY
>
> A small fee is charged to become a junior member (over fourteen) or senior member (eighteen plus). The club is a non-profit-making organization and is managed by a committee of volunteers from the village who ensure the smooth running of the business. All surpluses and fees are spent on more facilities and functions for the members.
>
> The club has continuously provided social facilities within the village including successful competitive teams for billiards, snooker, darts and pool within local leagues. It also offers weekly bingo, meat draw and Christmas club as well as many other events such as discos, live music, skittles and televised sport, yet it still retains a relaxed and casual social atmosphere.

Windmill Cottage *Oxford Street*

Windmill House *Oxford Street*

grandmother's knee when she was ninety-two. Her husband (Jim's great-grandfather) was born in 1789.

Beyond Windmill Close

Next to Windmill Close we find newly built *Windmill House* where Emma Colsell and her daughter, Tara, live. Then *Baydon Hill Farm*, worked by Michael Hale and supported by his wife, Jo, and their three children. Jo is well known for her cheesemaking.

The farm has served three generations of farmers; Bill who is Mike's father, can still be

> ### Good Old Pride of Aldbourne
>
> "I wonder if anyone can remember this song? I heard it coming back in a bus with the band after a contest at Fairford.
>
> 'Tis the good old pride of Aldbourne,
> Where no engine's puffer blows,
> And the fields are white with daisies,
> In the woods the bluebells grow.
>
> O'er the hills I love to wander
> Just to hear that sweet refrain,
> 'Tis the good old pride of Aldbourne
> Sing it o'er and o'er again."

Eventide *Aldbourne Road*

Baydon Hill Farm *Aldbourne Road*

Chapter Five

White Pond *Aldbourne Road*

East Leaze Farmhouse *Aldbourne Road*

> ### Aldbourne Road Farms
>
> *East Leaze* was part of the demesne lands when Thomas Bond purchased the Lordship of the Manor of Aldbourne in 1632.
> Ownership passed through several families and eventually became part of the Baydon Manor Estate in 1917. The land is now part of *North Farm*. The present farmhouse was built in the 19th century.

East Leaze Cottage *Aldbourne Road*

Greenhills *Aldbourne Road*

seen helping with the milking from time to time. He took over from his father, Charlie Hale, a great character who was a council member and school manager. The Hales were well known for their herd of Guernsey cows and the dairy that supplied milk to the village; some can remember glorious thick cream and proof that good rich milk helps you to live a long and energetic life. They gave up the dairy in the early 1960s. The herd is now Friesian (still excellent cream).

There is a tree half way up the hill which is known as Dare's Grave. A man was found hanged there and it is said to be haunted.

East Leaze farmyard is now mainly an equestrian centre founded by Emily Lovell (née Lawton). The land is farmed with North Farm on a mixed rotation.

East Leaze Farmhouse is divided into two flats, one occupied by Rod McKinnon who is in charge of the seed potato enterprise on the farm, and the other by a vet, Elisabeth Seidel, and her husband. *East Leaze Cottage* is the home of Jamie and Margie Lawton. Jamie runs the livestock side of *North Farm* but also delights in his garden which he has imaginatively landscaped. Margie is a farmer's daughter from South Africa where she and Jamie married in January 1999: she works at St John's School. Jamie trained at Seale Hayne College and the Royal Agricultural College and after travelling extensively worked for Kingshay Farming Trust for five years.

White Pond was, until her death in 1997 in her nineties, the home of Nora Pembroke who for many years ran *East Leaze Farm* on her own after the death of her husband Albert in the early 1960s. The house has extensive views over the Marlborough Downs and was originally two workers' cottages.

Greenhills is the home of Jack and Betty Pounds. After spending his youth as a huntsman, Jack worked for many years at *East Leaze Farm* and *North Farm*. He is famous for his ploughing, having won many competitions and now, in retirement, works on his vintage tractors and engines. Betty's father Len Ball was the faithful manager at *East Leaze* for Mrs Pembroke and was renowned for his hay – much in demand for horses.

CHAPTER FIVE

Windmill Close

Windmill Close was built in the late 1950s by Richard Stacey who, with his family, owned *Windmill Cottages*. He had previously built the houses in Oxford Street and this was to be a continuation before his retirement. In those days there was not a tree or a bush to be seen on the bank which is now well covered.

Ten houses and bungalows were planned but due to preference for the latter they ended up as all bungalows. The first buyers and occupiers were mainly young couples with small families, the only retired couple being Mr and

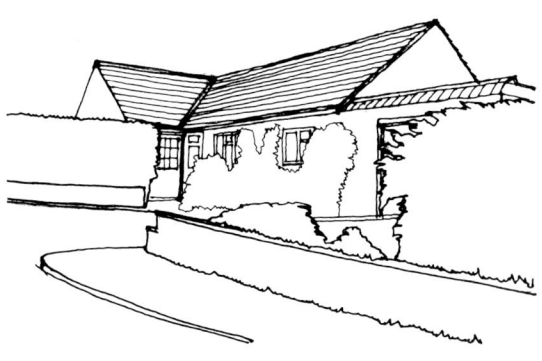

1 Windmill Close

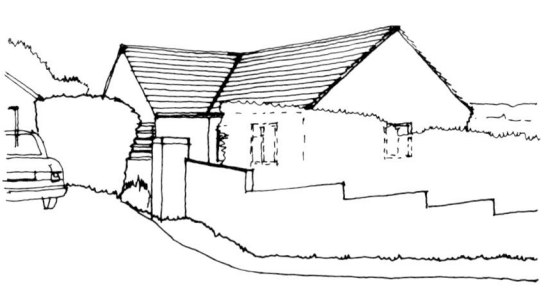

2 Windmill Close

3 Windmill Close

> ### CARNIVAL
>
> The year 2000 will see Aldbourne's eighty-fifth carnival. We are lucky to have a thriving carnival when many have been lost or are struggling to keep going.
>
> The first carnival was held in 1905 and consisted of decorated bicycles – a far cry from the large and heavily decorated floats of today. We still have Nancy Barrett, the original Carnival Queen, with us.
>
> There was a break in 1966. Since then the carnival has only once moved from its traditional first Saturday in September. This was on the occasion of the funeral of Diana Princess of Wales in 1997.
>
> In most years there are in the order of thirty-five entries, though we achieved forty-three entries in 1999. We have a thriving carnival which is well respected even by the organizers of Pewsey Carnival who have probably the largest procession in Wiltshire.
>
> Pewsey is the venue for the Wiltshire Carnival Queen Contest. In recent years Carnival Queens from Aldbourne have gone on to take first, second and third places at the county contest; our Princesses have also done well.
>
> 1999 saw Aldbourne Carnival Queen Shane Moreton (nineteen) crowned Carnival Queen of Wiltshire.

Mrs George Smith. He was a master baker who needs mention for the great contribution he made to village life, especially the printing of the combined churches monthly magazine.

A great sense of community spirit exists in what seems to be a secluded part of the village. During the summer we picnic and have barbecues with a bonfire which is almost on the same site as the celebratory bonfires that were held in the chalk pit in the past. We had one for the VE celebrations in 1995. In the winter, if the snow is bad enough, we have snow clearing parties; it only takes a small amount to make our road impassable and the

4 Windmill Close

> ### Shadow Council
>
> Sam recalls living next to Johnny Morris who they could hear laughing through the walls and how he always left his door unlocked so that if anything went wrong they or Reg Slocum, the landlord of *The Crown*, could get in. He also recalls when there was a fire in *Pond House* just before bonfire night. The roof space of *Pond House* and the shop is not divided and on the landing of the shop were £300 worth of fireworks. There were almost some early celebrations for November the fifth that year.
>
> He also remembers the 'shadow parish council' who were to be found on the bench near the phone box. They were members of the retired population of the village who watched village events and discussed village problems each day when the weather was fine.

5 Windmill Close

6 Windmill Close

hard work is great fun fuelled by Pauline's endless cups of tea and coffee. We all look forward to a Christmas party when we can relax and come together to chat about the year's events. Our Neighbourhood Watch policy is that we are here for each other when we are needed without being intrusive. It would seem people are unwilling to move from here and some have lived here for thirty or more years. We are a varied group of people in our work and hobbies; the younger members work from home and six households are retired but still very busy. We number an electrician, a mechanic, some DIY builders, excellent cooks and gardeners, a farmer with a good milking herd and a cheese maker. So we could definitely become self sufficient. We even have a pony and trap!

More about the residents

One family, the Moneys, have lived in the Close from the start. They have three children. Janet

7 Windmill Close

Poachers *(8) Windmill Close*

> ### ALDBOURNE SEES THE LIGHT
>
> When our electricity supply fails because of a storm or ill-directed digging, say, we realize how reliant we are upon it. We take it for granted though it was not until after World War II that mains electricity came to Aldbourne.
>
> In the early days of mains supplies, teams from the electricity companies toiled for days erecting new overhead lines supported by wooden poles. This enabled more and more houses to join the electricity revolution that was transforming everyday village life.
>
> Some of these lines still remain within the village but are being buried as opportunities arise, thus freeing historic views from disfigurement.
>
> Also many of the original line routes into Aldbourne are still operational bringing electricity from the power stations to the north to serve the twelve transformers in Aldbourne.

Money was a teacher who started working with Eric Strickland and continued to teach at the school for twenty-three years. She was well known for her interest in technology and for her work with recorder groups. Her hobby is driving horses and carriages and making their leather harnesses. This she does from a smallholding opposite Windmill Close.

Richard and Pauline Badger moved into No 3 in 1967 and very quickly established themselves in the village by joining in many activities. They also have three sons who can claim to be Dabchicks. Tom Port retired from the Navy in 1977, works hard in his home and garden, finds time to help with the church and can always be relied upon to give good advice or help in a crisis. He also takes a two- or three-mile daily walk occasionally accompanied by Marcus Rouse who himself is always busy with his numerous hobbies and is always ready to help others.

Jane Ebbut moved here in 1981 to live with her father; she has now retired from teaching in Newbury and enjoys leading walking parties

9 Windmill Close

Steyning *(10) Windmill Close*

Crops

Cropping is diverse having been through an era of continuous cereals in the 1970s and 1980s.

The most common crop is still grass in all its forms from ancient downland to grass seed production and a resurgence of clover rich leys. Crops that can be combined include wheat, barley, oats, triticali, peas, beans, linseed, clover and oil seed rape.

On-farm grain storage and drying is considerable at about 75,000 tons of cereals. Root crops such as seed potatoes and fodder turnips are grown as well as maize. Fodder is conserved mainly as silage although a little high quality hay is made for horses.

Compulsory set-aside, arable land required by the Common Agricultural Policy to be left fallow for one year in an attempt to cut production, is a feature; strangely it was common, for different reasons, at the beginning of the century.

over the Downs when she is not travelling the world. Dot and Sam Walls ran the shop by the Pond for many years and are still busy, especially with their endless work for the Prospect Foundation. Tess and Ian Standfast have the two young girls of the Close, born just after they moved here in 1992. Ian's hobby is flying and at times he circles above just to spy! They enjoy their life here and have fun on most occasions.

Vic and Eileen Naylor work hard growing their garden produce and numerous herbs and plants to help raise money for charity. Chaddy and George, who work so hard for the Red Cross, also help with many other village activities. They and Eddie and Stephanie Krupa live in the two cottages that were built on the site of the old windmill in 1902. The millstones are still around and some form the steps in the bank from the road.

Fatt Katt Cottage *Windmill Close*

Charities Begin at Home

Various village charities dating from 1818 onwards were subject to an enquiry in 1904. These were the Brown's, Goddard's, Poor's Gorse, John Brown, Wentworth, William Taylor, and they were added to later by the Aldbourne and Baydon Aid in Sickness Fund.

The Brown's Charity provided '3 Brown Cloth Great Coats for 3 poor men and any money left over for 5 gowns for 5 poor women'. This was still operative in 1904.

The Goddard's Bequest provided £2 per annum for coal and blankets for 'the oldest and most deserving poor'. The tenant of Upper Upham had to pay the £2 to the church wardens. Sixteen parishioners selected by the trustees all received 2/6d (12½p). This was redeemed at the last sale of the property for £15.

Poor's Gorse derives from the Enclosure Act of 1805 when 50 acres were given to the poor for 'furse and fuel'. A quarter of the area was cut each year and the poor had to carry the fuel back to the village. In 1829 a fire destroyed the Gorse and thereafter it was let for cattle and the rent from there went to provide fuel for the poor.

In 1856 John Brown provided £200 for the school to be used towards the 'cost of maintenance'. It is still in the school accounts.

The Wentworth Fund gave assistance to 'the two oldest Agricultural Labourers, born to the parish, resident therein and who had never received Parochial Relief'. The Fund still exists.

William Taylor's Gift for a Methodist minister created in 1894 had no movement by 1904 but the capital had increased in a bank account.

The Aldbourne and Baydon Aid in Sickness Fund is supported from the sale of the district nurse's house which was no longer required after the introduction of the National Health Service in 1948. The capital is invested with the Charity Commissioners and the income used to give relief 'in sickness with poverty' (that is, grants), and is also used for home nursing equipment.

Chapter Six

South Street & the Roads off it

South Street

South Street became the main entrance to the village from the south when the route from Ramsbury over Southward Down and The Butts became unsuitable for horse drawn vehicles. The road joined the route across The Green to the Swindon Road at Hightown. In 1814 the local Turnpike Act diverted the route round the bottom of the pond cutting off a small section of South Street. At the same time the stream was moved across to the east side of the main road, known locally as 'The Turnpike'.

To begin at the beginning

No 1 and No 3 were once occupied by the blacksmith and harness maker. Today No 1 is the library – open on Monday and Thursday afternoons and evenings. The constantly changing stock of 3,800 books are looked after by Trish Rushen who used to be 'helped' by Tiger the library cat. At one time the premises were used by a harness maker. The forge next door has not been used since the death of Alan Liddiard in 1982 who, in addition to general blacksmithing, had a considerable reputation as a maker of decorative ironwork. He

1, 2 & 3 South Street

> **The Surgery at Neals**
>
> The room was furnished with a desk, three chairs and a camp-bed upon which patients were examined.
>
> The cat, Harvey Pickle, slept under the camp-bed and once lost one of his lives when, due to the weight of an obese patient, the bed collapsed.

was asked to make a firescreen for the Queen Mother's Scottish home. The Smithy is still fully equipped and has a remarkable collection of traditional iron work, lamps and household items. Recently a complete peel of miniature bells has been installed to help train the bell-ringers. The small car park outside the forge was used for shoeing and fitting iron tyres on wooden waggon wheels. Len Liddiard, brother of Alan, and his wife, Elsie, live in No 3. It is thanks to him that each year there is a welcoming display of flowers along the edge of the road. When he left school towards the end of the War he became a builder with Jerram Brothers before doing his National Service as a 'Bevin Boy' in the coal mines in Arley. There he met his wife, who was born in a village near Nuneaton. At the completion of Len's service they moved to Aldbourne. Their first home was an ex-Army Nissen hut in Westfield Chase. No 2/4, on the west side by the brook, is a Georgian house, known as *Ivy House*. The house is now owned by Nick and Carey Josephy; they have two sons, Jack and William. They moved from Sussex to the village in 1997 when Nick's work brought him to Swindon. Nick's father is a resident in the Nursing Home and drives about the village in an electric carriage complete with his small dog, Poppy, to scare off road-hogs! No 5 was in turn the village workhouse, the last working malt-house in the village and also a brewery. The present owners, Ishbel and Andrew Sewell, arrived in 1959 with three children, the fourth qualified as a Dabchick. Ishbel accepted an invitation to join the WI while the

> ### THE FUSTIAN FACTORY
>
> Fustian was fabric rather like a heavy moleskin used for working clothes. It is thought that its manufacture was introduced by the Witts family in about 1660. It was an important source of employment in the village between then and 1880.
>
> The factory which survives as an outbuilding behind *Yew Tree House* dates from the early 19th century. It has a diaper brickwork façade on brick and sarsen structure with a slate roof. It was allegedly originally a three-storey building but is now two storeys.
>
> After the demise of the fustian industry the building was used for finishing chairs manufactured on the site of *One Ash* across the road.

Bay House *(5) South Street*

Ivy House *South Street*

furniture van was being unpacked and she is now president for the third time. She was elected a member of the RDC and became chairman of governors at St John's School in Marlborough. She restarted the Guides in 1964 and has run the village meals-on-wheels scheme for some twenty-five years. Andrew has maintained a long standing interest in local geology and archaeology. In 1980 while field walking near Ewin's Hill, he found the 'Aldbourne Hoard' of some five thousand Roman coins, now in the Devizes Museum.

From Strawberry Hill to Ford Farm Cottages

The Hensons moved to *Strawberry Hill* five years ago. John is a consultant radiologist at Princess Margaret Hospital and Ridgeway Hospital. Judy, a chartered physiotherapist, works part-time at the Nursing Home and spends some of her spare time gardening, a skill inherited from her late father, Bob Price, a TV gardening expert. Katie, ten, loves drama and hopes to be famous. Jonathan and Belinda Rayner and sons, Alexander, Niko and Hugh, moved to *Yew Tree House* in 1994 when they added further extensions to the three-hundred-and-fifty-year-old farmhouse, worked on the two-hundred-year-old fustian factory in the grounds and established a beautiful garden. Jonathan, from Lancashire, works as a local GP and Belinda, whose family originated in Ogbourne St George, comes from Australia. After a career in the Royal Navy, followed by a wardenship of St George's House in Windsor

> ### HOUSES
>
> *Yew Tree House* is a 19th century villa in the Gothic style. *Witts Piece*, named after the original owners of the fustian factory, was built in the vegetable garden in the late 20th century replacing a farm building. Behind *Barn Cottage* and *Lavender Cottage* lies Aldbourne Nursing Home on the site of Malthouse Farm.

Strawberry Hill *(7) South Street*

Yew Tree House *(11) South Street*

CHAPTER SIX

WHAT KATIE THINKS

"Being eleven years old and living in Aldbourne go well together. I can't imagine living anywhere else. Village life is special. It is great to walk or bike to friends without having to organize lifts.

There are loads of clubs and activities to fill our time. One of my favourites is ALEC as I want to be an actress when I grow up. I especially enjoyed being the Fairy Queen in this year's pantomime. I also belong to a group called Rock Solid which meets on Sundays. We have a great time each week doing different challenges and finishing in church.

Every year I always look forward to carnival and fairs. They're such fun. In summer a group of us had tennis coaching at the village tennis club which taught me lots of skills.

I've just started at St John's School in Marlborough. I feel really grown up catching the bus in The Square with my friends.

One thing I would miss if we ever moved is the friendly attitude of the people who live here. We're really lucky to have chosen such a fantastic village!"

Witts Piece *(11a) South Street*

Castle, Admiral Anthony Davies CB CVO retired to Aldbourne in 1972 and moved to *Witts Piece* after the death of his wife in 1980. In retirement he took a degree with the Open University and has been a regular supporter of church affairs. He has four children and ten grandchildren.

John and Marianne Adey, with their children Helen, Matthew, Francesca and Michael, have lived in the village since 1973, presently at *The Old Malt House*. John, a company director in healthcare, is chairman of the Tennis Club and, in 1990, was chairman of the village Festival. Marianne is a founder member

The Old Malt House *South Street*

The Old Malt House Barn *South Street*

of the Children's Book Group and a governor of St Michael's School. Both are involved with the Church. The garden and newly thatched nineteenth century barn are often the venue for village and charity events. Richard Miller and Jane Greve moved to *Barn Cottage* two years ago. Richard, from Guildford, works for a Swindon computer company. Jane, who is from South Africa, is involved in the travel business. Much of their spare time is spent on restoring their house but they enjoy sailing and scuba diving with the Marlborough Diving Club. Richard was involved with the Parish Appraisal.

Barn Cottage *(15) South Street*

THE EVOLUTION OF SOUTH STREET

The name was in use by 1553. It begins with a row of cottages called Blacksmith's Row, where a yeoman's cottage was probably built during the 16th century. Although it has been much altered and extended the divisions of 'one up one down' can still be seen.

There was a smithy here by 1692. In 1709 it included a dwelling house with a garden and barn. The Smith family were associated with the site for about 240 years until 1949. The disused smithy is still full of its old contents.

There was an alehouse at the south end of the row at the end of the 19th century; a few years later it was a chemist's shop. *Bay House* had close associations with the owners of Blacksmith's Row. There had been a dwelling converted from a barn at the top of the garden, burnt down in 1766. Two cottages were then built on the present site, thought to have been let to the Overseers of the Poor as a workhouse early in the 19th century. After another fire in about 1819 a dwelling house, bakehouse, malt-house and blacksmith's shop were built. A series of 1.5m high tunnels behind are thought to have been used to store waste from the brewing business until the brook ran to carry it away. Part seems subsequently to have been a cesspit.

The smithy returned to its present site in 1895; the malt-house was in use until the 1940s.

CHAPTER SIX

Aurum Cottage *(19) South Street*

Lavender Cottage *(17) South Street*

Nursing Home *South Street*

MEDICINE AT NEALS

From the mid-1950s until 1977 the Ramsbury practice held a surgery in Aldbourne, twice daily, six days a week at *Neals* in South Street, the home of the Alder family from whom the back kitchen was rented.

There was no receptionist, no telephone and no records were kept at *Neals*. Patients waited in the kitchen. The doctor rang a bell to summon the next patient. Hopefully, he would recognize them and remembered the nature of the problem. He then had to decide on the treatment.

The stock of medicines consisted of six bottles, the contents to be diluted 1:7 with water. They included aspirin in four colours – white, yellow, pink and mauve; if one colour did not work another usually met with success.

The doctor had to decide whether to prescribe from one of the six bottles or obtain a medicine from the main surgery. If the latter the medicines were left quite unsupervised in the glasshouse – the house was never locked. The dispensing charge, two shillings (10p), was left on the table when the patient collected the medicine. The occasional muddle occurred such as when a man took the contraceptive pill by mistake.

There was great sadness and indignation when *Neals* was sold and the surgery was closed in 1977. In spite of petitions for its continuance, a valued amenity and a favourite meeting place was lost.

Tony Hallows was a pupil at Marlborough College. After working in London and serving with the Wiltshire Regiment he joined the Indian Service Corps as major in charge of hospital transport. He and his late wife lived in her native New Zealand and in 1984 Tony moved to *Lavender Cottage* with son Giles. Tony's hobbies include sports and the University of the Third Age. David Bishop who moved to *Aurum Cottage* in 1998 is a musician and teacher and director of music at Cheam Hawtreys School. Following his first professional position as assistant organist at St-Martin-in-the-Fields, he has been organist at St Stephen's, Gloucester Road and at Chester Cathedral. He enjoys restoring his garden and walking with his dog, Ben.

The Aldbourne Nursing Home was opened in 1988 on the site of *Malt House Farm* buildings by John and Marianne Adey and the late Mollie and Tony Palmer, who lived in *Malt House Farm*. Mollie and Tony were involved in many village and local activities: they are greatly missed. Their children Richard and Karenza continue as partners in the Nursing Home with the Adeys. *Southleaze*, built in 1934 for the jockey Eric Brown, was considerably extended ten years ago.

Wyn and Cathy Hughes moved there in 1983 with their children Richard, who works in Swindon, and Claire, a student at Aberystwyth. Wyn and Richard play for the Aldbourne Band and Cathy sings with the WI Choir. Wyn is involved with fundraising and

Malt House Farm *(21) South Street*

Southleaze *(23) South Street*

A Barn with a History

There was a malt-house at the end of the present barn housed in the brick extension which can still be seen with its revolving cowl. The figure of the Malt Shovel Man on the vane was first mentioned in 1828.

In 1910 Charles McEvoy, who lived in the house, wrote a play called 'A Village Wedding' which was staged in the barn. The opening performance was attended by George Bernard Shaw, Granville Barker and Edgar Wallace among other celebrities. It was entirely a village enterprise with a cast of local people and later toured the country.

The play was well received in the village and in Devizes but the actors' Wiltshire accents made it hard to understand when it played in London.

Chapter Six

Jasmine House *(23a) South Street*

> **WILDLIFE MAMMALS**
>
> There are many mammals.
> Roe and fallow deer make use of woods as well as arable. The occasional muntjacs are less welcome. Badgers are plentiful, only cars cull them.
> Foxes and hares are fairly common, rabbits are increasing greatly, which may account for increased numbers of buzzards.

planning for the millennium festivities. 'Windlesham', now known as *Jasmine House*, was build by Donald (a builder) and Ann Barnes fifteen years ago. Their three children and one of their eight grandchildren are Dabchicks. Donald was on the Carnival committee and is now on the Millennium Festival committee. For many years he led the 'Beating the Bounds' which Ann has walked thirteen times. Ann is in the Church and WI Choirs and works for the Luncheon Club. Both are golfers.

Until recently Lindsey and Jennison Grey lived at No 25. Jennison is an electronics designer. Their children Kieran and Hannah attend St John's School where Lindsey is the librarian. Kieran and Hannah are Venture Scouts and Kieran also plays electric guitar in a band. All the family are involved in one or more types of bellringing and the Children's Book Club.

Richard (a Dabchick) and Joan Hale lived at No 27 for twenty years until Richard's death in 1997. Joan continues to live here with her mother and sons, Peter an analyst with a marketing consultancy, and David studying at Oxford Brookes. Joan ran a craft shop until 1998 in the Square where Richard, following three generations of his family, ran a grocery shop.

Jill Fremantle moved to No 29 in 1991, after forty years in Scotland, to be near her family. Her interests have included the Literary Club, Kennet DFAS and the Civic Society

Wyndmere *(25) South Street*

and she helps at St Margaret's Hospital Lunch Club. Jill often walks with her dog around the village and is amused to hear her nickname – 'Mrs Whippet'. George and Helen Labram moved to No 31 in January 1997 after thirty-two years living at *High Farm House*, Baydon. They have renovated the house and garden. George, a Cambridge graduate, was Director of Education in Swindon and Helen is a Guy's Hospital trained physiotherapist. Both served in World War II. Hobbies are quilting, upholstery and woodwork. They have three sons and seven grandchildren.

27 South Street

29 South Street

31 South Street

Chapter Six

Delivery by Pushbike

"Baydon Post Office didn't cash money orders whereas Aldbourne did so I had to take money up to the soldiers stationed there.

I got sixpence for going to Preston which I thought was quite good because it was flat all the way and yet I only got ninepence for going to *Upham House* or Russley."

Flatford *(33) South Street*

John and Peta Cook moved to No 33 in 1984. John retired in 1995 having been HM Inspector of Factories, an industrial health and safety adviser and, in his spare time, an area commissioner in St John Ambulance. Peta enjoys a variety of textile crafts. They both spend a lot of time working in and enjoying their large garden.

Steve and Carolana Whitaker came to No 35 from Dallas in 1996. When not travelling Europe for his work, Steve can be found on playing golf. Carolana had been in television for twenty-three years working with, among others, the Clintons and the Archbishop of Canterbury. She dived to film the wreck of the *Titanic* with its discoverer. Their son Jordan is the only known Texan Dabchick in captivity.

No 37, *White Gables*, was previously No 33, *Southeran House and Squin*. Musician and St Michael's Church organist Allan Keen, moved here in 1956 with his parents Esme (deceased 1996) and Graham, a retired aircraft designer who worked on the Spitfire. Allan is an enthusiastic campanologist as well as enjoying a passion for travelling especially within eastern Europe.

Tony and Greta Johnson have lived at No 39 for about thirty years. Tony loves sport,

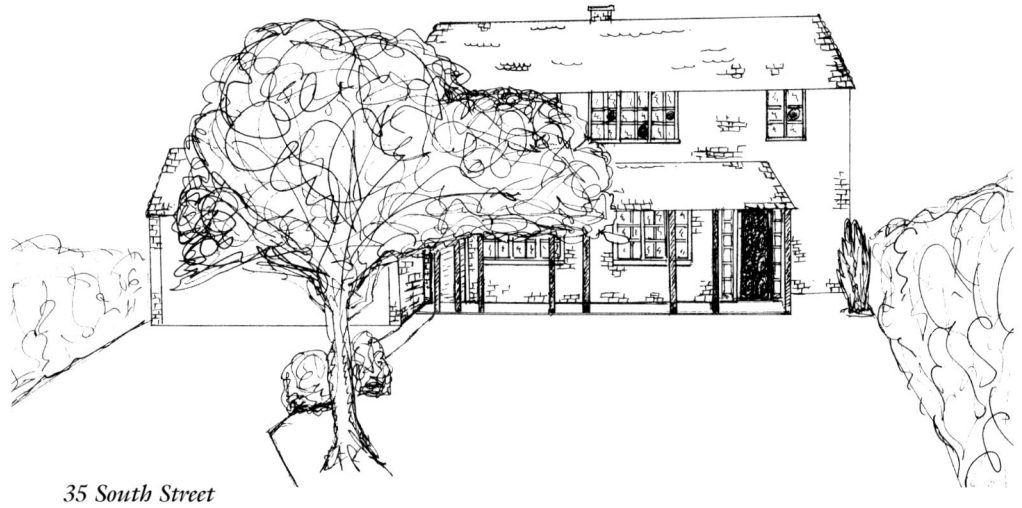

35 South Street

White Gables *(37) South Street*

gardening and horse racing. He worked for Peter Walwyn at his Lambourn stables, breaking yearlings and travelling to races with the horses. Greta was cook at *Ford Farm* and worked for Lady Black for forty years.

No 41 is the home of David and Beryl Phelps who moved to Aldbourne thirty-four years ago for David to work as gardener at *Ford Farm*. He still works for Lady Black at Goring-on-Thames. Their children Marilyn and Chris, went to St Michael's School and Marlborough. Beryl has been president and secretary of the Ladies' Group and WI president and drives for the surgery and hospital.

> ### The Feast
>
> "The Feast of St Mary Magdalen is held the first Sunday after 22 July. Before World War II on Feast Sunday the Methodist Band from Ramsbury marched through the village to the field on the hill behind the Memorial Hall. There several preachers would give an address and the band played hymns. It was repeated late in the afternoon. The day finished with the Aldbourne Band playing by the pond before the fairmen arrived to set up the roundabouts and side-shows.
>
> As a child I was thrilled with the fair. People who had lived in the village used to come back so it was one big reunion. The streets were full of people and the fair families were our friends."

39 & 41 South Street

Judith Sadler was born at Fox Hill and having travelled worldwide, returned to live at 1 *Ford Farm Cottages* with her children six years ago. She is sales and marketing director for a Malmesbury electronics company which began life in an Aldbourne back garden. Katy, a past Carnival Queen, is at art college and James, a zoology student at Edinburgh, plays rugby for the village. The second of the two cottages, built by the Pilkingtons in 1955, is the home of Margaret Cook. Margaret worked as nanny to their three daughters for about fifteen years. She moved into the house in 1971 and after the girls went to school she worked as a temporary nanny, returning during the school holidays before retiring in 1982.

Ann and Giles Currie came to *Ford Farm* from south-east London in 1991, but were married at West Overton in 1958. Giles is a retired stockbroker, now a Justice of the Peace and Commissioner for Income Tax, and Ann is a semi-retired historian.

From *Neals* to The Square

Moving north on the west side of South Street there are four old homes and two twentieth

> DISCIPLINE
>
> "The teacher in the little school, Miss Hawksworth, was a straight lady. We sat in baby chairs with little round arms and if we swung back on them she would roll up our sleeves and slap our arms.
>
> Yes, she was a very straight (strict) lady."

1 & 2 **Ford Farm Cottages** *South Street*

Ford Farm *South Street*

century homes which parallel the old stream from which Aldbourne acquired its name.

Neals (No 20) has been the home of Bill and Elisabeth Cooper since 1976 when Bill retired from the Army as Major General in the Royal Engineers. They moved to Aldbourne partially because Bill's cousin Betty Brown lived here. Elisabeth pursued her considerable talent as a painter and enjoyed gardening. In 1995 Elisabeth moved into the Nursing Home where, in 1999, she died. Bill is president of the British Society of Dowsers. Since 1965 identifying energy sources with dowsing rods has been a special interest. Their home was originally a thatched farmhouse built around 1650. At one time *Neals* was operating as a straw-plait factory; later it was the home of the local surgery.

Elizabeth House was built in 1953 and named because it was the year of the Queen's Coronation. It was the Police House until 1980. In the late 1990s Nancy and Neil Whittington from Chicago were renting the house while Neil was working for Lucent Technologies in Swindon. Nancy was very involved with the WI group here. During WI rambling events she developed an interest in the five thousand-year-old Ridgeway and walked the

Neals *(20) South Street*

> ### Barns
>
> There are also barns or conversions at *Alma Cottage*, Alma Farm, three in Back Lane, one in West Street, two in Castle Street and the converted *Whitley Cottage*, Corr's Barn, East Leaze, Eyres Barn at Upham, Ford Farm, Lodge Lower Barn, *The Old Malt House*, North Field, *Oak House*, Warren Farm.
>
> All barns originally had an exit opposite the entrance; one was tall for the laden carts to go in, the other lower for them to go out unloaded without turning round.
>
> There are still granaries on staddle stones at *Manor Farm* and *Ford Farm* and a 'skilling' at *Rose Cottage*.

Elizabeth House *South Street*

eighty-five mile path with Ann Lee. Peter and Gwyneth Bell came to Aldbourne in 1994 after living in Ramsbury for twelve years. *One Ash* was built in 1932 on the site of an old chair factory. Peter, a Devonian, worked in London for an insurance company and is a Fellow of the Institute of Actuaries. He is still a non-executive director for a medical insurance company. Gwyneth, who is from Scotland, has worked for *Woman* magazine and as an antiques dealer. Both have worked as volunteers for various local charities. They share an interest in gardening, historic houses and walking the dog. They have two sons, a daughter and a granddaughter living in London, Swindon and Hungerford respectively.

Turnpike Cottage has been the home of Patricia and Napier Collyns for twenty-one years. Much of their early married life was spent abroad working for Shell. They have five sons and ten grandchildren who love to visit Aldbourne. Some of the families live in America and Patricia is looking forward to the first visit of their latest grandson from Los Angeles. Patricia's interests are walking, opera music, photography, with a special interest in

Brook Cottage *South Street*

One Ash *(10) South Street*

> ### House Histories
>
> *Brook Cottage* reminds us the brook once ran on this side of the road. *One Ash*, built in 1932, is the site of a former chair factory moved from Castle Street by Thomas Orchard in 1887. *Turnpike Cottage*, dating from the 17th century, became a toll cottage when the road was turnpiked early in the 19th century. 18th century *Glebe House* was the farmhouse of the *Old Rectory*.
>
> Glebe Close stands on part of the old rectory glebe which was sold by the Neate family in 1963. The garden wall facing the main road was part of the barn. Willow weaving and blanching were carried out at *Neals* which dates back to the 18th and 19th centuries. In 1954 Mrs Edward Wentworth celebrated her 100th birthday there.

Turnpike Cottage *(8) South Street*

portraits of flowers and children, and working in the beautiful enclosed garden of the three hundred and fifty-year-old cottage.

Glebe House was purchased by Max and Jane Herbert in 1995. Max works for National Power in Swindon and Jane is with ComTel in Reading. They moved to Aldbourne when Alex was ready to attend Marlborough College. The Herberts are avid football fans; Alex is a goalkeeper at school and they all follow the Wimbledon football team. In the fifteenth century *Glebe House* was a farmhouse with a barn attached.

Preston Village

South Street continues towards Hungerford as the B4192 and, as it crosses the parish boundary at Preston, four houses fall within Aldbourne Parish.

Toll Cottage, featured in numerous books and calendars, has been the home of Rose and Ken Duddy since 1985. They have spent much of this time renovating the cottage, restoring original features like the big old fireplace. They enjoy meeting the tourists who stop to photograph their home, particularly in summer

Glebe House *(6) South Street*

Toll Cottage *Preston*

> ### What is a Dabchick?
>
> The answer comes quickly from those who proudly proclaim themselves true Dabchicks: 'someone born in the village'. The questionable alternative of being ducked in the pond to claim the coveted description is probably an insufficient qualification as well as being suspiciously embarrassing.
>
> Ida Gandy describes the well-known story of the strange bird appearing on the water and the oldest inhabitant being wheeled around the pond in a barrow to identify it. 'Wheel oi round agen' he demands before pronouncing the bird a dabchick. And there is even a grainy photograph to prove the truth of this!
>
> According to the Parish Appraisal in 1999 about 10 per cent of the current population claim to be true Dabchicks.

when it is festooned with hanging baskets. They spend many hours in the garden producing herbs and flowers, often sold by the roadside. *Preston Old House* has been lived in for the last twenty years by Peter Stibbard, a farmer, whose family have farmed locally for many years. The current owners of *Little Orchard House* are David and Jane Fanshawe, who moved here from Sydney, Australia, in 1992. David, an internationally acclaimed composer (*African Sanctus*), is also a musical explorer and ethno-musicologist. They have converted a garage in the grounds into a music studio and their business enterprise, Fanshawe One World Music, operates from *Little Orchard House*. Daughter Rachel attends Ramsbury Primary School and the family labrador, Trooper, loves his walks up Marridge Hill.

Nigel Palmer, of *Alma Farm*, was born at *Malt House Farm* – a true Dabchick. He moved to *Alma Farm* in 1969 with his late mother and sister. For fifteen years he ran his own agricultural contracting business but now he works for a Devizes dry lining company. He

Preston Old House *Preston*

Little Orchard House *Preston*

was a member of the Aldbourne Road Runners and has run the London and Rome marathons. His home-based hobby is gardening.

Turnpike and Rectory Wood

The ten houses in Turnpike were built by Hannick Homes of Swindon on the former paddock and kitchen garden of *The Old Manor* estate. Construction of these four- and five-

Alma Farm *Preston*

FORD FARM AND PRESTON

The houses on the north-east side of South Street beyond Farm Lane have mostly been built since World War II on land which was formerly part of *Ford Farm*. *White Gables*, No 37, was built in the early 1930s. There has been a settlement at 'Ford' since the Middle Ages, but *Ford Farm* house and grounds between the Hungerford Road and brook were only incorporated into Aldbourne Parish in 1934 when the boundary was moved from the brook to the road. The present house was largely rebuilt in 1873 and doubled in size in the mid-1950s. The farm land was sold for death duties in 1969. It is not clear where the ford was.

At Preston the brook is still the parish boundary, so only four houses fall within it. One is *Toll Cottage*, built about 1814 when the turnpike road was made. It is very picturesque and has figured in many books and calendars. *Preston Old House* was standing in 1773, when the first map was printed. The other three are 19th century although *Little Orchard House* has earlier origins.

10 *Turnpike*

CHAPTER SIX

> **TELEPHONES**
>
> The telephone service comes to Aldbourne by underground fibre-optic cable along the Ogbourne Road and then up to the exchange at Windmill Close. Here it is converted to digital pulse and thence relayed by copper cable to each household.
>
> Only the mobile telephone service is unsatisfactory. Coverage is patchy despite the installation of a new transmitter mast on Marlborough Road.

bedroom houses began in 1989. Many of the existing trees were retained, notably a wellingtonia, a mature horse-chestnut and a row of limes which border the adjacent Rectory Wood. An ancient wall constructed mainly of sarsen stones and chalk blocks, capped with tiles, forms part of the boundary of Nos 2 and 3 and extends to the gates of *The Old Manor*. The frontages were landscaped and laid out with grass areas, trees and shrubs. A show house was opened in 1989 and created a lot of interest to local inhabitants; a pond complete with goldfish was (and still is) a feature of the front garden. The show house was used by an

Glade House *(9) Turnpike*

Sylvan *(8) Turnpike*

7 Turnpike

Treneer *(6) Turnpike*

5 Turnpike

Wool Auction

"In Aldbourne there were twelve farms and about 6,000 sheep.

The sheep fed on the short downland grass in summer and were brought onto ploughed lands and water meadows in autumn to fertilize them. Shearing was done in the farmsteads.

The wool was sent to Marlborough and in order to get the wool there early the auctioneers offered a £1 prize for the first load. I've laid in bed in Baydon Hill and listened to the wagons from as far as Lambourn and Eastbury going past trying to be there first.

'Course it didn't do any good, you don't think they came back early from a wool sale? Oh no, they spent the £1 between 'em and the 'orses came back on their own with nobody holding the reins."

Chapter Six

Honeycomb *(4) Turnpike*

insurance company to make a security film which attracted much interest at the time.

The first residents moved into Turnpike in November 1989 and all the houses were occupied by August 1991. Soon after that a Neighbourhood Watch scheme was formed. The residents cover a wide age range from schoolchildren to the retired. Some of the residents moved to Aldbourne to be near to their relatives and others because their employment brought them to the area. The majority take an active part in village life and have joined those clubs and societies which appeal to their lifestyle.

In 1993 the site was extended by the construction of a further ten houses in Rectory Wood. When both developments were completed, the wooded area known as Rectory Wood was given over to the village by the developer together with sum of £10,000 for its future maintenance. This area forms a small haven for wildlife as well as for the enjoyment of the villagers. This land originally belonged to the Church with the rest of the *The Old Manor* estate, known then as 'The Rectory', but has changed hands many times since. During World War II, the first American soldiers in Aldbourne built a camp on the site of Rectory Wood and down towards Farm Lane. After the war the huts were taken over by the demobbed servicemen and their families because of the housing shortage.

Leather on Willow

Aldbourne Cricket Club dates back to before World War I. Until the 1950s the cricket ground was on West Street next to Woodley meadow but was relocated to the site of the current football field where the present pavilion, now used by the football team, was built by members of the club. During the 1960s the club ran two teams and gained national prominence when we became the first village club to play Sunday cricket.

Enthusiasm for cricket waned in the late 1960s. Because the pitch could not cope with soccer in the winter and cricket during the summer, the cricket club folded.

The club was reborn in 1997 with a fixture list of six matches.

It uses a pitch at Marlborough College as a home ground and trains weekly at the Allied Dunbar sports club. In 1999 the club had a full season and the diary is full once more for the year 2000.

South Street & the Roads off it

3 Turnpike

Riversdale (2) Turnpike

1 Turnpike

Growing up at Neals

"Grandma Penny kept *The Blue Boar* but bought *Neals* in 1922 for £400. They had no electricity, using oil lamps, and had an outside loo. Grandma Penny used to sew and darn by oil-lamp light and didn't wear glasses.

I was born in 1934 at *Neals*. At this time part of the house started to be used as a surgery. Before that the doctor used to ride over from Lambourn on a horse. The doctors from Ramsbury had a separate surgery on the Green.

After World War II Dr Osmond and Dr Mills went into partnership and then only *Neals* was used. People regarded the surgery as a meeting place.

I remember Auntie Wentworth living with us. She had come in 1930 after her husband died and never left. In 1952 we gave her a portable radio so she could hear the Queen's Christmas message. She thought it was terrible – the Queen speaking out of a box! She wasn't having that. Two years later when she was 100 she got her telegram from the Queen and was disgusted because it wasn't handwritten by the Queen! But we all celebrated. The Bishop of Salisbury came, and her sisters who were in their nineties, Miss Florence and Miss Grace.

She was a great lady."

Chapter Six

1, 2, 3 & 4 Rectory Wood

5, 6, 7 & 8 Rectory Wood

9 & 10 Rectory Wood

Eventually the huts were demolished, the Farm Lane council houses were built and the land to the rear was returned to private ownership.

One owner, Mr David Jackson, had an all-weather gallop built in Rectory Wood in the early 1980s and some trees were cut down to make way for it. It took three weeks to make, digging out a shallow trench, covering it with plastic sheeting and filling it with coke clinker from Swindon Gas Works. One of the people involved was Ron Morley. The horses came in through a gateway from Turnpike Field. Some beech saplings were planted and hence the start of the wood. So it has not been here all the time, as can be seen from the age of the trees.

Glebe Close

Built in 1973 on the site of a former barn and yard to provide a small development of seven four-bedroomed houses.

No 1 is the home of Mr and Mrs John Rendle. Mrs Rendle is always extremely busy with her own interior design business and John divides his time between work for various finance houses and continental travel. Michael and Sheila Wiggett and their son and daughter of school age live at No 2. Michael is secretary of Aldbourne's mini-rugger team and treasurer of the Scout, Cub and Beaver groups.

Peter and Sheila Gibson reside at No 3. Peter is a retired senior partner in a firm of

1 & 2 Glebe Close

BELLS AND CHAIRS

The manufacture of bells, from church bells downward, was an important source of employment. It began at *The Court House* in 1694 and continued at *Bell Court* on The Green and in the garden of *Pond House*, formerly Smith's Forge. Between 1781 and 1825 over 200 bells were cast. In 1825 Thomas Mears took over and transferred some of the workers to his foundry at Whitechapel. One of them, James Bridgman, later returned to Aldbourne and established a new foundry at High Town, which probably closed after his death in 1858. In several cases blacksmith's work was also carried out.

The manufacture of chairs was another local industry. Thomas Orchard is said to have opened a factory in Castle Street in about 1855. In 1887 he moved to *One Ash* in South Street where the business continued until 1927.

commercial surveyors and a former county councillor. He is active in voluntary, political and community affairs. Sheila directs local amateur theatre.

No 4 is owned by Colonel and Mrs Stephen Daniell who have three sons. Stephen, a retired army officer and diplomat, and his family are currently living in London whilst the house is temporarily let. At No 5 Derek Moore, a retired insurance broker, has taken on the role of chairman of the flourishing Theatre Club.

Paul and Dianne Lott, retired publicans who assist from time to time in hostelries in various parts of the country during the licensees' holidays, live at No 6. Paul and Pauline Beresford are the new owners of No 7 and recently married. They look forward to becoming active in the community.

> ### HEDGES AND WOODLAND
>
> The area always had few hedges but in the last few years there has been a trend away from hedge removal to hedge reinstatement and improvement.
>
> However, small copses have grown in number as areas difficult to use in other ways have been planted. Spinneys and clumps have been reinstated particularly after the great destructive storms of 1987 and 1991. The latter destroyed over 4,500 mature beech at *North Farm* alone. Three areas of ancient woodland survive at Wilding's Copse, High Clear Plantation and The Dean.
>
> Most timber produced is not processed in the parish except for firewood.

3 & 4 Glebe Close

5, 6 & 7 Glebe Close

Chapter Seven

The Farm Lane Area

Southfield

Southfield is a small close of six houses built in 1985–6. The leafy secluded setting with beautiful open plan front gardens gives it a feeling of great tranquillity. Perhaps this explains why all the houses, with one exception, are still occupied by their original owners. All residents have moved to Aldbourne from elsewhere.

No 4 is the home of Barbara Brownell who comes from York. After a very varied career in the armed forces during the war she was demobilized in 1947. She married an American and settled in New York. After her husband's retirement, they travelled around the United States, Canada and Mexico in a motor home for two-and-a-half years; they finally settled in

> **Daffodils and Lemonade**
>
> "We used to cycle to Coate Water to go swimming. We also collected daffodils and primroses from Daffy Copse and bring a whole basket full home to decorate the church font for Easter.
>
> Going up the hill to the Four Barrows for family picnics was a favourite pastime. I used take a bottle of lemonade and jam sandwiches. After church or chapel on Sundays families used to walk down Turnpike to Hodders Bridge.
>
> I've a photo of myself and my sister dressed as bride and groom in my father's sidecar as an entry in the carnival. Dad was dressed as a chauffeur."

2 Southfield

Sandwich, Cape Cod. Following her husband's death, Barbara returned to England in 1991.

John Symons lived in Bromley in Kent before moving to Thatcham in 1975. His wife Janet moved there in 1980 from Belfast. Her family originally came from Wales. John and Janet moved to No 6 in 1986. They both commute to London Heathrow where they work for British Airways. John has been a keen golfer since 1982.

Ambleside is where the Pryce family live. Malcolm originally comes from Malvern and is Group Scout Leader in the village. His work is primarily in the information technology and pharmaceutical industries. He is also a tennis player and private pilot. Linda comes from Cardiff and is an accountant in practice. She plays classical guitar. Daughter Laura has been a member of various organizations including ballet, Guides, ALEC and local music groups. Her brother Matthew takes part in Scouts, rugby, skateboarding and Youth Club.

Liz and Charles Bailey have lived at *Bonners* since moving from Winnersh in 1985. Liz has a part-time job in the village and enjoys swimming, yoga and travel. Charles advises farmers on growing crops. He also trades grain and other agricultural commodities. Their son Simon is now married and lives close enough to see them regularly.

Brian and Sandra Lincoln moved to No 1 in 1985 from Buckinghamshire and called it *Southfield Cottage*. They have two children, Simon and Tina, both married, and have two

4 Southfield

6 Southfield

BUILDING HOUSES

Richard Stacey started his building company before World War II but it really developed after the war when council houses were being built. He was responsible for those in Farm Lane and a large estate, St Margaret's Mead, in Marlborough.

He later built houses in Oxford Street and Windmill Close.

The Farm Lane Area

Ambleside *(5) Southfield*

Bonners *(3) Southfield*

Southfield Cottage *(1) Southfield*

Early Buildings

The first settlements were on the hills round about, but people gradually moved down into the valley. Early buildings of wood with thatched roofs were gradually replaced or altered.

The chalk, sarsen and flint of the local landscape make good building materials and can still be seen, mostly together with later brick.

Many fires have raged through the village, with two particularly disastrous ones in 1760 and 1777. Today most roofs are of clay tiles, with a few of slate or thatch.

There are still some old barns and other outbuildings such as granaries, but many have been converted to domestic use. Other buildings have switched from agricultural or industrial to domestic or retail use and sometimes back again, been divided up or joined together.

The Old Priest's House is the earliest and most complete existing domestic building; it probably dates from the 14th or 15th century, and the old hall construction can still be made out behind later additions. Several houses have parts dating from the 16th century but the older buildings date mostly from the later 18th and 19th centuries, many on earlier sites.

granddaughters. Since moving to Aldbourne Brian has worked for W H Smith and the Bible Society. He now works as a business consultant. Sandra works at the Princess Margaret Hospital. Both are members of St Michael's Church, Brian being churchwarden. He is also a Tennis Club member.

Farm Lane

Originally a lane running from Southward House to a farm on Southward Lane, Farm Lane is now quite busy with vehicles coming from the small estates and farms but residents still find it a relatively quiet and friendly neighbourhood.

The Evans family moved to *Southward House* from Wimbledon in 1995. Anthony, a retired Coldstreamer, and Jocelyn run a wine wholesale business from home. Anthony also works on 'Skylon', a reusable spaceplane project. Rosalie and Douglas are keen tennis players. *Penrose* was the home of the late Patricia Leigh who was working on both the text and the drawings for this book but was sadly unable to finish. Her sparkling ideas and

Southward House *Farm Lane*

Penrose *(1) Farm Lane*

enthusiasm were such an encouragement. She is greatly missed.

The small close of bungalows and houses, together with the adjacent playing field, was built at the end of World War II on the site of a British-American army camp of which only the two changing room huts remain. Doreen Pickworth has lived at No 2 for twenty of her forty-four years in Aldbourne. For fifteen years she cooked school dinners, at one time over a hundred meals a day. Now WI, Mothers' Union, Silver Threads and her garden keep her busy. Marjorie Rivitt moved to No 3 three years ago where she is often visited by her daughter, son and three grandchildren. She is restricted by poor eyesight but keeps active none the less. Peter and Dorothy Griffiths have lived at No 4 for four years and have a son and daughter, six grandchildren and two great grandchildren. Dot was in *The Masons Arms* darts team and undertakes sewing work. They both garden.

Iris Nutley lived at No 11 in 1954 and she and Frank moved to No 5 from South Street, with daughter Vanessa twenty-nine years ago. Both helped for many years in village affairs; the carnival, WI, and Luncheon Club are examples. Their garden is very beautiful.

2, 3 & 4 Farm Lane

5 & 6 Farm Lane

CHAPTER SEVEN

7 Farm Lane

Barbara and John Way moved into No 6 in 1999 when the dairy herd at Crowood Farm, which he had looked after for thirty-five years, was sold. He now works for Honda and they have two sons living locally. Arthur and Joyce Blake lived for ten years in Australia. They have now settled at No 7 close to their son and daughter in the village, their son in Swindon and the four grandchildren.

Ruth Beattie and her son Colin live at No 8 and were joined by Janet when she married Colin in May 1999. Nigel Keen, an HGV driver, has lived at No 9 all his life. Hazel, from *Chasewoods Farm*, works at St Michael's School where their son, James, is a pupil. The whole family loves sport, especially tennis and mountain-bike riding.

THE HISTORY OF FARM LANE AND SOUTHWARD LANE

By the late 18th century *Southward Farm* was the principal farmstead of *Aldbourne Manor*, with its buildings straddling the present Farm Lane. The house is 18th century with later additions and alterations. A date stone reading I H 1770 seems to have been reset later. The house next door was built in 1961 and those in Southfield in the 1980s. Cottages were built on the north side of the lane by Richard Stacey after World War II for Wiltshire County Council. They had large gardens at a time when villagers grew most of their own vegetables; some were pulled down to build Claridge Close at a much higher density.

There was a military camp in this area during World War II and the football changing rooms were the cookhouse. *Claypond Cottage* in Southward Lane originates from the 17th century with modern additions. No 2, originally *Southward Lane Farmhouse*, was resited in the 1950s by the Mildenhall family. The rest of the houses were built in the second half of the 20th century, apart from *Downside* – a good example of 1930s domestic architecture.

8, 9 & 10 Farm Lane

Joan Price moved to No 10 three years ago. She and her late husband lived for forty-seven years in West Street and their daughter is a Dabchick. Joan belongs to Silver Threads and has a granddaughter and grandson. Jean Davies was, with her late partner Cyril, landlady of *The Masons Arms* for ten years and held many charity events. She retired to No 11 in 1989 and now enjoys her involvement with Silver Threads, WI and Fellowship. Barbara (née Read) and Ernest Barnes, both Dabchicks, and their son Brian have lived at No 12 for five years. Apart from a period in Marlborough, they have spent all their lives in Aldbourne. Lily Newman, at No 13, spent World War II as a landgirl at Preston. Her late husband Ed was a butcher with 'Humphries'. She has a daughter, adopted son, grandchild and great-grandchild. At eighty-one, Lily is hampered by arthritis but is helped by neighbours and nurses. Julian and Antonetta Newton-Tyers have lived at No 14 for thirteen years. Julian works as a computer consultant from home and Antonetta in quality assurance for Vodaphone in Newbury. They have two children, Danielle, ten, and Stuart, two.

Southward Lane

The name Southward derives from South Wood Lane, probably altered over the years by dialect changes.

11 & 12 Farm Lane

13 & 14 Farm Lane

Pond Concerts

During the summer the band perform four concerts on the first Sunday evening of each of the summer months. They play in the Square next to the village pond.

Called the 'pond concerts' they are relaxed and entertaining, and extremely popular with hundreds of people coming into the village to enjoy an evening's music.

CHAPTER SEVEN

Douglas and Penny Hagerty built *Copper Beeches* in 1976–7 and extended it in 1979. Pottery, inkwells and spoons found during the excavations are believed to be from a World War II troop camp on the same site. Doug has lived in this area since he was six months old. Penny came here on her marriage in 1966. Their children, John and Leigh, were born at the Savernake Hospital. At the same time Doug's brother Roger built *Farefield*, a light modern house, next door. A lecturer, he had no expertise in building but proceeded during the driest summer of the decade, digging into solid chalk, then worked through the wettest autumn on record, wading in deep mud. In 1988 Roger and Krystyna extended the house to include a self-contained apartment. Both their children were born in Aldbourne. *Downside House* was built in 1934 for Colonel Collins by Arthur Stacey. Over the years it has had several owners including Ian Keel of Liddiards and Dr Lamb, an obstetrician at Wroughton Hospital. Since 1982 it has been the home of Duncan McPhedran, a local vet, Patricia and their two children. They have added a pond, patio doors and made a pony paddock in place of the tennis court.

On the parish boundary is *Brickkiln Cottage*.

Ewin's Hill Farm, the home of Guy Wentworth, appeared in a deed of sale in 1656. The various owners of parts of the farm are recorded on parchments until its principal

Farefield *Southward Lane*

Copper Beeches *Southward Lane*

> ### BUILDERS
>
> Charles Stacey started a building firm after World War I from a yard in Goddards Lane. During the depression in the 1930s his social commitment ensured that he employed as many men as he could. He knew what it was like to be poor as his father had died working in a well at Greenhill, leaving a widow with several children to bring up.
>
> He built many of the houses in the village but some projects were more distant. The men used to cycle there, live on site all week and cycle home for the weekend.
>
> When Mr Stacey retired the business was bought and continued by Mr Mantle and later taken over by Phillimore Construction. Liddiards took over the premises on the demise of Phillimores.

The Farm Lane Area

Downside House *Southward Lane*

> ### The Bourne
>
> Has the bourne, or brook as it is traditionally called, started to flow yet? Sometimes it starts early in the year, sometimes not at all.
>
> The average annual rainfall for the area is under 800mm with recent extremes of 440mm in 1975 and 1030mm in 1976–7. Rainfall in 1996 and 1997 was well below average; in 1998 it was well above.
>
> Our bourne is a typical chalk stream draining the dip slope of the Marlborough Downs. Winter rainfall percolates up to 100 metres through the soil and chalk to the underlying water table. This takes some months so the highest groundwater levels occur some time after the rainfall. Water levels in the chalk can vary by up to 30 metres a year depending on the amount and timing of winter rain.

Brickkiln Cottage *Loves Lane*

Ewin's Hill Farm *Southward Lane*

CHAPTER SEVEN

Broad Acres *Southward Lane*

union in 1867, when Joseph Wentworth bought two farms. The present farm, now increased to fifty-eight acres, is on clay-capped chalk. Originally, there were woodlands on the east, south and west and scrubland growing on chalk downland on the exposed northern slope. *Broad Acres* was built during 1996 on earlier (1970s) foundations and the site of a cottage shown on the 1828 OS map. Edgar Prentice was brought up in north London and spent his life in the steel industry and travelled worldwide. Carol spent her early life on her parents' farm at Ewin's Hill and worked mostly in the oil exploration industry in London, overseas, Scotland and Wiltshire.

Marion and Leonard Mildenhall moved into the newly-built *Southward Lane Farmhouse* after their wedding at the Methodist Chapel in June 1958. Marion (née Read) and Leonard both lived in the village and came from old village families. They farmed here since the early 1950s and have three sons all engaged in farming. The house enjoys lovely views across the Downs which the family farms. Leonard died in the late 1990s.

No 6, the last house in Southward Lane proper, was built by Mr McNaulty on the site of the tennis courts, part of Southward Farm. It is now the home of Mrs Nancy Barrett, Oliver Hawkins' daughter. Oliver was chairman of Aldbourne Parish Council for many years and representative on Kennet Council. He was a lay preacher in the Methodist Church.

No 5 is the home of Andrea and Peter West, and was built in 1961 on land which was a wedding present from Andrea's grandfather in 1960. Andrea's occupation and hobby was as a ceramic artist. Peter, who is a toolmaker and production engineer, started West Street Motors in 1976. Both now work for their

Southward Lane Farm *Southward Lane*

Greenacre *Southward Lane*

The Farm Lane Area

> ### Hot Quills
>
> "A precious memory of Aldbourne is of Emmy and Charlie Hale. One year just before Christmas when Emmy was dressing the turkey, the methylated sprits she used for burning off the quills exploded in her face and she was badly burnt. But this lead to a lasting friendship and many a long tale at their house *Eventide*.
>
> The most memorable was an invitation to tea which went on until 11.00pm."

6 Southward Lane

5 Southward Lane

Lamsden's Well *(4) Southward Lane*

3 Southward Lane

daughter Sarah at Southill Stables. Andrea was in the WI choir and drama group and enjoys line dancing. Peter was in the Aldbourne Band for twenty years.

No 4 was built by Oliver Hawkins on the site of his farm's broiler house. About a hundred years ago a cottage stood there. After his death Mr and Mrs Willis lived at No 4 and in 1992 it was purchased by Shirley and Howard Gibbs, who for twenty years, ran the Aldbourne Post Office and Stores. Shirley enjoys dancing, the WI and table tennis whilst Howard's interests are archaeology, local history and writing poetry.

No 3 was built in 1962–3 by William (Busky) Liddiard for his retirement. After his death Mrs Liddiard continued to live there until her death in 1997 when Graham and Jane Palmer bought it. They are each in different branches of the nursing profession. Their son Ian plays in the Aldbourne Silver Band and hopes to go to university.

Previously known as 'Southward Lane Farmhouse', No 2 was purchased by Mr Finnegan, who worked on local farms, and his wife. Their son and daughter continue to live there. Michael works at Aldermaston. The original cottage would have been over two hundred years old and carried thatch until about sixty or seventy years ago when it was enlarged to its present size and slated.

Roy and Manda Horton, who married in Marlborough, moved to *Claypond Cottage* in 1996. His hobbies are golf and swimming and hers are horse-riding and gardening. Roy

Chapter Seven

> **PETROL SALES**
>
> At one time there were very few cars in the village but four petrol outlets.
>
> Mrs Margery Barrett's father was the first to sell petrol in the village. It was in two-gallon cans. The other outlets were Mr Alsop, Mr Lunn and the Foundry.
>
> Now there are many cars in the village and no petrol station!

2 & Claypond Cottage (1) Southward Lane

added a greenhouse so that Manda can raise her own plants. She hopes to own her own horse. Ben, their young labrador tries to befriend everyone. The seventeenth-century cottage, with original inglenook and bread oven, was extended in 1960.

The Garlings

In the summer of 1960 Oliver Hawkins, who owned land off Southward Lane had a meeting with Mr Edwards the builder. It was agreed to erect a new development of houses, taking care to blend them into the hillside. The bungalows at the back were to be quite substantial, consisting of a split level building with a double garage and laundry room at ground level and upstairs a lounge, three or four bedrooms, bathroom, kitchen and dining room, opening onto a ground level garden at the back, and costing around £5,000. The smaller bungalows in the middle of the horseshoe would cost about £3,000 and consist of a living room, dining room, kitchen, bathroom, toilet and three bedrooms.

The original name given to this development was 'The Garlands' – a reminder of the days when young girls would come to pick wild flowers to make the garlands used for weddings or feast days.

On the left as you enter The Garlings are four new bungalows. The first two built by local builder Mr Ron King, about seven years ago. They are modern three- and four-bedroom detached bungalows, unusual in that they are built 'side on' to the street, the front door being at the back! *Cala* was occupied by the Faulkners, an elderly couple who died, one shortly after the other. The second is occupied by Stephen and Caroline Mitchell. Without a history as yet, it is worth mentioning the house was given its name, *Fiddlers Green*, which means 'Sailors' Elysium' as there was no number and normal names ending in 'house' or 'cottage' could not apply. It has subsequently earned itself slightly humourous connotations as Mr Mitchell works for the Inland Revenue.

The next two bungalows were built when The Downs estate was built about six years ago. Roy and Irene Dickens moved in two and a half years ago. Roy retired in 1985 having spent twenty-one years helping to build the business of Triumph International Ltd as their sales and marketing manager. Irene was involved in charity work for the blind for forty years and retired as chairperson of the Thamesdown Blind Association in 1992. The birth of their grandson brought them back to Wiltshire to be closer to their family and also to enjoy village life in Aldbourne.

Joyce and Don Webb live in *Brambly Hedge*, No 24. They moved in on 31 March 1993.

The Farm Lane Area

Cala & **Fiddlers Green** *The Garlings*

Brambly Hedge *(24)* & **Tregarth** *(22) The Garlings*

Metal Detecting

Ancient artifact recovery has increased hugely through metal detecting and local amateurs using this aid have added useful knowledge about Aldbourne.

For instance, not far from the boundary on the Hungerford Road, recently was found an Anglo-Saxon wrist clasp of a type believed to have been introduced from Norway in the 5th century. There have also been finds of ancient coins, including more coins detected in the area where the Aldbourne Hoard was uncovered. Other finds have told us of a general spacing of home sites.

We hope that there is more to be found that will add to our knowledge and the rich archaeological records of this area.

21 The Garlings

CHAPTER SEVEN

Don and Joyce came to Swindon with W H Smith when they moved their main warehouse from London to Greenbridge. Don was product control manager and took early retirement after forty-four years in the book trade. Joyce was a supervisor with Roussel Laboratories, a pharmaceutical drugs company, and retired in December 1988 after twenty years. One of their main interests is reading and recording news items for Talking Newspapers for the Blind, the other is their lovely pet collie, Tess. They love Aldbourne and have made many dear friends including neighbours since moving here.

Two families who were original inhabitants of The Garlings are Stanley and Joan Morton and Godfrey and Joy Parker. The Parkers realized what a bargain the new houses were – and they could choose their own bathroom fittings! They were not surprised when the builder subsequently went bankrupt. They extended their house to accommodate their growing family and put in a swimming pool.

The Craigs and their three children moved into their new house in 1963 at Easter, heavy snowfalls having prevented a planned move at Christmas. There was still some work to do inside and it was a sea of mud outside. The attic was later converted into a bedroom for their son. Harold Craig, who was headmaster of Commonweal School, Swindon, for a number of years, died five years ago. Gine was well known for her commitment to village organizations and her hobby of decorating eggs.

Clive and Elsie Crook and their two children, Fiona and John, lived at No 18 until

20 The Garlings

19 The Garlings

recently. They landscaped the garden and made extensive internal improvements. Jane and Jonathan Startin and their three children have now moved there.

Nos 17 and 16 changed hands in the last four years being bought by families who had been neighbours in Upper Upham. Vanessa and Anthony Butler and their two children, Nick, who is taking a year out before going to university and Lucy, who is at St John's School, bought their house from the Youngs who had lived there for many years. Vanessa is from an old village family being the great-granddaughter of Daniel and Sarah Cook (mentioned elsewhere). She was born here and has lived in the village for the greater part of her life. She has always taken an active part in village life and amongst other interests is a past chairman

> ### BUSINESS IN ADVERSITY
>
> There were two shoe menders in the village, Bill Palmer on the corner of Castle Street who had a bad stutter, and Percy Edwards who had a room on the north side of *Bay House*. He later set up business in Swindon and carried the shoes with him on the service bus despite having a false leg.
>
> Mr Teagle was a mat maker. He had been blinded in World War I, was retrained by the British Legion and had his business at 3 Lottage Road.
>
> Thomas Lunn had the shop which is now the 'Mini Mart' and sold hardware, tools, fancy goods and petrol.

18 The Garlings

17 The Garlings

Cricket Controversy

The Cricket Club was thriving and played its fixtures on the present football field. The enthusiasts wished to play on Sundays but the religious members of the community very much disapproved. There was a huge controversy and finally the Parish Council were called in to arbitrate. A plebiscite was held and to everyone's amazement the vote was three to one in favour of Sunday cricket. Whereupon the Almighty intervened and it rained every Sunday for the rest of the year!

of ALEC, organizes the senior citizens' Christmas dinner and is on the Millennium Festival Committee. She can remember when The Garlings was just a field and the great excitement of an influx of new people with the building of a new estate. Anthony came to Aldbourne when he married Vanessa and is an established carpenter and builder who takes an active part in village life, previously having helped the youth of the village with their football.

The Farr family now live in No 16. Steve, brought up around Newbury, is in agricultural sales. His wife Jean works in Baydon, one daughter, Jemma who is twenty-one, works

La Bauge *(16) The Garlings*

Avalonia *(15) The Garlings*

The Church and the School

(top) Bellringers: Katrina Lenton, Colin Mynett, Sheila Evans, Chris Barnes, George Newman, Allan Keen, Mark Hart and Lindsey Grey.
(above) Members of St Michael's Church Choir and Music Group: Marianne Adey, Ruth Pakenham, Pam Puttick, Charles Bland, Dee Pelham-Reid, George Rendell, Allan Keen (organist), Jenny Rendell, Ros Oswald (accompanist), Anthony Evans, Duncan McPhedran and Brian Lincoln.

(above) A representation of St Michael on the wall of the Primary School.
(top right) Gloria Passmore, the Methodist lay worker.
(above right) Rev Michael Forrer, the priest-in-charge at St Michael's Church.

(below) Feeding the ducks on the pond are Joseph Hedger, Kate Bunce, Molly Parmiter (a Dabchick), Lauren Beauchamp and Siobhan Casey.

(below) At St Michael's School Zachary Baker, Catherine Brown and Tom Rogerson make sure that Charlotte Startin gets it right.

Fuellers of the 'Inner Man'

(above left) Jocelyn and Anthony Evans of Southward Wines.
(above) Bob and Jackie Weedon who ran The Blue Boar until late 1999.
(far left) Tony and Ann Swinmurn outside The Crown Hotel.
(left) Jim and Mary Hannan at the entrance to 'Raffles'.

(left) Hugh and Sue Humphreys with Simon Trinder at The Masons Arms.
(below left) In The Blue Boar celebrating on Millennium Eve are Debbie Harding, Mickey and Jan Pattemore (who have recently taken over), Russell Martin and Ian Comley.
(below) Brian and Rosemary Buckler of Bucklers Banquets.

Service with a Smile

(above, from the top) Mandy Lawson and Robin Hayhurst at 'Alldays'; Rachel and Graham Browning, owners of the 'Mini Mart'; Bev and Ges Dolman who run the Post Office and Stores; Clare Knight, Sheila Jordan and Diane Perrett of 'Maxine's'.

(top) Neil O'Riordan, Ian Wright, Martin Hill and Roy Wood of NDS.
(centre) Framed at QED are Polly Halpin, Mark Messenger, Nicky Pearce, Nick Leigh, Stuart Toyne, Andrew Halsey, Cathy Wright and Jo Foxton.
(above) Leo Dopson, Tim Beattie, Beryl Gilligan, Martin Comley and Matthew Wakeham at West Street Motors.

Trades and Professions

(from the top, left to right) Sean Gilligan; Peter Lawler; Keith Evill; Ian Cowles; Roy Partridge holding the pattern for the Aldbourne Millennium Festival commemorative bell; Michael Beck; Sally Thomas; Trish Rushen; Francis May; Dave Rushen; Paul Newman; Michael Barnes.

VILLAGE EVENTS

(top) The start of the annual Beating the Bounds in 1999.

(above left) Carnival Queen Louise Hunt and chairman of the Parish Council, Chris Humphries, at the presentation of the 1989 Best Kept Village award.

(above) The Morris Men at the 1999 fête: Michael Barnes, Ron Morley, John Jepson, Anthony Butler, Chris Warrington and Ron Hacker.

(left) Susan Bailey opens the refurbished Old Schoolroom in June 1998.

A Wide Range of Jobs ...

(from the top, left to right) Sarah, Andrea and Peter West who run the local livery stables; Terence and Lionel Barnes, latest in the family line to run the business; Stephen, Keith and Barbara Sowerby, furniture makers; the men at Country Logs – Ricky Watts, Thomas Wells, Nick Turk and Andy Holbrow; Tom Barnes and A D Keen; Jo Hale and her cheeses; Andy Turner.
(left) Diana and Peter Ament with two of the cats at Cheldene Cattery.

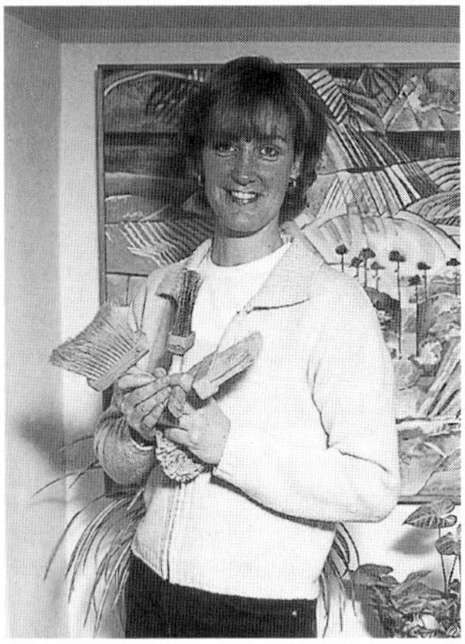

... Skills and Abilities

(above, top) John Adey, Guy Montezuma and Richard Palmer outside Aldbourne Nursing Home.
(above, middle) Sue French, Liz Bailey and the eponymous Linda of Linda Pryce and Co; Mike Nicholls (Nicky James), musician.
(above) Photographer extraordinaire, Brian Hale; Dowsers Bill Cooper, Peggy Delmé-Radcliffe and Marcus Rouse on an energy line, part of the Aldbourne hexagram complex.
(right, top to bottom) Composer and explorer David Fanshawe of Preston; Linda Jeffcoat, decorative painter; in the children's playground, Hebe and Fenella Elms (chair of the 1999 Parish Appraisal Working Party); Deborah Luck, physiotherapist.

The Village Celebrates the Millennium Moment

(above, from the top, left to right) Fireworks over St Michael's Church; the party in full swing in Barnes' coach garage; gathering on the Green at midnight; Donald Barnes getting into the spirit at The Blue Boar.

(left) A round of millennial drinks at The Crown.
(below left) Celebrations in The Masons Arms.
(below) Meanwhile, in the other bar at The Masons Arms …

for Virgin Atlantic and the other, Christy (eighteen) has recently completed her A levels. Jean belongs to the old Aldbourne Barnes family whose coach company was started by her grandfather, continued by her father and uncle and is now run by her brother and cousin. Her great uncle was Mr Oliver Hawkins, owner of the land on which The Garlings is built, and she remembers his farm when walking the common with her mother.

In 1982 Gwen and Roy Hazel moved into No 15 taking over from the Hamiltons. Roy and Gwen are both retired. Roy worked at British Rail as head of the apprentice school and Gwen was a school teacher. They founded the Aldbourne Table Tennis Club in 1987 and continue to organize and participate in league matches. Rosie and Tony Jarvis have lived at No 13, *Baker's Dozen,* since 1980. Tony is a life and pensions manager with an insurance broker. Rosie was a college lecturer for special education and is now a carer for two adults with learning difficulties. Their sons have now moved out and live in Swindon. Their outside interests include membership of a Lions club, a folk dancing club, the management committee of a day drop-in centre for adults and the quality assurance group for another day centre. They also run barn dances for people with special needs.

14 The Garlings

Baker's Dozen *(13) The Garlings*

Festivals

During Christmas 1969 a group of people got together to see how they could raise funds for improvements to the Memorial Hall. They proposed a number of events typical of a certain period in history. Activities might include theatre, music, dancing, exhibitions, and so on.

The 1970 Festival organized by Anthony Brown had a Georgian theme with no electricity for the weekend. Peter Ludlow's Victorian Festival in 1980 raised money for the hall and the band. The 1990 Festival was organized by John Adey and took us back to the Edwardian period. It raised money for the hall, the band and improvements to the pond.

These ten-yearly May Festivals have been an enjoyable and successful way of raising much needed funds.

CHAPTER SEVEN

12 The Garlings

11 The Garlings

10 The Garlings

Allan Cummings writes: 'The new school at Hungerford opened its doors in January 1963 and promptly closed them again – several times. The heating system was defeated by a frost which cemented snow to roads and fields for three months. This gave me the opportunity to benefit from the central heating of the show house at No 7. Over the weeks to Easter, No 12 was completed – one of the first in the estate on a greenfield site. Thanks to the welcome provided by Dabchicks like Oliver, Bob and Stella and subsequently others, my wife, mother-in-law and two pre-school children settled in quickly during the Easter holidays.' Allan taught at Hungerford and was a parish councillor for many years. Jean took an active part in village life, especially events connected with the Methodist Church. She was one of the founder members of the Aldbourne Young Wives which later evolved into Aldbourne Ladies' Group.

Geoff and Pat Eldridge have lived at No 11 since 1963. Geoff writes 'I came with Bert Edwards, the developer of The Garlings, in 1960 to see Mr Hawkins' field. I worked for Mr Edwards as a carpenter and started in 1960 on twenty-one bungalows. We got married on 20 July 1963 and moved into our new house which had just been completed. Our daughter Angela was born in 1965 and our son Richard in 1970.' Pat has been a firm supporter of village organizations such as the WI, Ladies'

The Farm Lane Area

Football

Aldbourne Football Club was formed in 1887 and the players that made up the first team were J Hawkins, G Witts, Tom Jerram, E Rodbourne, John Orchard, J Cook, A Perrett, S Howard, A W Aldridge, T Pembroke, F Bush and J Jerram (captain). The team played, as now, at Farm Lane on what was known at that time as the football meadow.

The team has had various names over the years. In 1902 they were called Aldbourne Divers; by 1904 they had changed the name to Aldbourne Thistle; and in more recent years they have been called Aldbourne Park and Aldbourne Ferndale.

The club has been very successful over the years playing in the Swindon and District League and the Wiltshire League, and has won numerous trophies including the Savernake Hospital Cup, Foxhill Shield, Wilts Junior League Cup, Harold Gwyther Benevolent Cup, Hungerford Cup, Greystone Cup and Wilts Senior Cup.

The club currently plays in the Wiltshire League Intermediate Division and in Wilts League Junior Division One.

Group and the Table Tennis Club over the years.

Others, too, have extended their properties. Keith and Anne Evill at No 9 built on a utility room and office. Keith, a corporate building surveyor, designed both the Methodist Church in Lottage Road and the Nursing Home in South Street.

Their neighbours, the Newhams, also built on a dinning room and kitchen, completely reorganizing the inside of the house to provide more space for their three children. They also have the benefit of a swimming pool in their garden. Daughter Clair, husband Andy and their small daughter set up home at No 6, one of the few bungalows still in its original form.

Until recently No 8 was occupied by Dudley and Dorothy Budden who spent a great deal of time decorating the house and doing up the garden. Dorothy or 'Dot' was a familiar figure at parish council meetings where she never missed an opportunity to question the decisions of the council but always with knowledge and the interests of the village at heart.

Vi Carr came to live at No 3 in 1979 with her husband. They were both retired and took over the house from the Warringtons of Back Lane after living in Cornwall for three years. Sadly Vi's husband died eight years ago. She continues to participate in village organizations such as the WI, of which she is a committee

9 The Garlings

8 The Garlings

CHAPTER SEVEN

1 The Garlings

2 The Garlings

3 The Garlings

WOMEN'S FELLOWSHIP

Originally, two meetings were held concurrently every Wednesday afternoon, the Sisterhood at the Primitive Methodist Chapel in West Street and the Women's Guild at the Wesleyan Methodist in Lottage Road. In 1955 a meeting was held to discuss whether the two meetings should combine. Presided over by Mrs R Stacey, the meeting opened with a hymn and a prayer that those present might be guided to put the work of God before personal feelings So the Women's Fellowship came into being and was held alternately in each Chapel. Membership fees were one penny per week, later changed to one shilling (5p) per year. Now in 1999 fees are £1.

In 1961 it was agreed to have a bring-and-buy sale for the East London Mission. This year £127 was raised in this way to go to the South London Mission. Since 1969 meetings have been held fortnightly and the format remains unchanged. They begin with a hymn followed by a prayer, a bible reading, a speaker, a bring-and-buy sale (usually for outing funds) and tea and biscuits. Members number forty-one, of all denominations or none, and everyone finds a welcome and 'fellowship'.

member. She has contributed an embroidered panel for the village map on display in the Memorial Hall and is working on a wall hanging depicting the village over the last thirty years. The bungalow has had one bedroom added and is much praised for its lovely garden, especially in the summer.

No 7, the show house, was completed before the terrible winter of 1962–3. The present owners, the Dymonds, relocated from Switzerland in the August of 1986 in time for the new school year. Their prime objective was to find a friendly environment in which to bring up their four children and Liz had not even seen the house she was moving into! Now, thirteen years later, they realize what a good choice it was! John and Liz have both been busy in local affairs. John was a parish councillor for five years and a founder member of the Aldbourne Housing Group. His claim to fame was to appear on the TV quiz programme 'Mastermind' and be immortalized in a ditty by the Aldbourne Buskers. Liz has served on several village committees such as the Friends of St Michael's School and the Ladies' Group. Their house has been the subject of many renovations over the years. Mr Gow, one of the former owners, was a well-known composer and pianist. He knocked down the interior wall to make room for his grand piano and built

4 The Garlings

Wide Stones *(5) The Garlings*

> ## Silver Threads
>
> In the early 1950s Mrs Sergeant of *Mowcop* in Oxford Street, and a group of friends, formed the first committee of the Aldbourne Silver Threads. The forty members met in the Old Church Room in Marlborough Road. In addition to regular meetings they formed a choir conducted by Mr T D Barnes to entertain themselves and other clubs. In the early years they won prizes, notably at the Aldbourne carnival!
>
> Now, in 1998, there are about seventy members paying £1 per annum. The president is Irene Jerram. The pianists are Ruth Pakenham and Jose Swash. In addition to their meetings on alternate Tuesdays, they have trips, mystery tours, a garden party, an annual holiday (to Falmouth in 1998) and, to finish the year, a carol service and tea.

6 The Garlings

7 The Garlings

> **BLACKSMITH**
>
> Eddie joined the army at seventeen and served for nine years, making 175 parachute drops – one in the Arctic at 40 degrees below with ice forming on his face as he dropped.
>
> Just prior to being demobbed he made friends with Alan Liddiard who ran the Aldbourne Forge. From him he learnt the blacksmith's trade.
>
> Eddie mainly produces gates and ornamental work using traditional 'fire welding' forging. At his forge at Littlecote he has made gates for many large estates and has also exported to Nassau in the Bahamas.
>
> Eddie stamps his work with an anvil shape and the letters EFP.

on a study and patio. The Dymonds have knocked down the garage to put in two bedrooms, a shower room and utility room.

The Downs

The ten houses of The Downs were built around 1992 on land formerly part of *Southward Lane Farm*. The owners, several from outside the area, find it one of the most picturesque developments within Aldbourne, situated on the edge of the village overlooking the Marlborough Downs from which it got its name.

No 1, *Mallards*, one of the three original houses, was owned by Mrs Pat Hood and changed hands in 1993. Henry Rees and Anthony Cain were the owners from 1993 to 1999. Henry, a chartered accountant with KPMG, read music at Magdalen College, Oxford where he was a scholar. Anthony studied at the Royal Academy of Music was elected ARAM in 1995 and also attended The Slade School of Fine Art. Mike and Linda Maggs moved from Wokingham to No 2 some seven years ago for a more rural environment for Emily, nine, and Nathan, five. The transition was easy for Emily but more difficult for Linda and Mike whose family and work remain in the Wokingham area. No 3 was finished in 1994 and in 1997 Peggy and Geoff Slater moved there from Baydon where they had lived since Geoff retired fifteen years previously. He was a chartered accountant with a paint company. Peggy still runs the Baydon Thursday Club and Geoff is chairman of Aldbourne Luncheon Club and president of the local National Trust Association.

The Farm Lane Area

Mallards *(1) The Downs*

2 & 3 The Downs

4 & 5 The Downs

1st Aldbourne Cubs

The Cub section of the Scout Association has existed for over 80 years although it is unknown how long an Aldbourne pack has been operating.

In order to join a Cub Pack the young person must be eight years old. The new Cub will spent his first few weeks learning about our ceremonies, activities and his Law and Promise before investiture. The Law and Promise is a solemn undertaking that the new Cub will do his best to do his duty to God and the Queen and help other people.

Through his Cub career we offer him a programme of progressive training that provides for challenge, adventure and excitement. Each stage completed earns a badge. Other badges are earned for skills and activities.

Cubs form into small groups called Sixes, each identified by a different coloured woggle. An older Cub known as a Sixer heads this group

A typical Cub night comprises our opening and closing ceremonies, some badge work and one or more games. We hold an annual camp under canvas which all Cubs may attend. Camp is a fun event for all that aims to broaden the individuals experiences and teach them outdoor skills.

Chapter Seven

Ann and Terence Rogers moved to No 4 'with panoramic views of *Southward Lane Farm*, the pig farm and stables' in 1994. In the beautiful east-facing suntrap garden they have created spectacular terraces to above house height using 8,500 bricks to include lawns, a water feature, a conservatory and a workshop. In 1996 Mike and Mary Knight came to No 5 and have a son and a daughter. Malcolm, an insurance manager, plays in the Aldbourne Band and is a keen runner having competed regularly over the last thirty-six years. Mary lived in Africa for fifteen years and is actively involved in the church. Kay Preston-Wilkes and Dyson Wilkes moved from Bedfordshire because of Dyson's work with a Swedish telecommunications company, buying No 6 when it was just a pile of earth. Working alongside the builders – and since – they have created a house and garden of character to their taste. Resulting from their Swedish travels they hold a 'Midsomer Fest' celebrating the summer solstice when friends and neighbours gather for a twelve-hour party, decorating with flowers a pole around which to dance. Everyone brings food and there is a barrel of beer – a wonderful way to celebrate the joys of summer!

No 7, the home of Peter Cotterill, was barely up to roof level in May 1993 but with the backdrop of the downs and a brilliant day it required little persuasion to purchase. While

6 & 7 The Downs

A Fair Fight

"When the fair came to the village trade in the shop fell because passing traffic did not stop. The fairground attractions were close up to the shop and the generators caused a constant noise and the house shook. The owner of the fairground was Mr Edwards and he ruled his workers with an iron hand. When one of the workers cheeked Mr Edwards over some incident on the dodgems, Mr Edwards threw a punch and flattened him."

8 The Downs

9 The Downs

dry weather during July was ideal for the move, the new saplings which are beginning to show as trees needed constant watering. Continuing building work and garden landscaping provided a sea of mud in the later months but have given pleasure in subsequent years. Michael and Julie Rycroft and their daughters moved to No 8 from Guildford in 1995. The downland reminded them of the Surrey Downs but they find the people much more friendly here and the village way of life, with their home, garden, views over farmland and beautiful sunsets far more agreeable. Julie works in Marlborough, Michael in Wootton Bassett, Jackie in Swindon and Suzanne is at Surrey University. David and Susan Latham at No 9 always admired Aldbourne during Sunday afternoon drives from Stratton St Margaret. They saw four completed houses in The Downs during summer 1993 and moved in that October. Dave says 'I get such a buzz from looking outside and seeing outstanding countryside. We are so fortunate! Sarah Jane, four, loves attending the local school.'

The Day family (No 10) were the first to secure a property. Mrs Day works at St Michael's School and has witnessed hundreds of local children progress from infants to adults. Son Peter attends Cheltenham College and daughter Sarah is employed by the human resources department of W H Smith.

Farm Lane

From The Butts to Claridge Close

This row of attractively designed houses, all south-facing, was built immediately after the war. They were originally council houses but several have been bought by their owners. All have large gardens with well kept lawns and a communal path in the front.

Perhaps because most of the residents have lived here for many years, there is a good neighbourhood spirit. The feeling that it is a safe environment for children was expressed

Oakwood *(10) The Downs*

15 & 16 Farm Lane

both by a long-time resident and the newest family.

Deborah and Darren Morgan moved here in August 1998 and look forward to lively two-year-old Bradley growing up here. Peggy Bendle has lived in her house for over fifty years. She now shares it with her granddaughter's family – Suzanne and John Gibbs and great-grandchildren, Michael, Matthew and Jonathan. For many years Peggy ran the village children's playgroup. Pam and Bill Puttick have been Peg's excellent next door neighbours for thirty-nine years. Pam is well known in the village, and nationally, for her poetry – often funny but full of well-observed comments on life. Pam's brother Ted Barnes, a resident for about forty years, is approaching ninety years of age, the eldest son of a village family of twelve children. He has been a chimney sweep and also a village baker. Ted and Cicely Gale moved into their house when it was built. Ted is over ninety but until recently was still riding his bicycle. Ethel Underwood is another genuine village lady. Like many others she spent some years away during the war but returned to Aldbourne and her new house in 1948. Reg Slade, now in his eighties, also returned after the war to a new home. He enjoyed participating in village activities and still speeds to local events in his powered invalid carriage. Michael Barnes, a Dabchick, and Grace have lived in their house for thirty-seven years. They have spent time working on both the house and garden to wonderful effect. The final two houses, built in 1929, belong to Keith and Ken Read, two of seven children born in the house where Keith has lived all his life. His wife, Maureen, made an emotional journey to Australia recently to meet her father for the first time. Ken, much in demand as a professional electrician, is modernizing the adjoining house.

Claridge Close

The Close comprises thirty houses of two, three and four bedrooms, built as social housing, much needed by the young of the parish. Built on the junction of South Street and Farm Lane it replaces eight original old style council houses built for war heroes. The adopted name 'Claridge' comes from Johnny Claridge who is best remembered for selling home-grown vegetables from a trolley pushed regularly around the village.

Kennet Housing Society built the first phase of ten houses, finishing in June 1993 when the first residents moved in. Later that year a very successful street party was held to celebrate, including flashing lights and disco, going on until midnight. Also that year, second prize was obtained in the Carnival with the first Claridge Close float, 'Claridge Corndollies', crop circles being much in the

17 & 18 Farm Lane

The Farm Lane Area

19 & 20 Farm Lane

21 & 22 Farm Lane

23 & 24 Farm Lane

Chapter Seven

7, 6, 5 & 4 Claridge Close

Water Supply

Thames Water, responsible for our mains water supply installed in 1960, inform us that our piped water supply comes from two boreholes in Ramsbury. Because it is rain water filtered through rock strata, it requires less treatment than water taken from rivers.

It is pumped to the Crowood Reservoir (capacity 680,000 litres) and flows by force of gravity through two mains, one four- and the other six-inch, to the village whose daily use on average is 650,000 litres. Supplies are adequate and it has not been necessary in recent years to ration water.

There remain a few working wells and our two public pumps are still in working order. Water from these pumps cost sixpence (2½p) a barrel in 1910.

3, 2, & 1 Claridge Close

8 & 9 Claridge Close

news at that time. Two years later a further fifteen families took up residence after completion of stage two. The final phase being built by Sarsen Housing Society when the last two remaining council houses were razed to the ground for that purpose.

The majority of the householders are under the age of thirty-five with a third of the residences having at least one adult family member who was actually born in the village. Of the remaining, all but a few have either family members who live in the village or have resided in Aldbourne themselves prior to moving into the Close. At the last count there were thirty-two children under the age of seventeen living in Claridge Close and although the numbers are due to increase later this year there is no knowledge of a millennium baby!

Crufts is very dear to one 'Closer' who has had some success over the years and still has an open invitation to attend. Meanwhile, two piglets, which took up residence in the garden shed, were the passion of another. Animals in general seem to occupy several households who have no fewer than forty-one pets between them; cats coming top of the list with fourteen, followed closely by dogs, various other furry friends, birds, fish and even a pony (not kept in the garden shed!)

Claridge boasts a musician in its midst whose band once used it as a location and all the children living in it as extras for the video

10, 11 & 12 Claridge Close

14, 15 & 16 Claridge Close

Ballet

"In 2000 I will have been teaching ballet in Aldbourne for twelve years.

I use the Cecchetti method, named after the dancing maestro Enrico Cecchetti. It is one of the two most well-known and internationally used methods of teaching ballet.

My aim is to introduce children to the art of dance to music. I teach children from the age of three years and I enter them for examinations, if their parents wish, every other year. This means that I take the children through the syllabus in front of the examiner in groups of between four and six because, in my experience, this gets the best out of them.

In the intervening years, I prepare the children to take part in a concert which I stage in aid of the charity Children's Aid Direct."

to accompany their re-mix of 'Blanket on the Ground', a Billy-Jo Spears classic. It also has a resident who starred as an extra in a 1984 Richard Burton film and another who is a friend of Ruby Wax.

Gardens are in the main well maintained with some added features – ponds, pergolas, decking, rockeries and some very attractive hanging baskets and tubs. The front of the houses being open-plan communal areas are kept trimmed and tidy by contract. With so many children it is good to have a well situated play area in the far corner between Claridge Close and Rectory Wood with gates for access from both estates. The equipment, five pieces in all, including a slide, a seesaw and a house are attractive and available to the under twelves.

The oldies meanwhile amuse themselves by playing for the local sports teams – Rugby Club, and so on. A lot of fishing takes place as the chairman of Hungerford Canal Angling Association is one of the residents. The reserve member of the Wiltshire Clay Pigeon Shooting Team also resides in Claridge. The Close has witnessed lots of joy with four weddings over the years, although one arranged for July 1999 had to be re-arranged as the groom, a

17 & 18 Claridge Close

19 & 20 Claridge Close

> ### Energy Lines
>
> Dowsing around Aldbourne has located a geometric pattern of mysterious energy lines in the shape of a hexagram some six miles in diameter. The accuracy of the complex suggests that prehistoric man mapped the whole of the county by equilateral triangulation.
>
> This hexagram is aligned with Newcastle (Tyneside), the Long Man of Wilmington in Sussex and Glastonbury via Avebury. Glastonbury is famous for the interlocking circles symbol in the Chalice Well which forms the early Christian mystic symbol of the Vesica Piscis.
>
> Through dowsing, an identical shape on a much larger scale has been found centred on Aldbourne pond. With the sites of three former stone circles these findings indicate the existence of an important religious centre.

31 & 30 Claridge Close

29 & 28 Claridge Close

> **PEELING ONIONS**
> **BY PAM PUTTICK**
>
> I was standing peeling onions
> To go in a nice beef stew
> When in came my next door neighbour
> Saying 'What is the matter with you?'
>
> I try to convince her I'm okay
> But I can't however I try
> 'Cause although I'm feeling happy
> My onions just make me cry.
>
> So we stand and have a chatter
> About the prices and the weather
> And I keep peeling my onions
> Then both of us cry together.

27, 26, 25 & 24 Claridge Close

British serviceman, had been posted to Kosovo as part of the KFOR peacekeeping force. With so many children it is not surprising that there have been several christenings. Unfortunately, also sadness with the loss of one much loved eleven-year-old and two serious house fires.

Chauffeur, gardener, builder, mechanic are all found in the Close. Also, there are a large number of carers with five residents currently employed at the local nursing home, one working with adults with learning difficulties, an occupational therapy assistant and one having donated bone marrow for the Anthony Nolan Campaign. Unfortunately, five people have suffered redundancies since living in Claridge but happily most are now re-employed.

When asked what is the most memorable thing that has happened since moving into Claridge Close, most residents listed having babies, getting married (not necessarily in that order!), the street party, meeting future husband/wife. But one said: 'Nothing memorable that sticks out, just that the village is so busy and the people are so friendly and it is set in such beautiful countryside'.

What more can you say?

23 & 22 Claridge Close

GEOLOGY

The geology of the parish has greatly influenced its appearance. Until recent times most of the buildings were made of material found locally; chalk, sarsen stone, flint and clay (tombstones being an exception). The outline of the downs and the crops and vegetation show that the parish lies in the belt of chalk land that stretches diagonally across England with surviving deposits of overlying clay with flints.

Between the upper chalk and middle chalk that form the steep slopes around the village, lies a band of chalk rock that was quarried, for example, where the cottages of The Butts now sit. This provided good quality masonry stone used in the church and many other older buildings. Ordinary chalk needs to be protected from rain and this accounts for the thatch and tile cappings on walls.

Sarsen stones found throughout the parish still provide good 'rubble' masonry for buildings which are sometimes decorated with framed areas of flint, providing a tough and well-dressed finish for outer walls. Flints, found in abundance in ploughed fields, were used before the introduction of tarmac to surface most of the roads.

Chapter Eight

Marlborough Road & Onwards

Marlborough Road

The Marlborough Road begins at the junction with Castle Street – the alternative route to Marlborough. It climbs up and up by 150 feet (45 metres) to the de-restriction sign, having taken a sharp right turn at the entrance to The Butts.

To the stables

Not surprisingly perhaps, the local hobbies reflect a fit, healthy populace with three households professing walking, gardening and biking as their main interests. Chris McGowan, as well as being church treasurer, is a keen tennis player whilst others admit to aerobics, swimming, diving, skiing, sailing and jogging. It is fortunate that Patsy Pringuer, a practising physiotherapist, lives in the road. Other more sedentary hobbies such as reading, music and sewing reflect alternative levels of activity.

Marlborough Road is a road beset by traffic which starts at 8.00am with the double-decker school bus to Marlborough and continuing thereafter with large industrial and agricultural vehicles. Most households, but not

1 & 3 Marlborough Road

Chapter Eight

Small White Ball, Four-inch Hole

The Dabchick Golf Society was formed during 1996 following a discussion in the village among three members of a local golf club and several 'hackers' keen to improve their skills.

Such was the enthusiasm among the novice members of the society that within two years over twenty had joined golf clubs in the area. The society currently consists of around forty paid up members – men and women of diverse playing standards, who get together six times a year to enjoy a game of golf and each others' company. Traditionally, five of the meetings take place at the weekend, after which players return to the village for a meal at 'Raffles' restaurant or one of the pubs. The remaining meeting is a midweek, all-day affair, when players stay at the club concerned for the evening meal. The organizers have always made the post-match meal a social gathering at which 'other halves' are welcome.

Three trophies have been donated by the public houses in the village and a fourth is sponsored by the society itself and is presented to the winner of the full day event. There is an additional trophy presented at each meeting which players do their utmost to avoid. The Buried Head comprises the grip and half shaft of a broken club and is presented to the player who has endured the most frustrating game of the day – just trying to get a little white ball down a four-inch hole!

5 Marlborough Road

Rectory Court *Marlborough Road*

Marlborough Road & Onwards

Duck Cottage *Marlborough Road*

Southill Farm *Marlborough Road*

Southill Stables

Equestrian Livery Yard was started in 1981 by Sarah West who had just completed her BHSAL qualification in Cirencester.

In 1991 a lease was taken out on some land at Southill and a new custom-built yard was constructed.

Initially the liveries were mainly hacks, but over the years the business has grown and now provides a service to a wide range of equestrian needs, including hacks, hunters, dressage, point-to-pointers, breaking, schooling and racehorse resting and preparation. Customers come from as far afield as Hong Kong.

The establishment consists of a large stable block, twenty acres of grassland divided into nine paddocks and an all-weather floodlit manège.

Sarah's mother and father help with the business which employs three other full-time staff.

all, own one or two cars and shopping practices are reflected by the use of Marlborough and Swindon for major items. Several residents stress the importance of the local shops to the livelihood of the village.

The houses at the village end of the road are the oldest. One, the home of Rupert Mayne, dates back to 1550 and was the original village Post Office. It is said to be the oldest occupied house in the village and when it was re-thatched in 1995, ships' beams were found under the thatch. Opposite is another old house where Audrey Gilligan lives. At the upper part of the road there is the quaint three-hundred-year-old *Duck Cottage* but the majority of the remaining houses were built in the twentieth century. The latest are four units at *Rectory Court*, a conversion from the stable block of *The Old Rectory*. The average occupation of houses is twelve years but varies from over fifty years to less than one. There are eighteen houses in the road but there are two other features worth mentioning. There are riding stables, not surprising in this part of the country. Also there used to be a mail-order company – previously an egg-packing depot –

Chapter Eight

Ex-Crowcastle *Marlborough Road*

14 Marlborough Road

Ash Lea *(12) Marlborough Road*

Fun! – and Profit?

The Aldbourne Investment Club was formed in October 1998 when about a dozen people agreed to get together once a month and begin to invest in the stockmarket. We meet in *The Masons Arms* – our first major decision. We aim to invest modestly but wisely not in big companies but in the riskier outer reaches of the market.

Luckily our combined democratic wisdom seems to be mysteriously enhanced by the liquid refreshment afforded by the congenial surroundings because we have so far contrived to make a smugly satisfying profit – on paper.

We subscribe £20 per month each and invest between £500 and £1000 per stock when we find ourselves with the appropriate funds and a consensus. Those proposing the next share certain to take the market by storm do so with a fierce confidence born of total ignorance. Yet somehow we continue to impress one another, we learn as we go and, above all, we enjoy ourselves.

But be warned! Passers-by who chance to overhear the urgent exhortation 'buy Bass!' should not make the mistake of rushing to their broker. This is probably not the high quality insider information they might think it is.

probably the largest employer in the village. It has the distinction of being built over a burial ground for victims of the Civil War of 1643. Next door is a more modern construction – the telecommunications mast.

A cosmopolitan mixture of people inhabit Marlborough Road – coming from Yorkshire, Norfolk, the Home Counties, the Middle East and India. Two are true Dabchicks, born in the village. The residents have a broad-based range of occupations, though eight are retired. There are two teachers, one of whom, Mary Cowan, teaches children with special needs. There is an accountant, a geophysicist, an engineer and a management consultant as well as a television producer and author, Ann Moir. Also in residence are a local government officer and our county councillor, Chris Humphries who is also the chairman of the parish council and a Kennet District councillor. One retired lady acts as a dog rescuer and there is a dental student in the road. Alex Cowan is in his fourth year at Guy's Hospital and his sister, Georgie, is a qualified ski

10 Marlborough Road

Windy Ridge *(8) Marlborough Road*

MARLBOROUGH ROAD

It appears the bottom end of this road was once called Butts Road. On the right are the backs of two houses in Castle Street. On the left, built in about 1890 by Daniel Cook of an old Aldbourne family, are Nos 1 and 3. They are now one house but were built as a pair with the main house in No 1 and the maids in No 3. They were all originally part of a block including 12 The Square which was a timber-curing yard and stables.

No 5 in the old Butts Road was at one time two cottages called 'The Retreat' and 'Eventide'. The property has a history going back at least to 1733. Rectory Close behind was built in 1990s in part of the grounds of *The Old Rectory*. *Duck Cottage*, No 7, is thought to have been built about 1700–1720.

No 10, *Southill Farmhouse*, was built in 1981 on land belonging to the farm of that name.

Chapter Eight

Combined Churches Fête

Prior to 1973 the Anglican Church Fête was held at various sites around the village; since 1972 a combined Methodist and Anglican Fête has been held on the Green with proceeds equally divided between the two churches.

Typically the sun shines and shade umbrellas abound; stalls are put up selling produce, books, jumble and much more. Other stalls challenge skills with games demanding imagination and luck. Refreshments are provided in the garden of a house on the Green. The Aldbourne Band plays, a Punch and Judy show entertains the children, the school gives a display of country dancing and the church is decorated with delightful flower arrangements. Untypically it pours with rain and then either dripping umbrellas are deployed or the fête is moved to *The Manor House* barns. The fête closes officially with a service held on the Green on the Sunday evening. In 1998, a rainy fête, the sum raised was in excess of £2,300.

Chalice Lodge *Marlborough Road*

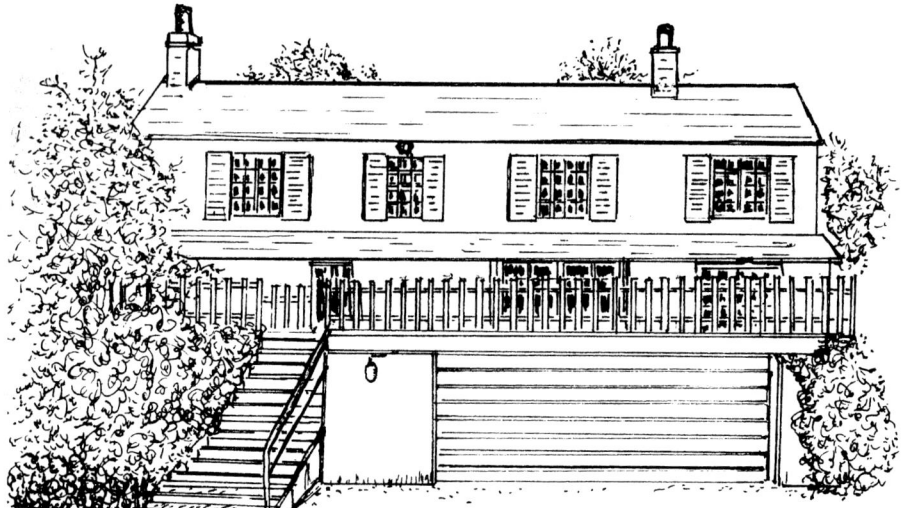

Box Cottage *(6) Marlborough Road*

Marlborough Road & Onwards

Southlands *Marlborough Road*

Little Paddock *Marlborough Road*

instructor and has just started a university degree course at Durham. Most of the Marlborough Road children attend local schools though there are several away at boarding school.

Dogs outnumber cats and there are no admitted exotic pets unless one counts a donkey. The stables naturally house a number of well cared for horses. When the wind is in the right direction the residents are reminded of the nearby pig farm.

And so the road proceeds out of the village further uphill to Axford and Marlborough.

Aldbourne Light Entertainment Club

ALEC came into being in 1983 growing out of a WI drama group performance of *White Horse Inn*. The cast was drawn from a wide range of people – those who could sing, those who liked acting and people who just wanted to have a go. The production was a huge success and soon afterwards ALEC was born with Howard Gibbs as its first chairman.

Since then ALEC has staged thirty-four productions, including revues, plays, pantomimes and musicals, ranging from low farce to high drama, from Gilbert and Sullivan to rock opera. Each has had the ALEC hallmarks of tremendous enthusiasm and the consistent delivery of a better show than anyone could reasonably expect from a village drama group. High points have been the gritty social comment of *The Matchgirls*, a powerful staging of *Jesus Christ Superstar* in the church, and *It's a Lovely Day Tomorrow*. This revue of songs and sketches from World War II won ALEC a regional drama award. All of these provoked strong emotions in their audiences which, after all, is what good theatre is all about.

Over time ALEC has called on the talents and skills of over 300 different people, nearly all from within the village. The faces change but the show goes on!

Chapter Eight

Hampstead Cottage & Castle Cottage *Marlborough Road*

Castlemaine *Marlborough Road*

The Butts

Archery practice was probably carried out on or near this site in the Middle Ages; chalk was also quarried here. Most of the cottages are 17th to 18th century and several were originally two dwellings. Indeed No 4 may have been three dwellings as it has three wells. Nos 5 to 10 form a terrace rebuilt on earlier sites. These cottages are built of sarsen, flint and chalk; all are still thatched, with brick chimney stacks and casement windows. Most have 20th century additions.

The interior of No 8 has a round pole spine beam. Nos 11 and 12 were also probably once thatched but have been altered and extended. No 14 was originally two farm cottages for *Southill Farm*.

1 The Butts

> **Snap**
>
> The history of the village known as Snap is well documented. A pleasant walk from Woodsend leads to the ancient spot where, at the right time of the year, it is still possible to see the vestiges of the foundations of dwellings last occupied in the 1920s.

2 The Butts

3/4 The Butts

The Butts

The Butts was originally concerned with archery but its original role in defence is no longer appropriate and there is no modern sporting association in the village. It was also the first road from Aldbourne to Marlborough but that has also been superseded. The original, doubtless muddy, road surface is now metalled and carries a wide variety of through traffic.

The houses at the village end of The Butts are principally those that were built first – in the seventeenth century – of chalk, flint and sarsen stone with a thatched roof. Time has

Chapter Eight

19 The Butts

meant much modification with the addition of modern services though some still have wells in their gardens, albeit covered. Anne and David Robertson's house at No 3 (now incorporating No 4) has two staircases and two wells. Rita and Tony Stapleton at No 9 have a priest's hole by the main fireplace. Several houses enjoy an inglenook fireplace with an open fire. One old cottage, which has now been demolished, was at one time the home of the author Hammond Innes who wrote 'Air Bridge', centred on Membury airfield. At the southern end of The Butts, in contrast, is a small modern development of detached brick bungalows. Here one of the few remaining local workshops in the village can be found –

Faneuil *The Butts*

Briary Wood *The Butts*

a furniture-making business run by Keith Sowerby assisted by his son Stephen.

The residential profile of The Butts has changed considerably with time. In 1850 it was mostly occupied by agricultural and manual workers and there were several small shops. It is also said to have housed the local 'blaggards'! Nowadays the residents would claim to be somewhat more upmarket – Paul Williams, an engineer; Roger Hill, a business director; Nick Kennedy, an airline pilot; his wife Bev, a MacMillan nurse at the Prospect Hospice. Our latest residents in No 17 are recent arrivals Stephen McEntee, a selector of books for W H Smith and Diane Scarlett, an editor. Of eight retired persons there are included a marketing director and a doctor. Four persons admitted to being housewives. The Butts can also boast involvement in village life. Sandy Martin is clerk to the governors of St Michael's School. Paul Williams is a scout master. David Robertson is chairman of the Civic Society. Malcolm Shuttleworth is closely involved in ALEC and *The Dabchick* as well as being chairman of the Aldbourne Investment Club and co-editor of the Millennium Book of Aldbourne.

Living in The Butts are thirty-eight adults and eight children – Lisa and Nathan Williams, James and Nick Wilmott, Alison and Louise French and Catherine and Christopher Martin. Seven of these young people are at St

Rosemount *The Butts*

South Down *(18) The Butts*

Chapter Eight

17 The Butts

South Cottage *(16) The Butts*

15 The Butts

Ring out Proud Bells

Aldbourne is proud of its bells. From its former foundries, bells all over the country echo the sound. Handbells, invented here, take their big brothers' solace to the old.

The names of those who ring now mean nothing. That we chanced to be here while the millennium changed means less. In the 500 years our bells have rung there are many far more deserving of mention than us. All of them we remember with affection because, whatever the reason they are no longer with us, they are still part of our band.

Our duty is to those who have gone before, better men who taught us what we know. Our commitment is to those who come after, better people, that we pass on what we were taught successfully.

We could tell you we are important. But the bells know different. For it is they that are the epitome of English life.

So, on a summer's morn, surrounded by the verdure and the fragrance of the blossom, listen for the bells. For this is England. And think that but for those past, present and yet to come, it would not be the same. If our bells should fall silent, part of it is lost.

'You are now home' sing the bells of Aldbourne.

Marlborough Road & Onwards

The Aldbourne Ladies' Group

A meeting was called of known interested parties at 12 The Garlings in September 1963 to explore the possibilities of forming a young wives' group in the Aldbourne area. The Rev R Delap presided and the ladies present were the Mrs Delap, Cullis, Palmer, Liddiard and Cummings. Invitations were sent out to ladies 'personally known' to those at the first meeting and a programme drawn up. To start with the group was very much a Methodist Church organization and meetings started and finished with a prayer.

However at the AGM in April 1974 a Mrs Perrett suggested that the Young Wives be renamed with a view to encouraging all age groups. Aldbourne Ladies' Club, with a more secular image, was born. By the 1977 Jubilee celebrations it was being referred to as the Aldbourne Ladies' Group.

Today the group follows the same formula agreed at that far-off meeting. For a while meetings were held in the Scout Hut but now we meet in members' houses on the third Monday of each month except August. We have guest speakers who talk about a variety of topics some cultural, some informative, some to do with health and some to do with hobbies. We fundraise and donate to charities; we go on outings and have barbecues in the summer. At a committee meeting in 1968 it was decided to enter the Aldbourne carnival. Members and their children entered as 'Quality Street Assortment' and won first prize in their class and a long standing commitment to the carnival has continued ever since.

John's, Marlborough and one at St Michael's. The small number of children is, however, made up for by the plethora of grandchildren – one family boasting twelve.

People have lived in The Butts from twenty-four years to less than one. Three residents have been the only occupants of their house. A number of people now living in other parts of the village spent part of their lives at The Butts whilst the newest residents, Diane and Stephen, moved from Stephen's parents home in Cook Road.

The majority of people are originally from London and the Home Counties though there are also incomers from Cheshire and South Yorkshire. Several people have lived abroad for a significant period of their lives – in South Africa, Malaya and Hong Kong. Barbara Sowerby is a survivor of four years imprisonment by the Japanese during World War II.

There are twenty residences in The Butts with thirty-one cars, three bicycles regularly used and one motorcycle. Two residents confess that they actually prefer to walk from A to

14 The Butts

Chapter Eight

St Benions (12), Ollerton Cottage (11), 10 & 9 The Butts

8, 7, 6 & 5 The Butts

Flora

The downs, before they were ploughed, were grazed by sheep and the sides were a mass of chalk-loving plants which fortunately survive in some areas, notably High Clear Down below Upper Upham which is managed by the Wiltshire Wildlife Trust. This area has many special plants including cowslips, rockroses, milkwort, scabious, knapweed and vetches, several species of orchid and tiny gentians which attract numerous butterflies.

The Parish Council has two wildlife areas on the Southward. One is a small area where the three byways meet and where chalk-tolerant shrubs, such as thorns, spindles, guelder rose and dogwood were planted in the late 1970s making a dense area of shelter next to which downland flowers luxuriate among the grasses. The other on the clay/flint top is Aldbourne Gorse, an indigenous woodland with a sizeable central patch empty of trees that is a carpet of bluebells and Solomon's Seal in spring but choked by bracken in summer. The clearance of some of the bracken near the track, has allowed natural oak regeneration and some ash and cherry has been planted.

These areas and a beech plantation at Rectory Wood are managed on behalf of the Parish Council by the Aldbourne Conservation Volunteers. Several landowners have planted mixed chalk-tolerant trees in groups on the lower downland slopes to provide new habitats.

B. Shopping expeditions are undertaken to Reading and Bristol as well as to local shops. Travel is mostly for pleasure though there is some for business, including Jimmy Joy who works for the EU in Belgium and Nick Kennedy a BA pilot.

The views from The Butts cannot be described as outstanding. At the village end is a row of five concrete garages which have replace earlier cottages. The trees between The Butts and the gardens of Turnpike however constitute a fine, tall boundary. The houses at the southern end have an inspiring view over Ewin's Hill and Southward Down – and the local football pitch.

Hobbies are varied and include collecting cheese dishes, tapestry, music and studying the life of Lord Nelson. Albert Pennington is a gifted watercolour artist. The road boasts two members of the WI Choir – Daphne Williams and Anne Robertson. Sporting activities among residents include rugby football, tennis, cycling (seriously by the Hendricks family) and the less strenuous activity of bowls.

There are as many dogs in The Butts as there are children, and there are also cats, gerbils and a rabbit. Nobody admitted owning a bird, though there are many wild varieties including our constant companions the rooks and, in the winter, numerous tits, blackcaps, pigeons, sparrows and wrens waiting to be fed. Despite the tall trees very few squirrels seem to have taken up residence.

Beyond the village boundary

The area

Beyond the outskirts of the village Marlborough Road eventually becomes Stock Lane. One can take a magical drive through the countryside and, by taking a right hand turn at *Stock*

Hill View *Marlborough Road*

> ### Spitfires
>
> In 1940 Florence Sherman enlisted for war work. She went to the factory at Shaw which assembled Spitfires.
>
> She worked in the stores handing out the hundreds of parts needed to make a Spitfire.
>
> After the war she was transferred to Vickers at South Marston and stayed there in charge of the stores until she retired.

Little Acre *Marlborough Road*

CHAPTER EIGHT

THE GAS SUPPLY

Aldbourne is fortunate in that for almost fifty years it has been supplied with mains gas, thanks to the large Swindon to Hungerford gas supply pipe which passes through the village.

Under the roads lie Transco's network of pipes, some of metal and others of bright yellow polyethylene plastic. The village is also home to three governors which reduce the pressure for onward transmission through smaller pipes to people's homes. Since mid-1998 customers have had a choice of gas supplier but all gas delivery is done by Transco.

Westdown *Marlborough Road*

New Cottages *Marlborough Road*

Stock Close Farm *Stock Lane*

Stock Lane Cottage *Stock Lane*

Hillwood Stud *Stock Lane*

> **STOCK LANE AND LAINES**
>
> During and soon after World War I Henry Brind Shepherd bought Prospect Farm in West Street with land up the Marlborough Road. At the time he was able to take his cattle up to the fields in safety, but by the 1930s this was no longer so. Frederick, his son, sold the property in West Street and built *Hill View*, which was sold in the early 1960s when *Little Acre* and *Westdown* were built.
>
> In 1327 Thomas atte Halle lived at Hillwood Farm. By the middle of the 20th century it was deserted, and only the ruined foundations are still there.
>
> In 1971 John and Joy Hobby built a fine house and set up a stud farm. The Victoria County History says Laines may be the farmstead with the longest history of occupation. Certainly a farmstead stood there in 1773.

Lane Cottage, arrive almost at the top of Ogbourne Road – which by turning left and left again would bring you to Chasewoods.

The first part of the journey involves a drive past a pig farm with at times the smell of natural country air and by looking right the views stretch over to the Ogbourne Road and the houses that are scattered there.

The autumn colours of the trees are spectacular and well worth the drive. Laines is a very narrow road used most frequently by farm vehicles and householders travelling from A to B. From this road you get an excellent view of Snap.

People

There are surprisingly quite a number of houses on this half-circular route and families have lived in the area for varying amounts of time. One family have been here for two years whereas the Lampard family have lived in the Parish since 1949 – two generations.

What a varied list of hobbies and pastimes these local people have. They take part in village activities such as WI and ALEC and other pastimes include needlework, cookery, icing cakes, beekeeping, metal and wood-turning, keep-fit, horses, gardening, playing squash, horse-racing, psychology and music. The car plays an essential part in these peoples' lives not only to enable them to participate in their hobbies but also for general shopping and other essential visits.

A Duke of Edinburgh Bronze Award is held by one of the people living in the area and the parents of another family dined with the Queen in 1991. Very royal connections.

One couple who were both employed by British Airways have spent a long time restoring their cottage and have revealed an inglenook fireplace – just right for the long, dark, cold winter nights.

Some people live in this area because of their work – perhaps in local farming – whereas others are required to travel for their jobs which include cooking, childminding, office worker, company director, housekeeping and gardening.

One person still travels a lot for his work as cabin crew for British Airways. His wife held a similar position but gave it up to become a mother and a student. Others like to go away on holiday though mainly in this country and also travel to see friends and relations. All seem to love living in the parish and envisage staying here.

Hillwood *Stock Lane*

Laines Lodge *Laines*

Chaseside *Laines*

Laines *Laines*

Chapter Eight

The Marlborough Banana

We live in the Marlborough Banana! So the BBC said to someone complaining about poor radio and television reception in the parish. It is an area which it is difficult to beam transmissions into and as a result radio, TV and mobile phone reception is poor. Those who enjoy BBC Radio 4 can still get it on Long Wave unless driven off by Test Match coverage but the other radio programmes are all on FM reception which, in parts of the village, is patchy without a special aerial.

Tuning the car radio to pick up the different wavelengths of the same programme as the car moves out of the parish is a skill that has passed many by but can usually be supplied by a handy grandchild. They are also useful when faced with a computer problem or working the video recorder.

Bruce Titcombe has for two decades applied his skills to erecting aerials that ensure good reception. He says that the Queen's coronation in 1953 saw the first commercial surge in television. Huge H-type aerials were fitted and neighbours and friends were invited round to watch the ceremonies and celebrations, though only in black-and-white; it was magic. It was not long before the BBC's monopoly was broken by independent television, the 405-line system replaced by 625 lines and UHF. Early colour was not satisfactory; the sets were expensive and very fragile, installation took two hours and reception was poor. This problem was partly overcome in 1985 when a sub-transmitter was built on the Marlborough Road to relay picture signals from Hannington to Aldbourne. The disadvantage is that we are limited to one commercial TV station, currently Meridian. Satellite TV is also received, beamed down from space and received via dish aerials. The day will perhaps come when all programmes are received through dish aerials and our sky and roof lines will no longer be disfigured.

Aldbourne and Parliament

From the perspective of our Member of Parliament:

'Aldbourne is almost on the edge of my Devizes constituency. In terms of the concern of its community it is right in the heart of the politics of rural communities in general and Wiltshire villages in particular, but with the added interests in the economy of Swindon as many Aldbourne folk work there. Per head of population I probably get more letters from Aldbourne than from any other community within my constituency. They are not letters of complaint, but rather of suggestions as to how things can be improved and seeking my help or advice in doing so.

Aldbourne took on its own affordable housing problems, raised them with me, but through their own effort secured the action which was needed. I am contacted, often with constructive suggestions, about schooling, small village shops, new technological ideas, the agricultural economy, the industrial sector, and so on. However I have always felt that Aldbourne pulls together, that it is a proud and hopeful community, that its varied interests and backgrounds are a source of strength. I am proud to represent Aldbourne in Parliament.

I have two particular views of and unique to Aldbourne. One is from the pulpit when I spoke in the church one Sunday on "Christianity and politics", and learned how long a sermon should be! The other was from a dust cart when as part of seeing all sides of my constituency I spent a morning on a refuse collection vehicle collecting Aldbourne's rubbish! My perception of Aldbourne genuinely stretches from the sublime to the ridiculous.'

Chapter Nine

Via Castle Street to Snap

Castle Street

Castle Street begins its narrow journey curling upwards at its junction with Marlborough Road. On the right hand corner is the Post Office and Stores and on the left a private dwelling which used to be the cobbler's shop. There are no pavements and at times the residents have a hazardous walk to the shops, negotiating parked vehicles and dodging fast moving traffic. Castle Street winds on – to the left a small track to the local tennis courts, to the right a tile hung single dwelling that used to serve as homes of four families. Further up to the left a meadow, once belonging to the farmhouse opposite, now houses the largest estate in the village built in the 1970s. It widens now and opposite the entrance to Westfield Chase is a field – the subject of controversy a few years ago when planning permission was sought for a housing estate. From here there is a fine view of the church and its surrounds. Just around another bend and Castle Street ends at the Aldbourne sign.

5 & 7 Castle Street

> ### Artists and Writers
>
> The forty or so local artists whose drawings illustrate this book are by no means all those who paint and draw and also live here. Poetry is similarly strong, not merely in numbers but also in quality.
>
> One Dabchick has rightly earned her place with a poem in a national anthology of poetry published in the 1990s.

Chapter Nine

Inhabitants – age and time

It appears that Castle Street is becoming populated with older people. Only four families have children and all told there are seven of school age or under. Those aged sixty and over account for 45 per cent of the residents, whilst under-twelves account for 15 per cent. Interestingly, there are no teenagers and no twenty-somethings. Those in their thirties and forties account for 12 per cent each and people in their fifties 16 per cent. It would appear, though, that all residents integrate well.

Six residents claim to be Dabchicks and one-fifth have been in Aldbourne – if not resident in Castle Street itself – for more than fifty years. Another fifth have lived in Castle Street for

11 Castle Street

Half Moon Cottage *(13) Castle Street*

Swan Cottage *Castle Street*

Wartime Memories

"We were in the flight path for Coventry and with the airfield at Ramsbury felt vulnerable so daddy decided to build a dugout in the garden.

As he dug the hole filled with water. Grandmother Penny was about eighty and she couldn't understand why with a war on he wanted a swimming pool!

She also thought that all the soldiers were her sons coming home from World War I. She would rush out of the house to welcome them back. The soldiers had to start to return to camp via the Butts rather than risk being accosted by her.

On VE Day we had a bonfire by the pond. Everyone danced and drank and many had sore heads the next day."

less than five years, whilst a quarter have resided here between ten and twenty years. Of the seven households who have moved here in the last seven years, four are of pensionable age and two have children.

Work and school

Of the six school-age children, four attend St Michael's School, one attends the local comprehensive and the other is educated privately. There is no uniformity among those who work, although of the five (two women and three men) who have occupations in Aldbourne, the two women are domestic workers and two of the men are gardeners or

15 Castle Street

Whitley Cottage *Castle Street*

19 Castle Street

> ### HARK! THE HERALD
>
> Each Christmas morning the band has the honour or waking up the village by playing carols, starting at 4.00am, touring each road around the village, often joined by supporters. They need to remember which particular carols have been asked to be played outside which houses.
>
> The event finishes at 6.30am, with carols being played from the roof of the church tower before the bandsmen go home for some much-needed sleep prior to the day's real festivities.
>
> This enduring and endearing tradition, like many in the village, has been a long-standing engagement since about the turn of the century. It never fails to surprise Chistmas visitors and families new to the village.

handymen. Of the four mothers, two work outside the home, one in full time employment. Only one other woman has a full time job outside the home. Two men travel extensively worldwide, whilst the rest work within a reasonable proximity to Aldbourne. Occupations are as diverse as pharmacist, journalist, business proprietor, airline pilot, office administrator and social services care manager. Only in two families is there evidence to suggest that they relocated to the village for employment purposes.

Shopping and transport

All except two households shop in the village and three families buy the bulk of their shopping here. Half shop in Marlborough, while only a quarter travel to Swindon. Hungerford is next in popularity followed by Newbury. People travel in the family car (only two families have more than one) to do their shopping. Two elderly single ladies do not have any form of vehicle, so travel on public transport. A younger gentleman said he would like to travel thus if it were user-friendly.

Leisure activities

Most residents enjoy more than one hobby or interest, with gardening heading the list for men and women of all ages. Craftwork (that is, knitting, sewing, cross-stitch, flower arranging, and so on) is also extremely popular. Participation in various sports – hockey, tennis and rugby – keep a few bodies fit, but a few more

Whitley Lodge *Castle Street*

> **STRICT SUNDAYS**
>
> "My grandparents and mother were Primitive Methodists who were particularly strict about doing very little on Sundays except walking sedately to church and reading the bible, but no other books.
> Church or chapel music was the only music they were permitted to listen to."

23 & 25 Castle Street

Castle Street

Maurice Crane said there were houses here in the 16th century but most are much later. No 1 was a farmhouse, built in the 17th to 18th centuries. No 2, *Hampstead Cottage*, is 18th and late 19th century. Nos 3 and 5 are now one. No 11, once known as 'Little Cottage', is in a terrace with *Half Moon Cottage*, No 13, which was originally three. They date from the 18th century and are still thatched.

Part of No 17, *Whitley Cottage*, was a barn. Between 1945 and 1949 it was inhabited by Jankel Adler, a noted artist, who made the gargoyles on the front and back.

There were originally four thatched cottages where No 21 stands; it was built on their foundations in about 1919. *Barn House* was converted from two cottages in the 1930s by Doctor Varvill; the barn beyond belongs to it. *Pudley Cottage* was once four. The next house with its farm buildings was set up as a smallholding for World War I returners.

Careless Cottage, No 33, was converted to one in 1989 from two brick and flint cottages built in 1873, one of three pairs. The flint is said to have come from the abandoned village of Snap. Both parts have been owned by long-standing Aldbourne families.

Flint Cottage *(27) & 29 Castle Street*

Careless Cottage *(33) Castle Street*

Chapter Nine

> ### Joints
>
> "Just before Christmas the farmer at Woodsend would kill a sheep and the families in the village could walk up and collect a joint – one per family.
>
> My brother and I went and he said 'I'll get ours and you get one for Gran'. When we got there he said 'Sherman' and got his joint. Another girl was told 'If your gran wants a joint, she must come and fetch it'. I thought, 'what shall I do'. Anyway I said 'Wilkins' – my Gran's name – and I got a lovely piece of meat for her!"

enjoy sporting activities from the sidelines! (Or armchair!) The older residents keep active with country walks and all ages enjoy reading and crossword puzzles. Unusual hobbies are 'comedy' and leaded stained glass work. Castle Street boasts two talented musicians. Local organizations are well attended – WI, the Band, the Sports and Social Club, the pubs, Women's Fellowship to name a few. One quarter of the residents attend religious services either at St Michael's Church or the Methodist Church. Children also belong to the various clubs and play tennis and swim. Two are learning to play musical instruments (the recorder and flute) and two girls ride ponies.

35 & 37 Castle Street

39 & 41 Castle Street

Via Castle Street to Snap

20 Castle Street

Pudley Cottage *Castle Street*

Barn House *Castle Street*

Sculpture

Roger Leigh was a sculptor and he and Pat organized a National Sculpture Exhibition in the garden of West Leaze in 1969.

The Arts Council sponsored the exhibition which included Henry Moore amongst the eighteen exhibitors. Five thousand people visited the show that summer.

Chapter Nine

Cobblestones *(8) & 6 Castle Street*

4 & 2 Castle Street

Holidays

The most avid holiday travellers appear to be in the forty to sixty age group, taking holidays at least twice a year, both in Britain and abroad. Two families take two foreign holidays per annum. Six more families take one annual holiday – five preferring to spend their holidays in Britain. Of the over-seventies, 70 per cent say they do not travel far.

Interesting collections?

Only three residents admitted being collectors. Two collect ornamental animals – pigs and cats, and the third has a few vintage motorbikes carefully and lovingly restored by himself. The same person will admit to collecting anything!

Where did they come from?

Apart from the dwellers of Castle Street who are Dabchicks and have family ties in Aldbourne, the rest have come from far and wide.

From Wales, Newcastle, Sussex, Lanarkshire, Chorleywood, Jersey and Manchester. Our furthest travelled family originated from the island of St Helena, which is in the South Atlantic.

20 & 19 Westfield Chase

18 & 17 Westfield Chase

Westfield Chase

In the mists of time

Eighteen Reema houses were built in 1950–1 by Marlborough and Ramsbury District Council on the campsite which, during World War II, had housed soldiers of the Searchlight Battalion. The houses were pre-constructed concrete sections of three- and four-bedroom semi-detached post-war houses to accommodate young village families.

This small estate built around a circular grass area was named Westfield Chase, being in the vicinity of Westfield Cottages and The Chase from Snap.

The community

During the first decade there were thirty-four children under the age of sixteen of whom one became a doctor, some became teachers and nurses and one became a Mensan (high IQ). At least two families emigrated to Australia. This young and energetic group supported village events, belonged to the Scout and Guide movement and the children attended St Michael's School before going on to the Marlborough Secondary School on the Common or to Marlborough Grammar School. The annual Carnival float with most of the children participating was on a loaned Barnes coal lorry. The 'Green' was a wonderful play area

CHAPTER NINE

16 & 15 Westfield Chase

14 & 13 Westfield Chase

12 & 11 Westfield Chase

FIRE IN THE FIELDS

It was in the late 1970s or early 1980s and harvest time. The field next to Westfield Chase had been baled and two men were preparing the field for ploughing. They were gathering the odd bits of straw and burning it. They started a fire near the houses and a householder was concerned the fire was too near. The ploughmen explained that there was only a small amount to be burnt and they were looking after it so there was no danger.

The next thing they knew Ramsbury Fire Brigade was racing down the field all bells ringing. The fireman jumped out and said 'Where's the fire?'

'Here it is.' says the ploughmen 'What have you come for?'

'We've heard there's a fire out of control.'

'Well you can see how out of control it is.'

'Yes' says the fireman 'it's hardly worth getting our stuff out.'

Then they noticed some smouldering straw under the fire engine was beginning to burn. The flames licked up and set the fire engine alight and it was completely burnt out.

The outcome was that the firemen had to walk down to the village and catch the bus back to Ramsbury! It was the talk of the village for weeks.

and facility for holding fundraising events arranged by the youngsters with help from the parents.

Currently, residents include ten Dabchicks and others who were born in other areas of Wiltshire, Berkshire, Dorset, Essex and Oxford. Ages range from two years to seventy-eight years, there being ten senior citizens but only eight children who attend St Michael's, St John's and John O'Gaunt Schools. There are still three original residents.

Hobbies and interests

Several people have more than one interest and they are varied: gardening, music, reading, knitting, sewing, darts, walking, line dancing, photography, swimming, horses, trains, bell-ringing and church activities.

Collections include trophies, cuddly toys, elephants and Elvis Presley records.

Only one family travel abroad regularly but others enjoy occasional holidays and visit family and friends.

Memorable events

Derek Holmes, a retired Coldstream Guard, was bitten by an adder whilst working in his garden on a cold spring day in 1986, causing him to be off work for several weeks with a poisoned hand. Derek also remembers that during the winter of 1983 he brought milk down from Snap Farm through the fields on a

10, 9, 8, 7, 6, & 5 Westfield Chase

4 & 3 Westfield Chase

Bump and Bounce

"I remember Tommy Barnes' blue carrier van used to go to and from Hungerford – in the morning to catch the train to London; again at lunch time to meet the 1.30pm from London; then home; then back again for the evening train.

We travelled with a variety of things including chickens. People put a notice in their window if they wanted him to stop.

It took a time to get there and it was very bumpy and bouncy."

Chapter Nine

2 & 1 Westfield Chase

Briar Farm *Castle Street*

> ### Leighs and West Leaze
>
> Pat and Roger bought *West Leaze* in 1965 from Lady Ruth Dalton, widow of Lord Hugh Dalton. They had had the house built in the 1930s and had imported tons of soil for the chalk garden in order to plant the six and a half acre garden of trees. Lord Dalton and Roger belonged to the 'Men of the Trees', and Roger continued tree planting. He renamed the house *Sorbus* in recognition of the many species of sorbus which Hugh Dalton had planted.
>
> Lord Shinwell and Hugh Gaitskell frequently visited the house to discuss Socialist policy. The Leighs met Anthony Crossland, Barbara Castle and Roy Jenkins who separately came on pilgrimages to West Leaze.
>
> Lord Dalton did not possess a car and would walk from the station in Hungerford.

tractor as the Ogbourne Road was closed by a heavy snowfall. Large amounts of milk were wasted as there was no collection possible.

Alf Blackall and his family saw Amy Johnson take off from Mingladon Airport in Burma on her solo flight to Australia in 1934. Although only four years old he remembers the occasion vividly.

Joy Keen is proud of her son Peter's record-breaking throwing of an egg (without it breaking) which took place on the the Green. One of five children, Joy enjoys her childhood memories of Aldbourne and has a twin brother living in the village as well as her family of three sons and two daughters. One of her sisters, Molly, married an American soldier and lives in America.

One resident claims to have met Jesus and is concerned with the way we are polluting the world.

Occupations

For those who work their jobs are varied: car mechanic, care assistant, hairdresser, lorry driver, bar steward. Among the retired is a machine designer.

West Leaze *Castle Street*

Ulmus *Castle Street*

Continuing up Castle Street

When travelling from the village to Marlborough most people tend to take the main route which leads up the Ogbourne Road. They do not realize just how steep this road is unless they have also cycled or walked it.

Just outside the village on the right hand side is a very well placed seat providing a welcome respite. During the spring daffodils can be admired whilst resting and during the summer months one very kind villager keeps the grass cut under and around the seat.

West Leaze to Woodsend

West Leaze, or *Sorbus*, was designed in 1930 by Frederick McManus of Burnet, Tait and Lorne for Mr and Mrs Hugh Dalton. He was later Chancellor of the Exchequer in the Atlee government. It has a very fine collection of rowan, or sorbus, trees.

There was a house called *Dudmore Lodge* early in the 16th century which appears to have been held by the Keeper of Aldbourne Chase. The earliest deed, of 1689, shows by then it was owned by the City of London following the sale of Aldbourne Manor by Charles I in 1625. The deeds trace the owners from then on and show farm lands being added and sold.

The existing house of this name is thought to be early 19th century and is probably on the same site. Frederick and Nellie Gentry bought the house and farm in 1927 and their daughter Betty still farms it.

Lodge Lower Barn was rebuilt in the 18th century of 17th century timber framing with weatherboarding, but with a corrugated iron roof. It is rare to see outfield barns around here.

CHAPTER NINE

The few residential properties that scatter this road afford far-reaching views of the surrounding countryside and the homeowners all tend their gardens with loving care.

This area is farming country and a wide variety of arable crops can be found in the fields – corn, wheat and barley grow along with oil seed rape – though occasionally the fields are 'set aside'. Combines and tractors are a common sight on this road during harvest time and the fields are a hive of activity from dawn to dusk.

On reaching the area of Woodsend, or Snap as it is commonly called, you find another farming element – a dairy. There are farmworkers' cottages here along with other residential properties and all the occupiers obviously enjoy the country life as borne out by their hobbies which include horse riding, gardening and breeding cats. Several people enjoy railways and indeed own model railways.

A car is essential when living in this area, particularly for coming down to the village centre for various activities and local shopping facilities.

The children living here go to a range of schools – St Michael's, Kingsbury Hill in Marlborough and Pinewood at Bourton. Yet another reason why people need a car.

Residents have lived in this area from anything between three and fifteen years and most moved here because of their work.

Dudmore Lodge *Castle Street*

Cheldene *Woodsend*

Chasewoods Farmhouse Cottage *Woodsend*

Chasewoods Farmhouse *Woodsend*

Snap Farm *Woodsend*

Woodsend

Woodsend was a considerable hamlet in the 19th century, with about sixteen cottages, a chapel and school.

These were abandoned in the early 20th century, but there was some rebuilding later using building materials recovered from the deserted village of Snap nearby.

Chapter Nine

Woodsend 2 *Woodsend*

Brads in his Mouth

"Our cobbler, a gentleman named Mr Billy Palmer, lived in the house at the bottom of Castle Street right on the corner.

The two little windows are still the same. You would see Billy sitting at the window with the door always open. I spent many a happy hour just standing by his side watching his skilful hands hammering in the brads around the soles of the shoes He kept the brads in his mouth, for quickness I suppose.

Billy always wore a felt trilby hat, a thick woolly jumper and a leather apron. His workshop was always neat and tidy. The shoes which had been repaired were labelled and stood in rows ready for the owners to collect. Real leather was used in those days and I can still remembers the smell. The little oil lamp on the floor was the only heating he had."

Woodsend 3 *Woodsend*

Christmas Cottage *Woodsend*

Woodsend Farm *Woodsend*

The Chase *Woodsend*

Dudmore Bungalow *Castle Street*

Aldbourne Dabchicks Rugby Club

The club is now one of the most well-established sports clubs in the village. Formed during the 1993–4 season by a few local enthusiasts and playing three games in this first year, the club has gone from strength to strength. It is a matter of pride that the teams that take the field are always made up of no less than 75 per cent of individuals from the village. Considered to be one of the strongest village sides in the area, the Dabchicks have the reputation of a side who are physical on the field and friendly off it. Games take place on both Saturdays and Sundays, which emphasizes the Dabchicks' commitment to remain a social side playing only friendlies. This is despite numerous offers to join various leagues.

The club also has a well organized and committed team of 'minis' whose ages range from six to thirteen. They can be seen training every Sunday often with both sexes participating. This side too is regarded with envy by other larger villages and towns.

The Dabchicks have ambitions to erect a purpose-built changing facility on Ewin's Hill where they have been playing since the club started. Every effort is being made to achieve this goal with work potentially starting in the summer of 2000.

Chapter Nine

Lawn Tennis Club

The club developed from a group of friends meeting regularly in the 1920s. Notable amongst these were: Capt Brown (William's grandfather); Major Bland (Henry's father); W J Osmond; Henry Billington (Tim Henman's grandfather) who was a Wimbledon and Davis Cup player; Violet Owen, Wimbledon and international player; and Arthur Smith, a club stalwart who later became a life member.

The first recorded minutes are dated 1936. With so many quality players the club had a formidable reputation, winning numerous county trophies. The war produced a quiet period, tennis being kept alive by the ladies and veterans. As the men returned in 1945 the club revived under the leadership of Messrs Anthony Brown, Henry Bland and Arthur Smith.

The 1960s saw a large group break away and form the Aldbourne Hard Courts. The Tennis Club recovered from this blow and membership gradually increased and Ralph Harding became chairman. In 1968 Mr Neate, the landlord of ground in Castle Street, died and Anthony Brown, then president, purchased and donated the property. Several years of concentrated fundraising followed. The new pavilion was officially opened by Mrs A Brown in 1977 and in May 1983 the new courts were ready for use, and they have helped considerably in the coaching of juniors wherein lies the future of the club.

1988 was Ralph Harding's twenty-fifth year as chairman and he was able to hand over to John Adey a thriving club with a membership of over 100 seniors and juniors. The club has changed a lot in twenty-five years. Today the hard courts are used throughout the year, other private courts are used when needed and the floodlights extend playing time. The club plays about fifty competitive matches but it never forgets that it is a village tennis club and anyone of any standard is welcome.

The Skies over Aldbourne

We are used to the sound of aircraft over the parish and the sight of condensation trails crossing the sky. We live under a busy piece of airspace through which both military and civil aircraft fly.

What the military aircraft, in particular Hercules transporters, helicopters and sometimes the noisier fighter aircraft are doing at low level, we can only guess. The military manoeuvres on Salisbury Plain, the Army Air Corps training base at Middle Wallop and RAF stations to the north of us and at Lyneham generate much overflying.

Occasionally smaller aircraft are spotted perhaps when the few local residents with private licences circle us. On summer evenings we are overflown by noisy micro-lights. On still days at any time of the year we watch the peaceful passage of hot-air balloons and in summer see hang gliders launched from Sugar Hill.

It is however commercial aircraft that are most common. Twice daily we hear and often see the supersonic Concorde on its scheduled service to New York. At more sedate speeds the subsonic Jumbos pass over daily on their flights to and from the USA. The common trans-atlantic route to and from international airports both in this country and Europe takes them over Wiltshire, Wales and southern Ireland. However, commercial traffic tends to be over 10,000ft when passing us and usually it is the military aircraft that most disturb our peaceful existence.

An exception, to be welcomed, is the police helicopter on its patrol, pursuit or rescue duties. Parishioners coming a cropper on the downs have been rescued.

Chapter Ten

The Whitley Estate

Whitley, Hawkins & Hillwood

The estate was built over a period of approximately fifteen years and in several stages. The first houses were built by Kennet District Council, now owned by Sarsen Housing Association, and were for the elderly and retired. Hawkins Road (named after the late Oliver Hawkins who was for many years chairman of the Parish Council) and Hillwood Road were then added and a number of family homes were built.

The third phase included three houses and two bungalows for first time buyers, enabling young Aldbourne couples to stay in the village. The cost for a two-bedroom house in 1981 was £19,750. In the early 1980s the final phase of houses was built comprising two- and three-bedroom homes again for first time buyers; and also a self-build scheme which

1 & 3 Whitley Road

1, 2 & 3 Hawkins Road

Oliver Hawkins

Oliver Hawkins played a prominent part in village life in the middle of the 20th century. He was chairman of the Parish Council for many years and a county councillor for twenty years. In 1963 he was made an alderman.

He became a household name in the village and sorted out many problems for the village as a whole and for individuals in particular.

Hawkins Road was named after him and his daughter planted a tree by the pond in his memory.

consisted of twelve three- and four-bedroom houses. Only one of these houses is still occupied by an original self-builder – Andy Pickford along with his wife and two children.

The surroundings are very pleasant with grass areas and plenty of trees. Most residents list gardening as one of their main hobbies and throughout the summer months many gardens are a riot of colour.

The residents

They vary in age from babies to a much older generation, some being in their nineties. Many have lived here all their lives, others were born here, while some have come to live in Aldbourne because the village is quite central to their work.

Children are very well catered for in this area. They have the use of a small swing park and a large playing field for ball games. Their leisure activities are very varied but a large number of them enjoy the same things, music, horse riding, football, handbell ringing and cycling. Drama plays a large part in their lives and in 1998 four of them were involved in the local pantomime produced by ALEC. The majority of children go to local schools – Aldbourne pre-school, St Michael's School and

4, 5, 6 & 7 Hawkins Road

Wired to the World

According to a recent survey, 29 per cent of British homes have a personal computer. In Aldbourne, it is twice that figure (Parish Appraisal 1999). And half of our PCs are connected to the Internet.

With over 160 satellite TVs in our midst, we are indeed wired to the world.

8 & 9 Hawkins Road

The Whitley Estate

10 & 11 Hawkins Road

5, 7, 9 & 11 Whitley Road

13, 15, 17 & 19 Whitley Road

Chapter Ten

1 & 2 Hillwood Road

> #### Damn Lies
>
> The Parish Appraisal conducted in 1999 tells us that we have 400 cats and nearly 300 dogs.
>
> There are, it seems, just enough personal stereos to ensure that each cat can have its own.
>
> Dogs are even luckier; they can have two mobile phones each.

3 & 4 Hillwood Road

5, 6, 7 & 8 Hillwood Road

The Whitley Estate

9, 10, 11 & 12 Hillwood Road

13 Hillwood Road

Adam and Eve

The two fire engines now kept in the church were bought by public subscription after a calamitous fire in 1778. They were inherited by the Parish Council together with fire fighting responsibilities in 1894 and were used until 1924 when they were replaced with a rather more modern appliance.

They were not so inefficient as they might appear. They could be manhandled at a run to the fire, if necessary hoisted over the garden hedge, and positioned close to the conflagration.

It was in 1906 that the Parish Council's Fire Engine Committee became concerned about the state of the fire engines but they were not replaced for some years.

In 1915 modernization started – a Minimax fire extinguisher was purchased!

21 & 23 Whitley Road

Chapter Ten

25 & 27 Whitley Road

Pudley Byre *(29) & 31 Whitley Road*

Tannenbaum *(33) Whitley Road*

then St. John's School in Marlborough. A small minority travel to Hungerford and Newbury.

Several children have used their hobbies for further achievements.

Oliver Kent was named Player of the Year in 1998 for Ramsbury Junior Football Club.

Trevor Clarkson has played rugby for the Wiltshire league.

George Baker was selected for three consecutive years, from the age of twelve, to run in the Berkshire (Junior) Cross Country events.

Oliver Kimber took part in 'Joseph and The Amazing Technicolour Dreamcoat' at the Palladium in London and was also in The Royal Variety Show at The Dominion Theatre in 1992 in the presence of Prince Charles and Princess Diana.

Hobbies and pastimes

Gardening and sport are the most popular hobbies of the Whitley residents. Most properties have their own gardens and keen gardeners can be seen busying themselves all year round. Among the younger element football is the most popular sport with rugby, tennis, badminton and rifle shooting as other interests. Many listed cycling as an interest with the majority owning their own bicycles and using

35 Whitley Road

Cromwell House *(37) Whitley Road*

Guiding

Guiding has been taking place here for many a year. There is never a shortage of girls wishing to join one of the groups.

Rainbows were first started some four years ago for girls aged between five and seven. They meet every Monday after school, wear a coloured tabard and make a small promise. They enjoy craft and activity games and generally have fun.

Brownies are aged between seven and eleven years and wear a yellow and brown uniform. They do interest badges and craft and activities. They also go away under a roof, not canvas, to have fun and adventure and come home with new skills and more badges to be sewn on.

Guides are aged between ten and a half and fourteen years and are expected to be self-thinking and able to plan and carry out simple tasks with the guidance of their leaders. They go on hikes and to camps and do backwoods cooking. Girls from Aldbourne went to Sherwood '98 and camped with some 7,000 other Scouts and Guides from all over the world – an experience to tell younger girls about.

So Guiding thrives with approximately fifty girls currently involved. We are of course eternally grateful to the trained leaders who run the weekly meetings.

Chapter Ten

39 Whitley Road

them to travel around the village and further afield. Cultural activities such as art and history were mentioned as well as creative writing and sketching.

Local resident Julie Kent has put her hobby of sketching to good use by drawing houses for this book, while her husband Chris visited the site of the Battle of the Somme as he has a particular interest in World War I. This comes in very useful for teenagers studying history for GCSE as they also visit this area for their studies.

Motorsport plays a big part for several residents with one owning a racing car and one a racing motorbike. Chris and Cheryl Phelps often spend weekends watching road-racing

41, 43 & 45 Whitley Road

46, 47, 48, 49, 50 & 51 Whitley Road

The Whitley Estate

52, 53, 54, 55, 56 & 57 Whitley Road

58 & 59 Whitley Road

60 & 61 Whitley Road

Housing

Of the 770 occupied dwellings in the parish 667 are privately owned, the majority owner occupied, and 103, known as affordable or social housing, are owned by three housing associations.

Back in 1988 it became obvious that young couples with modest means were being priced out of the village so the Aldbourne Housing Group was formed to encourage the building of affordable houses. The group's first success was to attract Hastoe Housing Association. With the help of local farmers who responded generously to an appeal for land and by getting exceptional planning approval, Hastoe Housing Association built six houses in Lottage Road just outside the village perimeter.

Aldbourne's lively interest in housing also encouraged Kennet Housing Society and Sarsen Housing Association to build thirty houses in Claridge Close. Our current housing need appears to have largely been met since there is not always an Aldbourne 'take up' when housing becomes available. It is also possible that the need is changing.

Forty-two tenants took up the right to buy their housing but except for former council tenants this right no longer exists in rural villages such as Aldbourne.

CHAPTER TEN

CHAIR MAKING

"Thomas Orchard started a chair factory at *Barn House*. Parts of chairs were also made at *Hightown*. My grandfather, George Hale, was head turner and also worked a lathe. Bill Dean cut out the seats with an adze. Old-fashioned foot lathes were used to turn the legs. John Cook cut out the patterns and the spars for the chair backs. Now when I was a little boy my grandfather took me to the factory and sat me up on the bench. He put a bit o' wood in the vice and said: 'Now you can learn to be a chair maker. Here's a spokeshaver', and he gave me the spokeshaver and showed me how to use 'un. I looked in my shed t'other day and I found 'un. One of my grandsons was there and I told him he could have the spokeshave I was given when I was about eight. Chair makers made all their own tools.

There were between thirty and forty men employed in the business. The men stayed at the factory all day and didn't go home for their tea. In the mixed school Miss Lawrence the headmistress used to say to the children: 'It's quarter to four. The boys and girls who have to go to the chair shop with teas can leave'. We would go home, pick up a can of tea and a bit of food and take the men their teas."

62 Whitley Road

63, 64 & 65 Whitley Road

66 Whitley Road

The Whitley Estate

67, 68 & 69 Whitley Road

where they have seen Ian Clarkson Cowles racing his motorbike. Ian also rode sidecar for Aldbourne resident Dennis Keen many years ago.

There are quite a few dog owners on the estate and one couple have three leonbergers the youngest of which has qualified for Crufts two years running.

So varied are the interests of local people that one has practised healing and another has a collection of items associated with the Spanish Armada.

Achievements

The wide cultural scope of Whitley Road residents is reflected in the range of achievements reported.

A bandsman for forty-five years, Cyril Barrett started playing at the age of thirteen and mastered the cornet, euphonium and E-flat bass and as a member of the Aldbourne Silver Band took part in many concerts and contests. His wife Audrey (an avid fundraiser for various village societies) was WI president

42, 40, 38 & 36 Whitley Road

The Motor Car

According to the Parish Appraisal done in 1999, there are on average 1.4 cars per household.

Since the last parish survey in 1976 the numbers of cars and bicycles have nearly doubled; but the number of cars needing to be parked on the roads has increased by nearly eight times.

for three terms of office, whilst local girl Cheryl Phelps was head girl at St Michael's School in 1983.

Further afield Ken Warren sailed a thousand miles up the Amazon, and staying on a nautical theme Nigel May was World E Boat Class Champion in 1981.

Adam Woodrow used to play football alongside England player Paul Ince. In a different sphere he is very proud of his wife Rhoda's first class honours degree.

The left-hand side of Oxford Street (on the old chalkpit) and the bungalows in Windmill Close were built by Nancy Keast's father – Richard Stacey.

Staying in times past, Tony Edwards was proud to return home safely from Burma after World War II to his wife Pat who was also doing her patriotic duty working in a Spitfire factory. Constance Turner was also in a man's world, becoming one of the first draughtswomen when in her early teens. Constance has also travelled extensively and spent time living in the Far East.

Collections

China and antiques are frequent collections particularly teapots, wall plates, majolica, Lilliput Lane cottages, coins and stamps.

Engravings and badges are also collected as well as an unusual collection of *Autosport* magazines. More cuddly collections include pigs and

34, 32, 30 & 28 Whitley Road

> ### REFUGEES
>
> "In 1940 many children came from Dagenham as refugees.
>
> At first we were terrified because they all seemed so much bigger than us, I remember one boy called George Bull, he looked like 'Just William' and he was a proper bully. He took me under his wing and I felt highly honoured but the teachers took an instant dislike to him."

Staceys House *Whitley Road*

The Whitley Estate

26 & 24 Whitley Road

22 Whitley Road

20 Whitley Road

Women's Institute

The WI movement came to the UK from Canada in 1915. It had been started by a woman who felt that if she had known more about hygiene and childcare her baby would not have died. She wanted to improve countrywomen's knowledge of homemaking, hygiene and childcare.

The WI in Aldbourne was formed in 1918 and for many years we have been the largest Institute in Wiltshire. Besides our monthly meetings with a speaker and social time in the Memorial Hall, our Home Economics Group meets monthly when there are demonstrations of crafts, gardening and flower arranging. Our WI Choir meets weekly in the Methodist Church and we entertain at many venues as well as entering festivals and competitions. Our Ramblers meet in the Square on the first and third Saturdays walking locally and further afield; non-members are always welcome to join us. Members also take part in the county Skittles League. We have a bi-monthly group which discusses current issues raised by our national executive.

The aims of the WI are: to improve and develop the quality of life, particularly in rural areas, for women and their families; to advance the education of women in citizenship and public issues, national and international; and to enable women to work together to put into practice the ideals for which our organization stands. Nationally, the WI has been at the forefront in the 'Keep Britain Tidy' campaign and in bringing sanitation, piped water and public telephones to all villages – making a big difference in rural areas.

The WI is often referred to by detractors as 'all jam and Jerusalem'. Yes, in Aldbourne, we do make jam and we do sing 'Jerusalem' but we do a great deal more besides. Mainly we offer friendship, skills and fun to anyone who cares to join us. Our motto is: today's women working for tomorrow's world.

Chapter Ten

teddies with one resident extending her teddy collection to the supporting of real bears in the world via the World Society for the Protection of Animals' Liberty charity.

Occupations

Occupations range from the traditional to the hi-tech!

Whitley Road boasts a real abundance of office workers in personnel or administrative functions.

Outdoor workers include builders, a farrier, a landscaping contractor and an aborculturalist, and in order to help these people a meteorologist keeps an eye on the weather for them. Other practical jobs include a driver, a packer and a female welder.

Cars can be well looked after by both a mechanic and an AA rescue worker. A police officer is on hand to deal with any emergencies and we can call on nurses or a health visitor.

Problems with computer hacking? Then bring in our information technology security officer!

Two people run hairdressing businesses and another is an antiques dealer.

Many of the residents are now retired and it was interesting to find out that among the younger element most mothers stayed at home to bring up their children.

18 Whitley Road

> ### Pre-School Nursery
>
> "I remember vividly attending Miss Aldridge's pre-school age 'nursery' at her house next to the village school. There was a multi-hole 'toilet shed' at the bottom of the garden with child-size seats.
>
> One day I escaped and went home. I was made to return but was allowed to ride my scooter back. It was very different to the motor scooter of today. Your leg got quite tired scooting it along."

16 & 14 Whitley Road

The Whitley Estate

Aldbourne Road Runners

Currently there is only one active member resident in the village but there are three in South Wales and one in Calne. In the mid-1980s the club had over forty members and they had completed many marathons between them.

The club was founded by Dabchicks Trevor Davis (Senior) and Cyril Liddiard and the best runner in the club was Trevor Davis (Junior), also a Dabchick, who was in the top ten in the country in his age group. The annual Ridgeway run of 40 miles draws back the distant members each May.

12 Whitley Road

10 Whitley Road

Chapter Ten

> ### Dissenters
>
> In 1669 about 300 Dissenters used to meet outside *The Court House* on Thursdays and Saturdays to hear sermons. The Methodists and other dissenting churches put down strong roots in the village.
>
> The present church in Lottage Road replaced a Wesleyan Methodist Chapel built in the 19th century and demolished in 1968. A Primitive Methodist Chapel in West Street was pulled down in 1982.

The wide range of jobs and almost full employment is encouraging for the many teenagers about to enter the job market.

Whitley Road is a diverse area catering for the elderly and young families but is a jolly place to live with most people knowing one another and helping each other out.

Street parties have been held to celebrate two royal weddings – Prince Charles to Lady Diana Spencer and Prince Andrew to Sarah Ferguson. We are now looking forward to the day of another royal wedding. Who will be first, Prince Edward or Prince William?

8 & 6 Whitley Road

4 & 2 Whitley Road

Chapter Eleven

West Street to Upham

West Street

From the centre to Sixpenny

The buildings in this street have changed little since World War II, apart from the two cottages which replaced the Methodist Chapel and a family house erected in a builders' yard.

Nos 1, 2 and 3 are joined and date from way back. A curving road brings to this mixture of homes and gardens a fascinating pattern of boundaries. Wells used to be the only source of drinking water and it was hard work when the copper needed filling for the Monday wash. Lavatories were well away from the houses; one resident remembers how her mother was in shock after finding a tramp had been sitting in her privy all night. He needed firm persuasion to move on.

Rose Ware lives at No 5; her father, Christopher Hawkins, was a Dabchick and her late husband, Peter, a village postman. After school in Aldbourne, Rose left to work in Slough but returned to the district in 1947.

Michael Palmer was born at No 19 in 1943. On marrying Sue Green from Ramsbury in 1968, he moved a few yards into what was then known as Lower Sixpenny, next door to the authoress, Ida Gandy; later they moved to No 9. Daughter Stephanie and son William were born in the village. In 1998–9 Mick and Sue ran the local tea-room called 'Palmer's'.

It is believed that No 11, *The Masons Arms*, had once been a coaching inn. Chris Wheare

1, 3 & 5 West Street

7 & 9 West Street

Chapter Eleven

The Masons Arms *West Street*

has lived at *West Street House* (No 13) for twenty-one years. Her two daughters, Catherine and Jane, were already at university when the family came to the village and so remain 'visitors', but her sons, Michael and David, attended St Michael's School and St John's School, Marlborough. Born in the West Riding of Yorkshire, Chris worked on eight provincial newspapers during her career as a journalist, ending up with the *Wiltshire Times*, *Newbury Weekly News* and finally the *Wiltshire Gazette and Herald*. She has been a member of the WI since coming to the village and also the Aldbourne Children's Book Group and the Civic Society. She is a former booking secretary of the Theatre Club. Her interests include

West Street House *(13) & 15 West Street*

Kin y Cart?

Prior to 1968 Margaret only spent holidays here. She remembers her grandfather's strong Wiltshire accent. When asking if she could carry some apples, he said: 'kin y cart?' (can you carry it?).

She thought of Aldbourne as magical and always cried when it was time to return to London.

17 & 17a West Street

painting, gardening and the organic movement. She runs an organic vegetable box scheme from her home. The date of the house is unknown as the deeds only go back to the 1930s when the block consisting of *The Masons Arms*, *West Street House* and No 15 was divided into three.

Clive and Hazel Morris live at No 15. Now retired, they ran a picture-framing business at this address from 1982 to 1997. No 17a was once a wash-house for the family next door but became a fish-and-chip shop, 'The Village Plaice'. Mabel Beckingham now lives at No 19, the Palmer's old family home. She went to the village school and spent her working life in preparatory and public schools. Since returning to the village she has enjoyed the many activities offered by this friendly, well balanced community of young and old.

Gladys Greasley lives at No 21. Her late husband George left the village to join the army but later came back to his roots; generations of his family have lived here. They shared an interest in the church, the Band and a love of gardening. Their daughter, Sheila, runs the hairdressing business in the village. Two grandchildren both used to play in the village band.

No 23 is the home of Peter and Joan Biggs who came to Aldbourne in 1983. The house is next door to the now-demolished chapel and has been made comfortable by renovation and the addition of an extension at the back. They

19 West Street

Briar Dene *(21) West Street*

1 & 2 **Chapel Cottages** *West Street*

23 West Street

have enjoyed designing the garden and later picking the fruit and basking in the sun – when available – with the odd glass or two.

Honeypot was built in 1992–3 on the site of a builders' yard for Andy, Sally, April and Jack Matthews. Andy has lived in the village for thirty-one years and Sally moved here from Marlborough fifteen years ago when they married. Nos 25 and 25a were a farmhouse where Harry Sheppard farmed and also cut men's and boys' hair. He wore a pair of gold-rimmed glasses on the end of his nose and, in the evening, worked by the light of an oil lamp; you were well advised to keep your head still.

Mr A V Jerram bought the house and its outbuildings in 1936 to carry on business with his brothers as builders, decorators and undertakers. His son Vincent lived here until 1948, apart from army service from 1939 to 1945, and entered the family business. He moved to Westfield Chase in 1948, but later returned and inherited the house in 1969. He and his wife Pearl are both retired. Their daughter Heather, a PA administrator at Shrivenham College of Science, and son-in-law Ken, a self employed electrician, live next door at 25a which was formed by extending and dividing No 25.

To the edge of the village

This group comprises fifteen houses to the north and south of West Street. In the mid-nineteenth century these households were entirely engaged in agriculture and the three

Honeypot *West Street*

25 West Street

25a West Street

farmhouses (with yards) had about twenty-five attached cottages in all. A courtyard of fourteen cottages was partially burnt down about 1910; only six remain plus two rebuilt cottages. Of the present fifteen households, eight are owner-occupied, three are tied to the farm and therefore rent free, and four are let by the farm. Now there is one working farmhouse and only two of the cottages house agricultural workers; otherwise the residents are from various backgrounds, many retired and others working outside the village. Trades and professions include regular soldier, dealer in oriental ceramics, professional skater, doctor, solicitor, accountant, social worker, builder, maker of medical equipment, sculptor and film maker, computer engineer, garden designer and aromatherapist. The cottages would all have

Thrupenny & Sixpenny *West Street*

35 & 37 West Street

> ## NOT JUST KNOTS
>
> 2000 is the 92nd year of scouting. We have no record precisely when Scouting started in Aldbourne but in 1910 The Marlborough Times contains a reference to Aldbourne Scouts Jack Penny and Wilf Jerram attending a Scouts Sports Day. The scoutmaster was Mr Lewis in 1914 and Miss Peterson in 1921. When she left in 1923 the troop was forced to close. In the 1919 Scouts' Roll of Honour Frank W Stacey and Richard Loveday were both remembered for giving their lives in World War I.
>
> The present troop dates back to 1989 when Jane Palmer restarted scouts with the help of Sue Palmer. In 1992 Mike Waters took over and kept things going with Graham Browning until Paul Williams was persuaded to take up the reins in 1996. Since then it is thanks to Mick Hills, Malcolm Pryce, Peter Dinwiddie and previous scouters that we still have a troop.
>
> The Aldbourne Scouts cater for boys from ten and a half to fifteen and a half years old with the majority coming up from the Aldbourne Cub Pack. When they are too old for the troop they have the opportunity to continue scouting with the local Merlin Venture and Ranger Unit. As well as the traditional skills such as knots and first aid, the scouts also undertake cultural and social projects, go on expeditions, develop outdoor activities and go camping where they learn a range of abilities including how to pitch a tent and how to cook a meal.
>
> Scouts currently meet on Monday nights between 7.00pm and 9.00pm and on a number of weekends for full-day activities including climbing, canoeing, night hikes, dry skiing, pioneering, clay pigeon shooting, ice skating, go-karting and orienteering.
>
> Last year ten scouts went to the District Camp at Youlbury near Oxford and later in the year a group went to Longridge Scout Activity Centre.

had their own vegetable gardens with a pigsty at the end and chickens; now there are only a few plots of vegetables (one with traditional chalk block walls thatched with wheat straw) and most of the gardens are purely decorative, often with paving stones in place of grass. Dogs in the nineteenth century would mostly have been working ones – sheep-, guard- or gun dogs. Now there are two sheepdogs and one gundog in the group; the rest are pets, together with many cats and a flock of fantail pigeons.

Thanks to thoughtful management in the past, this road running west from the village is the only one without ribbon development and it therefore retains its agricultural character throughout with the main grain store of the farm close to the village. Within walking distance of the centre of the village there is a field where cricket and football were played before the present sports field was opened, and where communal events such as gathering for the carnival procession are now held. Two large houses south of the road lie at the foot of the hill and have substantial cellars with drains that carry away the spring water that pours in. They have main drainage now, and during its installation traces of Roman drains were found. There are also two ice-houses; one partially collapsed in about 1960 and the other is now used for potato storage. There are two granaries on staddle stones standing within the farm complex to the north of the street.

William Walter Brown (born 1954) is current 'Lord of the Manor', a title inherited from

> ### West Street History
>
> The first mention of West Street can be traced back to 1614.
>
> There were farmsteads beside the road in the 16th century. In 1780 the present *Masons Arms*, *West Street House* and No 15 formed the stage for the stage-wagon. No 15 has been a fish shop, a greengrocer's and a picture-framing gallery and is now a private dwelling. Modern houses stand where the Primitive Methodist Chapel was pulled down in 1982.
>
> The yard of *Prospect Farm* was sold in 1936 to the Jerram brothers and became a builders' yard. *Honeypot* was built there in the 1990s. Beyond is the old farmhouse and a group of 17th and 18th century cottages known as *Sixpenny* (originally four cottages), *Upper Sixpenny* and *Thrupenny*. All the cottages from No 29 on the south side and No 20 on the north were originally for agricultural workers.
>
> *Westfield Farmhouse* and *The Manor House* date from the 19th century. The Browns of *The Manor House* have farmed hereabouts for hundreds of years. There is an ice-house in the garden and another can be found in the field behind *Westfield Farmhouse*.

Westfield Farm *West Street*

Westcott *West Street*

three generations and bought by his great-grandfather William Brown in 1892 when West Street Farm became known as *The Manor House*. This one remaining farm now has two regular workers, with some work, such as bale-wrapping done by contractors, and some seasonal workers at peak times for lambing and harvest. The boundaries have changed over the years, with additions and reductions in acreage, which now stands at roughly 1,000 acres in total. In addition the farm 'share-farms' with another property for cereal growing, whereby the other owner supplies land, building and seed and the Aldbourne farmer supplies the machinery and labour. Thatching has become almost prohibitively expensive but the farm retains a few listed thatched buildings and walls.

Three pumps on the farm produce water (regularly government-tested) for nine properties and for the animals reared on the farm. At present a fuel tank is permitted for diesel for the tractors, and so on. The farm produces cereal for seed, animal feed and malting, and also has a beef unit with calves bought in for fattening and finishing in thirty months. A flock of sheep produces two harvests, wool and meat. Trees and hedges are carefully managed by pruning, harvesting and replanting. Supervision by government inspectors of sheep dipping, farm safety, movement of animals and VAT registration engenders much paperwork.

At present there are twelve children under the age of twelve in the group, most of whom attend the school or the pre-school nursery.

Fish

15 West Street was a wet fish shop and sold fruit and vegetables. It was started by Clifford Brown and run later by Mr Trap and Mr Ansel. Later Mr and Mrs Morris ran a picture-framing business there.

Next door was a fish-and-chip shop connected with the fruit-and-vegetable shop but later managed separately. The most recent owner was Ron Hacker who ceased to trade in 1998.

41 West Street

The Manor House *West Street*

CHAPTER ELEVEN

Warren Farm Cottage *Aldbourne*

Warren Farm *Aldbourne*

SUNDAY SCHOOL OUTING

"Sunday School Anniversary was a great occasion; the chapel was packed and we sat on a platform above the congregation. I, like the others, always had a new dress and usually black patent-leather shoes and a straw hat. The hat came from Mrs Palmer's shop in the village.

Our anniversary was on Whit Sunday and several weeks before we had to learn special songs composed by Jo Alder. I still have the music. We also gave recitations which we learnt by heart.

The Sunday School outing was usually by bus. We started at 6.00am and went to places like Weston-super-Mare, Bournemouth or Weymouth.

On one special occasion we travelled by train – from Ogbourne to Teignmouth!"

Sugar Hill Cottage *Aldbourne*

Residents are involved in home care, pastoral visiting, the Parish Council, point-to-point meetings, the school, the churches and the WI. One erstwhile resident, Ida Gandy, wrote several books, including one about Aldbourne, while she lived here. There is one privately owned tennis court upon which energetic exercise is taken. The players are all members of the Tennis Club which flourishes in the centre of the village. Residents also enjoy shooting and swimming.

Aldbourne Warren

John Bland has lived at *The Warren* all his life and still runs the poultry farm keeping the Post Office and others supplied with eggs. His great passions are Vauxhall Crestas and jazz and he used to ski. His nephew Hugh lives at *Sugar Hill Cottage* with his wife Anna and their three children aged three to eight. The cottage was converted from two in 1975 and recently extended. Hugh is fully involved in farming having qualified as a Chartered Accountant in London. He plays tennis for Aldbourne, enjoys most sport and looks after the finances of various village organizations. Anna is interested in antiques.

John and Jackie Lee live at 1 *Warren Farm Cottage* with two children and several dogs. Jackie is a dedicated horsewoman. Yorkshire-born John has worked on the farm since 1989 and enjoys shooting and mountain-biking.

At No 2 live Andrei and Ellen Plocki, newly married in July, who both work in computers in Swindon and who also have a menagerie of animals which keeps them busy.

1 & 2 **Summerdale Cottages** *Upham*

3 & 4 **Summerdale Cottages** *Upham*

CHAPTER ELEVEN

Upper Upham

Upper Upham is within the Aldbourne Parish boundary but being some three miles from the village itself, it has its own identity and is a community quite distinct from Aldbourne village.

The large house which dominates the landscape as visitors approach Upham was originally an Elizabethan manor and is now divided into four dwellings; the main house being divided into two and *The Gatehouse* and *The Chapel* being the others. In addition there are another fourteen dwellings which make up the community. Nine are housed in *Summerdale Cottages*, built by the estate owner, Hugh Somers (hence *Summerdale*), in the 1960s. In the same decade a detached house was built for the farm manager and *High Clear House* was built with kennels for the breeding of boxer dogs. There are also *The Coach House, Eyre's Barn* and *Upham Gardens* built in the early 1990s.

The population is currently mainly adult although that was not always the case. At one time during the last decade as many as eleven children from Upham attended St Michael's School – except when it snowed! Now the Barnes coach comes up the hill every day to collect just two children for St John's. There are seven other young residents, either too young for St Michael's or at school elsewhere.

5 & 6 **Summerdale Cottages** *Upham*

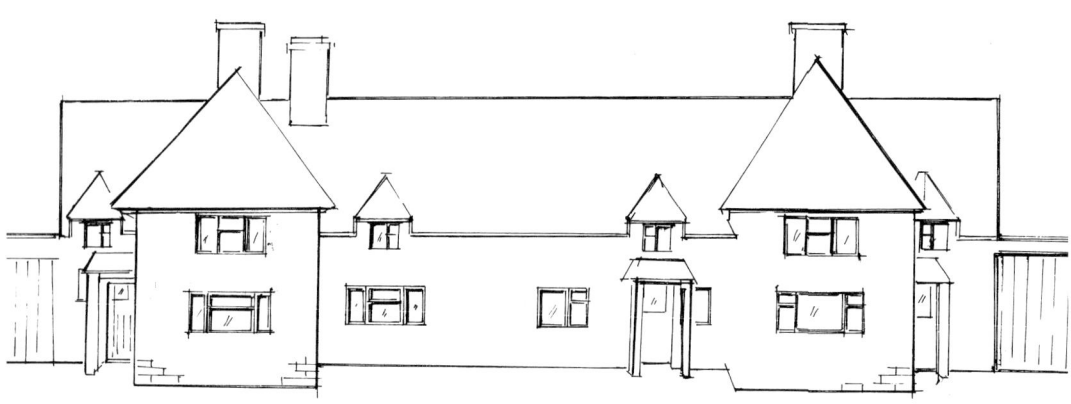

7, 8 & 9 **Summerdale Cottages** *Upham*

Upham Farmhouse *Upham*

Farm Labour

Labour and mechanization have shown the most startling changes over recent years particularly on arable farms.

It is common for one man to work 500 or more acres with the help of large machines representing an increase of ten fold over the century. A combine harvester is capable of harvesting up to 2,000 acres per season while the driver sits in sound-proof air-conditioned comfort, linked to his colleagues by radio.

So the trend has been for fewer farms, farmers and staff.

The Coach House *Upham*

Eyre's Barn *Upham*

Chapter Eleven

Upham

Some of the earliest settlements were in this area. When Henry VIII privatized the monasteries in the 16th century, John Goddard acquired the old timber house and his son Thomas remodelled it, encasing the walls with flint and ragstone. His son Richard continued the work. The initials of Thomas and his wife Anne Gifford are on the central gable and those of Richard and his wife Elizabeth Walrond on the south porch. There are some fine chimneypieces. In 1641 this branch of the Goddards died out and the house fell into decay. For a time in the 19th century only two rooms were occupied, by a shepherd. In 1909 it was bought by Hilda Hanbury, later Lady Currie, and was remodelled and rebuilt by the architect Biddulph Pinchard. It was described in *Country Life* in 1922.

In 1967 it was divided into two. Its gatehouse, also by Pinchard, the building known as the *Chapel*, and *Eyre's Barn* are now houses. An earlier cottage stood on the site of *High Clear House* between the 17th and 19th centuries. *Summerdale Cottages* were built in the 1960s. *Lower Upham Farmhouse* dates from the late 16th century, but is now mostly 19th century with 20th century additions. Down on the Swindon Road lies *Warren Farm* and its associated cottages and outbuildings. The farmhouse is early 19th century, with a barn and granary of the same date. The cottages opposite are slightly later.

Upham Gardens *Upham*

All the residents share a great love for the countryside and are seen out walking in all weathers, enjoying this very beautiful part of Wiltshire. Many of the households have dogs and/or cats. In the six houses around the Green alone, there are no fewer than eight dogs, nine cats and one ferret! As well as domestic animals we enjoy regular visits from squirrels, foxes and badgers, not to mention a very varied bird population which includes woodpeckers (four lesser spotted woodpeckers visit one garden daily and devour large quantities of peanuts!), nuthatches and even buzzards. There is a large population of roe deer too, although they do not often venture into the gardens.

The Chapel *Upham*

Upham Hall *Upham*

Upham estate was owned until fairly recently by the Electricity Board Pension fund and the six houses around the Green were sold privately by the Board in the 1970s and 1980s. Three of the cottages still belong to the estate, now owned by a German landowner and leased locally. Some of the farm buildings have been converted into two small businesses, and George Davies, the florist, grows some of his flowers in the area. Three or four residents work locally but most have to leave the hill daily to go to work. That is particularly hard to do when Upham is bathed in sunshine and Aldbourne is shrouded in fog! An eight-year-old visitor to Upham recently exclaimed as she

The Gatehouse *Upham*

Our Farming Heritage

Until recently farming was the main occupation and source of employment. Many farms or smallholdings were centred in the village and many associated buildings survive.

In addition to the remaining farms there were *Southby Farm* on the east of the Green, *Prospect Farm*, *Westfield Farm* and *Cor's Farm* in West Street, Upper and Lower Upham, farmhouses at the present *Orchard Cottage* in Oxford Street, *White Pond House* on the Baydon Road, 1 Castle Street, *East Leaze*, *Malt-house Farm* in South Street (now the Nursing Home) and *Neals* opposite, *Ford Farm* and *Alma Farm* on the Hungerford Road, *Aldbourne Farm* at the present *Southward Farmhouse*, *Southill Farm* on the Marlborough Road, *Kays Cottage*, 27–9 Lottage Road, *Lottage Farm* and one at *Alma Cottage* up Lottage Road.

Chapter Eleven

High Clear *Upham*

Lower *Upham*

Lower *Upham*

went up the hill on such a morning, 'Oh, it's like being in Heaven!' Upham claims to be marginally higher than Baydon, Wiltshire's so-called highest village, and it does therefore have quite different climatic conditions and not always advantageous ones! It does get cut off from the rest of the world when it snows heavily and often has snow when Aldbourne is experiencing rain. Many times there has been a snowman on Upham's Green when there is no hint of snow in the village! However the snow does bring out the community spirit, as does a power cut, when all residents rally round and help each other. The male members of the community tend to get restless after a couple of days of isolation and soon form a band of workers to clear a way out down the hill!

When there were more young residents the community spirit prevailed at Carnival time and great fun was had by all preparing the Carnival entry. Even the adults without children joined in enthusiastically, as we did before Christmas when we formed our own carol-singing group and went from house to house sampling sherry, mulled wine and mince pies! The singing was the rather poor excuse to wish each other the compliments of the season! For several years we were privileged to have the Aldbourne Silver Band visit Upham on Christmas Eve but their services

Lower Upham

28 West Street

are now much in demand elsewhere! Father Christmas sometimes appeared in person on Christmas morning – but he hasn't done so recently!

Back To The Centre

On West Street *Gladstone House* (No 14), named after the Victorian Prime Minister, is over two hundred years old and still has its original hearths, fireplaces and inglenooks. Sandra Barnes lives there and works at the village school in the classrooms. She enjoys music, singing and ringing handbells in a group with her son Russell. He also plays the piano and has accompanied village musicals and pantomimes, the church group and school productions. Sandra's late husband Bob was joint proprietor with his brother, Jim, of the family business, Barnes Coaches. Bob conducted and played in the Aldbourne Silver Band and was the musical director for various choirs. Vic and Sue Smith, next door, come from Wroughton and Lambourn, although Vic's family were originally Dabchicks, connected with East Leaze farm. They were married in Lambourn in January 1966, and on the same day moved into their present home. Over the years Vic, a builder, repaired and extended the nineteenth-century cottage. Together he and Sue carefully

26, 24 & 22 West Street

Rose Cottage *(20) West Street*

West Street Motors

In 1976 Mr McKeon's car repair business became West Street Motors. Mr and Mrs Peter West, the directors, later decided to concentrate their energies in helping at their daughter's riding stables.

The current directors are Tim Beattie and Martin Comley.

renovated the interior, uncovering many original features including fireplaces, beams and roof timbers remaining from the time the house was thatched – thus restoring the house to its original character. The well still provides water when needed. Daughter Lesley and sons Ashley and Christopher have all left home but come back often to the house where they grew up and which all the family love. Further along Elizabeth Webb lives in a cottage that she and her husband bought in 1972, first as a weekend retreat from the pressures of her husband's work as a parliamentary official. It became her permanent home after her husband died. Much of her time initially was spent looking after her increasingly infirm parents. The garden and

18 West Street

Glebe Cottage *(16) West Street*

WEST STREET

No 4, originally a dwelling house, was the *Queen*, later *Queen Victoria Inn*, from the mid-19th century until 1968. No 6, *Oak House*, was probably built in the 17th century as a farm or yeoman's cottage and its outhouses ran through to what was then known as Church Street. The Cor family owned it in the early 18th century.

No 8 was a barn of *Bell Court* on the Green.

Gladstone House *(14) & 12 West Street*

CHAPTER ELEVEN

house have been replanned in recent years. Elizabeth has taught herself to be a botanical artist and is involved in voluntary work in the church and the community. With many friends and relatives outside the British Isles, she travels widely, most frequently to Canada and France, but is always happy to return home to Aldbourne.

Marian Deuchar, the widow of a Royal Marine captain, lives further along West Street. As a small child she saw Pavlova dance, watched the airship R101 pass overhead, went on a journey with Christopher Robin – but not, sadly, with Winnie-the-Pooh – and joined in the celebrations for King George V's Silver Jubilee. She served in the WRNS during the War then lived in Portsmouth and Malaya before moving to *The Court House* in the village in 1955. After leaving the marines, her husband worked for Plessey and the Confederation of British Industry. The careers of her daughter and four sons include army colonel, chief executive of The Albert Hall, lawyer and archbishop's envoy in succession to Terry Waite.

Nick and Nicky Leigh have lived in No 4 for seven years in what was once a public house. They have two very young children and a dog. Nicky graduated in fabric design and became a fabrics buyer for Harrods where she met many well-known people who were customers of the firm. She hopes to return to working with fabrics when the children are older. Nick runs a framing business in the

10 West Street

Coach House *(8) West Street*

OLD SCHOOLROOM

From 1990 the building deteriorated rapidly due to a shortage of funds and a lack of a kitchen and other facilities. Then in November 1996 with ivy creeping through the walls and plaster falling from the ceiling, representatives of the trustees and the community formed a committee to secure the future of the building. The plan was to renovate and redecorate the existing building and add an extension with kitchen and toilet facilities.

Voluntary work started in April 1997 and much was achieved. £80,000 was raised from a generous grant boosted by local fundraising.

The *Old Schoolroom* was reopened for community use to a fanfare from the Aldbourne Band in June 1998.

Oak House *(6) & 'Mini Mart' West Street*

4 West Street

The Old Bakehouse *(2) West Street*

> ## THE CIVIC SOCIETY
>
> Aldbourne Civic Society was founded in 1970 and has a membership of about 100 people. It is registered with the Civic Trust and is affiliated to the Council for the Protection of Rural England. The Society is managed by a committee and membership is open to all residents of Aldbourne at £5.00 for family membership and £3.00 for individual membership.
>
> The aims of the Society are 'to help safeguard, enhance and promote the character, environment and heritage of the village for the continued benefit of all'. To meet these aims the Society undertakes the following activities:
>
> • reviews all proposed local planning applications and, where necessary, comments on them to Kennet District Council and Aldbourne Parish Council,
> • where appropriate, prepares and gives evidence at public inquiries relating to planning matters,
> • liaises with Aldbourne Parish Council on matters of mutual interest,
> • arranges visits and meetings for members and, where the subject is of wide interest, for the general public,
> • facilitates relevant projects within the village, for example, The Millennium Book of Aldbourne and the 1999 Parish Appraisal.

village; he collects antiquarian books and plays golf. Previously he was a record buyer in London. Both love music; he plays the piano and she used to play the cello when she had more time! Both are well travelled; he in Spain, while she has lived in Nigeria, Norway and the US. Friends and socializing are important.

Sheila and David Jordan live at the *Old Bakehouse*. Sheila was born in Kent but two of her great-grandparents lived in the village. There are frequent visits from daughter Amanda now living in Marlborough, and son Simon in London. Simon plays and teaches the drums. While he lived in Aldbourne a room was specially soundproofed for him! The bakery had closed in 1966 and when Sheila bought the house in 1979 it was gutted and restored before its present use as a hairdressing salon.

St Michael's Close

St Michael's Close is a small group of houses off West Street.

Julie Alder, a Dabchick, is a paraplegic living in a specially-adapted bungalow. She is an expert needlewoman. Her mother came from an old village family, the Pennys; her father, Joe conducted the village band for many years.

Constance and Kate Liddiard are true Dabchicks, as were their parents. In the early 1900s

1 St Michael's Close

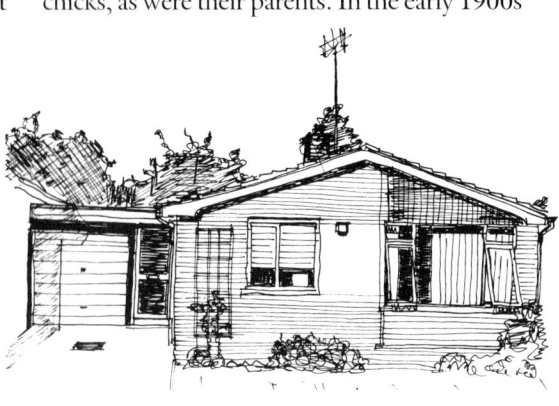

2 St Michael's Close

3 St Michael's Close

4 St Michael's Close

both their grandfathers were farming here. Connie followed a nursing career mainly in London, becoming a matron, while Kate, now a widow, went as a GI bride to the US, where her children still live.

Bob and Margaret Lawson have lived here for twenty-three years. Bob was an engineer working with Frank Whittle on jet engines at Farnborough. He was also a keen fly-fisherman both in Scotland and on the Avon. Margaret was a teacher. They enjoy frequent visits from their daughter and three grandchildren who live in Weybridge.

Mrs Alice Willis moved to the village from the north with her husband nearly thirty years ago. In their retirement they travelled widely in Europe in their motor caravan. In the Prospect Hospice in Swindon there is a lovely memorial window to their son Roger who died in 1979. Alice now keeps busy with her handicrafts, especially her fine needlework.

Back Lane

Chris and Jean Warrington live in an old house in Back Lane used as a blacksmith's shop by the Aldridge family from 1811 until the late 1960s. The house is named after the 1928 Derby winner 'Felstead' who was shod there. The old forge and stables still remain. In part

5 St Michael's Close

1 Back Lane

> ### EGG THROWING CHAMPIONSHIPS
>
> International renown came to Aldbourne on Easter Monday 16 April 1990 when, with the encouragement of Anne and Bill Moir and the brilliant showmanship of Peter Ludlow, the Egg Throwing Championships were held in the village. The aim was to see who could throw a raw egg furthest without catching or breaking it, and whether the world record held by a Canadian could be beaten.
>
> The competition started diagonally across the Green but the increasing distances that eggs were being thrown required the finals to be moved to Woodley Meadow. There were many competitors who threw eggs which landed, bounced and rolled unbroken on the grass. Such was the strength of the eggs, supplied by the Egg Packing Company, that some survived to be thrown twice only to meet their end in the frying pan at the barbecue in the evening.
>
> The eventual winner was Peter Keen from Hungerford who achieved a distance of 285 feet 10¾ inches, a world record which may well still stand. The umpire was Rear Admiral Anthony Davies, a retired Royal Navy gunnery officer with great experience of trajectory and ranging.

CHAPTER ELEVEN

Felstead *Back Lane*

BACK LANE AND WEST STREET

Back Lane runs along the back of the properties on the west side of The Green. Most of the buildings on the east side of the lane are therefore barns or conversions. *Felstead Cottage* was once a blacksmith's, where the eponymous Derby winner of 1928 was shod. The old forge and stables still stand.

On the corner, 10 West Street, like many others, seems to have been two cottages, and was occupied for many years by Thomas Brind, of an old Aldbourne family. A row of 17th century cottages follows. *Glebe Cottage* was part of the glebe lands, with a barn which was demolished in 1967 as part of the development of St Michael's Close. *The Old Priest's House* stands behind *Rose Cottage*, which was formerly called 'Cor's Farmhouse' after the ubiquitous family. The earliest part dates back to the 17th century. An 18th century stable and carriage house were originally attached to Cor's barn to the west. This had to be rebuilt after an elm crashed through it in 1974. Another outhouse in front, a skilling, is 18th century. The garden walls of *Rose Cottage* are listed as of historic interest, as is a granary on staddle stones beyond the barn. There was once a school in a small thatched building in the grounds. The cottages beyond belong to *The Manor House*.

of the garden stood the 'Strict and Particular Baptist Chapel' until it was demolished in 1915. The burial ground can still be seen. Chris and Jean came from London thirty years ago. They have an unusual business, growing oxygenating plants in various lakes and ponds in the district. They are strong supporters of the Prospect Hospice and hold an annual fund-raising sale and party at their house. Their son and two daughters have now left the village but they are still near enough for visits to the nine grandchildren.

Duncan's Barn *Back Lane*

The Vicarage *Back Lane*

BAPTIST BURIAL GROUND

The small grassed area in Back Lane, enclosed by walls and railings, with several tombstones leaning against the back wall, is the Burial Ground of the demolished Baptist Chapel that stood in what is now the garden of *Felstead Cottage*. With the help of The Strict Baptist Historical Society and local records the story of this peaceful and attractive spot can be told.

A Chapel was built in the early 1840s for a small congregation, rebuilt in the 1860s when the congregation had enlarged to about 80, but was finally sold in 1914 after the congregation had dwindled. Only the Burial Ground was left in the possession of Baptist Trustees, to which it still belongs. It is currently cared for by a neighbour and is a reminder of an inspired, zealous and devout group of Christians living in the village who had the courage and spirit to meet and worship in a manner that more greatly suited their spirituality than did the existing churches.

Two men involved in the formation of the Baptist Church have left vivid records of those times. Thomas Barrett, son of a fustian weaver, recollected that he was a dissolute youth in the 1830s, when 'the poor people in our village rose in a mob and broke all the machines on the farmers' premises and then demanded a sovereign for every machine they broke and spent the money in drink'. He then felt a sense of penitence. This led him, via the Primitive Methodists, to the Baptists at Baydon, where the Minister baptized him and four others in a pond upon confession of their faith in the Lord Jesus Christ. Later with five others, baptized in the brook at Preston, he came back to Aldbourne to set up the Chapel in Back Lane having earlier held prayer meetings in his own home. He related that a man named Alder made sport of it and Mr Tiptaft the preacher spoke very solemnly to him and said 'perhaps before another Sabbath you may be in eternity'. In the following week this man went out with a wagon and the horses ran over him and killed him. Secondly William Taylor, an Anglican and then a Weslyan, was moved by a sudden sense of God's love and judgement to join with the Baptists and subsequently to raise the funds to convert the cottages in Back Lane into a chapel in the 1840s; he is buried in the Burial Ground.

The Viburnum Bodnantense by the gate was planted in memory of Mrs Ida Gandy, the authoress.

Chapter Eleven

St Michael's School

St Michael's School was founded in 1857 and is a Church of England Aided Primary School. It was given grant-aided status under the 1944 Education Act enabling it to remain faithful to its original church foundation. The ethos of the school is based on Christian principles and this is reflected in its daily act of worship. The majority of the Governors represent the Church and traditionally on St Michael's Day the Parochial Church Council presents inscribed Bibles to all new Key Stage 2 children in the school.

The school was originally housed in what is now the *Old Schoolroom*. The present school building was opened in 1963, with an Infants area being added in 1974. The school became locally managed by the Governors in April 1994 and in 1997 Aldbourne pre-school moved on-site and work closely with the reception class teacher to smooth the transition to school for the rising fives.

In the 1970s there were over 200 children at the school; there are currently 107 in four classes with a head teacher, a deputy and three other teaching staff supplemented by four educational support assistants and other staff. In 1999 'Woodleys' out-of-school club was opened in the *Old Schoolroom* providing after-school care and a range of activities.

Recently the school has discovered log books dating back to 1863 which provide a fascinating record of school life in the past and changing attitudes in education.

St Michael's School *Back Lane*

Old Schoolroom *Back Lane*

Index

Adam and Eve (fire engines) 16, 219
adult education 100
aircraft 214
Aldbourne
   Children's Book Group 22
   Civic Society 89, 105, 249
   Cricket Club 140, 160
   Dabchicks Rugby Club 213
   Football Club 163
   Housing Group 223
   Hoard 72
   Investment Club 180
   Ladies' Group 189
   Lawn Tennis Club 214
   Light Entertainment Club (ALEC) 183
   Luncheon Club 84
   Road 113–15
     farms 114
   Road Runners 229
   Silver Band 38, 96, 113, 151, 199
   Silver Threads 165
   Sports and Social Club 98, 112
   Toddler Group 76
   Warren 239
ALEC *see* Aldbourne Light Entertainment Club
Alma Road 79–83
appraisal *see* Parish Appraisal
archaeological survey 29
artists and writers 197
astronomy 77

Back Lane 251–4
   history of 252
bakers 106
ballet classes 173
band *see* Aldbourne Silver Band
Baptist burial ground 253
Barnes Coaches 11, 207
barns 133
beating the bounds 24
Beech Knoll House 30–1
bell
   foundry 99, 143, 188
   ringing 188

birthdays 87, 90
birds and butterflies 81
black market 27
blacksmith 166
Blue Boar, The 23
bombs 42
bourne 153
Brenan, Gerald 21, 22
Brind, Thomas 111
brook 153
Brownies, Guides and 221
builders 146, 152
bump and bounce 207
businesses 159
butcher's shop 13
butterflies, birds and 81
Butts, The 185–91
   history of 184

café in The Square 12
carnival 116
carrier service 207
Castle Street 197–204, 209–10
   history of 201
cats and dogs 218
celebrating 87
chair making 53, 143, 224
Chandlers Lane 68–71
changing tastes 58
chantry 20
charities 120
church *see* Methodist Church *and* St Michael's Anglican Church
churchyard 34
Civic Society 89, 105, 249
Claridge Close 170–6
cobbler 159, 212
Combined Churches Fête 182
Cook Close 87–8
Cook Road estate 79–96
   history of 85
Cook Road 84–96
Court House, The 26, 30
crib 71
cricket 140, 160
Crooked Corner 27–8, 33
   history of 30
crops 119

Cubs 167
cycle repair man 21

Dabchick Golf Society 178
Dabchick, The 108
Dabchick?, what is a 135
daffodils and lemonade 145
dances 103
delivery by pushbike 130
discipline, school 132
dissenters 230
do you remember? 110
Downs, The 166–9
dowsing 80, 174
dynasties 37

early buildings 147
egg throwing championships 251
electricity supply 118
energy line 174

fair 168
family dynasties 37
farm labour 241
Farm Lane 148–51, 169–70
   history of 150
farming heritage 114, 243
   in the parish 40
feast 131
festivals 161
fête 182
fire
   engines (Adam and Eve) 219
   in the fields 206
   service 93
fish shops 237
flora 190
food 58
football 163
Ford Farm, history of 137
foundry site, Lottage Road 43
funerals 59
fustian factory 122

Garlings, The 156–66
gas supply 192
geology 176
Glebe Close 143–4

— 255 —

INDEX

Goddards Lane 63–7
  history of 65
golf 178
'Good Old Pride of Aldbourne' 113
Grasshills 27–33
grave digging 88
'Grazells Inn' 30
Green, The 15–27
  history of 16
Guides and Brownies 221

Hawkins Road 215–17
Hawkins, Oliver 215
heavens 77
hedges and woodland 144
Hillwood Road 218–19
home working 50
hot quills 155
housing
  building of 146
  costs in the past 17
  group *see* Aldbourne Housing Group
  prices today 109

Jerram brothers 59, 67, 88
joints of meat 202

Kandahar 70, 71–8
Katie's view 124
kin y cart? 232
Knoll, The 67

Laines 191–4
  history of 193
law and order 55
Liddiard family 91
line dancing 68
livestock 79
local government 94
Lottage Road 37–62
  businesses today 41
  history of 39
  in the 1920s
    – I 46
    – II 49
    – III 54
    – IV 60
  roads off 63–78
Lottage Way 70, 78
Lutwyk 39

Marlborough banana 196
Marlborough Road 177–83,
  history of 181
meals-on-wheels 107
medicine
  now 61
  at *Neals* 126
Member of Parliament 196

memories of 1945 92
Men's Luncheon Club 75
metal detecting 157
Methodist Church 35, 200, 230
millennium celebrations 66
monuments and trees survey 29
Mothers' Union 104
motor car 225

Neals 121, 126
  growing up at 141
newspaper shop 69
North Farm 57
nursery 228

Old Malt House barn 127
Old Manor, The 8
Old Schoolroom 248, 254
Oxford Street 97–105
  buildings 102
  shop 101

Paddocks, The 105
Parish Appraisal 50, 216, 218, 225
parish magazine *see The Dabchick*
'Peeling Onions' 175
petrol sales 156
police 55
pond 7, 63
  concerts 151
post 44, 111, 130
Post Office and Stores 10
prehistory 95
Preston Village 135–7
  history of 137

Rectory Wood 140–3
refugees 226
research 89
Ridgeway Crib League 71
Romans, the 72
Royal Mail 44
royal wave 83
rugby 213

school 132
  history of 25
  memories of 48, 132
Scouts 235
sculpture 203
shadow council 117
Shane's view 36
shops
  in Oxford Street 101
  in The Square 14
Silver Threads 165
skies 214
Snap 185
South Street 121–35
  house histories 123, 134

  the evolution of 125
Southfield 145–8
Southill stables 179
Southward Lane 151–6
  history of 150
Spitfires 191
Sports and Social Club 98, 112
Square, The 7–15
  café in 12
  history of 9
  shops in 14
St Michael's
  Anglican Church 34
  on the site of 19
  today 18
  Close 250–1
  School 254
Stock Lane 191–4
  history of 193
strict Sundays 200
Sunday School outing 238
surgery 61
  at *Neals* 121, 126
Symingtons Soup 73

Table Tennis Club 34
telephones 138
tennis 214
Theatre Club 62
tree survey 29
Turnpike 137–43
TV and radio reception 196

Upper Upham 240–6
  history of 242

vicarages 96

wartime memories 92, 198, 226
water supply 172
West Leaze 208, 209
West Street 231–9, 246–50
  history of 236, 247
West Street Motors 246
Westfield Chase 205–7
Whitley Estate 215–30
wildlife 81, 128, 190
Windmill Close 116–20
wired to the world 216
Women's Fellowship 164
Women's Institute 227
woodlands, hedges and 144
Woodsend 210–13
wool auction 139
workhouse 97
working from home 50
writers, artists and 197

Zeppelins overhead 32